HISTORY OF INDIA

FROM 1206 TO 1773

VOLUME II

N. JAYAPALAN

ATLANTIC PUBLISHERS AND DISTRIBUTORS

Published by
ATLANTIC PUBLISHERS AND DISTRIBUTORS
B-2, Vishal Enclave, Opp. Rajouri Garden, New Delhi-27
Phones : 5413460, 5429987

Sales Office
4215/1, Ansari Road, Darya Ganj, New Delhi-110 002
Phones : 3273880, 3285873, 3280451
Fax : 91-11-3285873
e-mail : info@atlantibooks.com
web : www.atlanticbooks.com

ISBN 81-7156-914-5 Vol. I
ISBN 81-7156-915-3 Vol. II
ISBN 81-7156-916-1 Vol. III
ISBN 81-7156-917-X Vol. IV
ISBN 81-7156-928-5 (Set)

Typeset at
APD Computer Graphics, Delhi

Printed in India at
Mehra Offset Press, Delhi

PREFACE

It gives me great pleasure to place this book in the hands of the readers. The book is quite comprehensive and covers the entire syllabus prescribed by various universities. I have narrated all the events chronologically from the beginning to the end. I have also made a serious attempt to present the matter in a simple manner.

There is a plethora of books on the 'History of India from 1206 to 1773.' Most of them are bulky. Hence, I have written this book in a sizable Volume *i.e.*, neither too small nor too big. In addition to this, I have given importance to the Social, Economic and Cultural conditions of the period.

My experience of teaching the subject at the college level for several years has prompted me to write this book for the students of our universities mainly to meet their requirements. In addition to this, it has been designed to meet the requirements of the examinees of Civil Services Examination in History and Political Science. I hope that the present book will prove to be more useful to the students than any other book on the subject available in the market.

I am thankful to the M/s Atlantic Publishers and Distributors, New Delhi for readily agreeing to publish this book and bringing it out expeditiously and efficiently.

Suggestions, if any, for the improvement of the book in the next edition will be highly appreciated.

N. JAYAPALAN

CONTENTS

PART I
DELHI SULTANATE

PART II
MUGHAL EMPIRE

PART I

DELHI SULTANATE

1

Slave Dynasty

(I) QUTUB-UD-DIN AIBAK (A.D. 1206 TO 1210)

Introduction

The Indian rulers did not learn any lesson from the frequent invasions of Mahmud Ghazni. They were disunited and engaged in incessant internecine warfare even on the eve of Muhammad Ghori's invasions. North India was ruled by many Rajput Kings during the last quarter of the twelfth century A.D. They were Prithviraj Chauhan III of Delhi and Ajmer, Mulraj II the Chalukya ruler of Gujarat, Jaichandra the Gahadvala King of Kanauj and Lakshmana Sena of Bengal. Punjab was under Khusru Malik, the last member of the Ghaznavid dynasty. No two Indian Hindu rulers joined hands to resist the impending invasion of Muhammad Ghori.

Second Battle of Tarain 1192

Muhammad Ghori conquered Peshawar, Sialkot, seized and captured Lahore and thereby became the Lord of Punjab. Then he marched towards Delhi and on his way he seized Bhatinda. Prithviraj Chauhan III the ruler of Delhi met Ghori on the historic battlefield of Tarain in the year 1191 and won a resounding victory over Ghori. But in the very next year Muhammad Ghori launched another formidable attack on Prithviraj defeated and killed him in the second battle of Tarain in 1192. Muslim Dominion was established in India. Ghori appointed Qutub-ud-din Aibak the Viceroy of his conquered territories.

Significance of the Battle of Tarain

(1) It laid the foundation of the Delhi Sultanate and thereby heralded the inauguration of the Muslim rule in India. "From the days of Muhammad Ghori to the catastrophe of the Indian Mutiny, there was always a Muhammadan king upon the throne of Delhi."

(2) The blow in the second battle of Tarain was an irreparable one to the Rajputs. No one did even think of recovering the lost territories from the hands of Ghori.

(3) Dr. V.A. Smith considered that this battle to be a decisive contest which ensured the ultimate success of the Mohammadan attack on Hinduism.

Qutub-ud-din Aibak's early career

The first Sultan of Delhi and the first Muslim ruler of Hindustan was Qutub-ud-din Aibak. He was born free but became a slave when he was a boy in Turkistan. He was purchased by the Gazi of Nishapur. When his master died he was sold to Muhammad Ghori. His courage, manly bearing and generosity attracted the attention of his master. By dint of his ability, he rose to the position of the master of the stables. He became the trusted General of Muhammad after the second battle of Tarain for his further conquests in Hindustan.

Aibak as Viceroy (1192-1206)

1. As Viceroy Aibak had to consolidate the conquests of his master. The Rajputs were struggling hard to overthrow the Muslim rule. An uprising at Ajmer against Prithviraj's son for surrendering to the Muslims was suppressed. Aibak waged series of wars against Rajputs and thereby conquered Bulandshahr, Meerut, Aligarh and Delhi from them. Then he made Delhi his metropolis.

2. Mohammed Ghori wanted to make his conquest of Hindustan to be complete and hence marched against Jaichandra

of Kanauj. Aibak had an equal share in the conquest of Kanauj as a result of the war of Chandwar on the banks of the Yamuna.

3. Aibak suppressed a rebellion at Ajmer and captured it. He defeated Sulakshanapala of Gwalior and occupied the fort in 1196. He conquered Paramardhideva of Kalinjar and seized Bundelkhand.

4. The Rajputs of Ajmer and Bhima II, the Chalukya King of Anhilwara joined hands to drive away the Turks from India. In the war that ensued in Mount Abu in 1196, Aibak got a decisive final victory over them and plundered the city of Anhilwara. Thus, Aibak consolidated the Turkish dominion in Hindustan.

5. The only powerful ruler left unconquered was Lakshmana Sena of Bengal. He too was defeated by Ikhtiyar-ud-din Muhammad Bhaktiyar, one of the adventurous generals of Aibak in 1197 and his capital Nadia was easily occupied. Because of his marvellous feats in the establishment of Turkish Dominion Aibak was offered the title of 'Malik' in 1206 by his master Muhammad Ghori. Ghori was killed in his expedition against Khokars in Punjab.

Aibak as the First Sultan (1206-1210)

Ghori did not have a male heir to succeed his throne. When it was referred to him, he was said to have one or two male heirs, but he had thousands of heirs the Turkish slaves. They were not only his heirs but also would read his name in Khutba. Aibak proved to be worthy of the trust that was placed upon him by his master. After the murder of his master he ascended on the throne as the Sultan of Delhi on 24th June 1206. His accession was approved and was freed from slavery in 1208 by Giasuddin the successor of Muhammad Ghori.

Aibak strengthened his position long before his accession to the throne by matrimonial alliances. He married the daughter of Taj-ud-din Yildiz the Governor of Kirman who later on had become King of Ghazi. He gave his daughter in marriage to Iltutmish and his sister to Nasir-ud-din Qubachah, the Governor of Multan and Uch.

Slave Dyansty

The dynasty founded by Aibak was called as slave dynasy

because it was founded by Aibak, a slave and ruled by most of slave kings and their kins. But Prof. Srivastava defies this concept saying that the rulers of this dynasty do not belong to the same lineage and also that they ascended on the throne after they were freed from slavery. Hence, it is a misnomer to call that a slave dynasty.

Achievements of Aibak

The infant kingdom of Delhi Sultanate was surrounded by dangers on all sides. Taj-ud-din Yildiz who occupied the throne of Ghazni also claimed the control of Hindustan. Shah of Khwarizm also was plotting against the Delhi authority. The Chandellas and Gahadawalas regained their lost position. Bengal and Bihar were already caught up in the grips of a revolution. Aibak saved the kingdom from all these menaces.

1. Taj-ud-din Yildiz was forced to leave Ghazni in 1208 owing to the pressure from the Shah of Khwarizm and he sought assylum in Punjab. Anticipating danger from Taj-ud-din, Aibak took effective steps to prevent Taj-ud-din from getting a foothold in Punjab. Besides he marched towards Ghazni and occupied the vacant throne. But since the citizens of Ghazni preferred Taj-ud-din to Aibak, he returned to Delhi without opposing Taj-ud-din. Afghanistan remained separate from the frontiers of Hindustan till the establishment of Moghul dynasty after 320 years.

2. He restored order out of chaos in Bengal. Ali Mardan Khan tried to succeed Ikhtiyar-ud-din who had already established the authority of Turks in Bengal. But the Khilji Lords raised a rebellion against Ali Mardan Khan. Aibak appointed him Governor of Bengal and brought peace in Bengal.

Aibak fell down from his horse while playing the game of polo and died in 1210 A.D.

Architecture

The Indo-Muslim architecture commenced from the short span of regin of Aibak. Vincent Smith infers that Aibak might have demolished at least twenty-seven Hindu temples and with those materials he built two mosques one at Delhi known as Quwat-ul-Islam, and other at Ajmer known as Dhai Din Ka Jhompara.

Religious Policy

Aibak did not possess religious toleration. During his campaigns against Anhilwara and Kalinjar, thousands of Hindus were enslaved and forced to convert to Islam at the point of sword. Vincent Smith explains this attitude as something natural for numerically inferior Muslims who tried to suppress the numerically superior Hindus.

Estimate

Even though Aibak ruled the Kingdom with full sovereignty, he neither issued any coin in his name nor ordered to read Khutba in his name. Anyhow his sovereignty is proved beyond doubt. His munificance earned for him the title of "Lakhbaksha" (giver of lakhs). In the midst of his preoccupations he found time to extend his patronage to men of letters like Hasan, Nizami and Fakruddin the historian of his period. His greatest achievement was that he severed India's connection with Ghazni and founded the first Muslim State with its base in India.

(II) ARAM-SHAH (1210-1211 A.D.)

Immediately after the death of Qutub-ud-din Aibak, in order to avoid any possible confusion, the Amirs and Maliks of Lahore placed Aram Shah, the son of Aibak on the throne. It is a point of doubt and dispute whether Aram Shah was the male heir of Aibak at all. For Minhaj-us-Siraj has clearly mentioned about three daughters only for Aibak. Abul Fazl considers Aram Shah to be a brother of Aibak. Aram Shah was an incompetent person to occupy the throne at that critical juncture. Nasiruddin Qubachah of Multan and Ali Mardan Khan of Bengal had already established their sway of independent power in thier regions. The kingdom began to disintegrate. Aram Shah was unequal to the task for which he was placed on the throne. In order to save the infant kingdom from its abrupt decline, the nobles of Delhi invited Iltutmish, the Governor of Badaun, to accept the crown. Iltutmish proceeded towards Delhi and routed and killed Aram Shah who opposed him on his way and ascended on the throne of Delhi in 1211.

(III) ILTUTMISH (1211-1236 A.D.)

"The greatest ruler of the Slave Dynasty," was the estimate of Prof. Iswari Prasad about Iltutmish who was a slave of the slave. His master Qutub-ud-din Aibak was a slave of Muhammad Ghori. Having been able to read out the greatness of Iltutmish from his face Ghori was said to have predicted about it to his slave Aibak. Shamsuddin Iltutmish, born in a Turkish family was sold to a merchant Jamaluddin by name, who in turn sold him to Qutub-ud-din Aibak in Ghazni. Iltutmish was both handsome and energetic. By dint of his ability he rose from position to position. After the capture of Gwalior, Iltutmish took charge of the fort. Subsequently he was appointed the Governor of Bulandshahr. Later on he became the son-in-law of Aibak and was made the Governor of Badaun.

Accession of Iltutmish

Since Aram Shah the successor of Aibak was incompetent to maintain and administer the kingdom, Iltutmish was invited by the nobles of Delhi to occupy the throne. Hence, Iltutmish marched towards Delhi and defeated Aram Shah, the Sultan at Jude and crowned himself in 1211 as the Sultan of Delhi.

Initial Impediments

Iltutmish had to face a number of formidable difficulties as soon as he ascended on the throne.

(1) The founder of the slave dynasty, Aibak ruled the country only for a very brief span of four years and he was mainly preoccupied in wars to consolidate his position. Hence, he was not able to establish a good administration in the country. It was entrusted upon Iltutmish to offer an efficient and stable Government to the Delhi Sultanate. Moreover, Iltutmish realised that the throne of Delhi was not a bed of roses.

(2) Tajuddin Yildiz, the ruler of Ghazni declared his claims over Delhi and treated Iltutmish as his vassal.

(3) Ali Mardan Khan of Lakshmanavati made himself up as an independent ruler of Bengal and thus, severed his connections with Delhi.

(4) Nasiruddin Qabachah of Sindh captured Multan and entered the Punjab. He also seized the city of Lahore.

(5) The Rajputs of Ranthambhor, Ajmer, Jalor and Gwalior threw off the Turkish yoke and asserted their independence.

(6) The Turkish nobles refused to obey the dictates of Iltutmish decrying that he was a slave of a slave. The supporters of Aram Shah brought out a rebellion in Delhi itself. Hence, Iltutmish's sway did not extend beyond Delhi and Badaun.

Achievements of Iltutmish

(1) At first Iltutmish took stern steps of suppression of the supporters of Aram Shah and Muslim Amirs around Delhi and in the Doab region through his tactful displomacy and thereby brought Delhi under his complete control.

(2) Iltutmish pretended to be subordinate to the ruler of Ghazni, Tajuddin Yildiz. But the moment when he was driven out from Ghazni by the Shah of Khwarism of Central Asia and took shelter in Lahore, Iltutmish marched against him and inflicted a crushing defeat upon him in the battle of Tarain in 1215. Yildiz was taken captive and subsequently put to death. Thus, he got rid of the danger from Ghazni.

Mongol Peril : Chengiz Khan

Tanujin, popularly called by the name of Changiz Khan was a mighty Mongol leader and was considered to be the Scourge of God. He posed a threat to the infant Delhi Sultanate in 1221. The Mongols had ravaged China, Central Asia and Western Asia. They pulled down the Khwarism Empire too and made Alauddin Mohammad its emperor to flee to the Caspian coast. His successor Jalaluddin Mangbarni sought asylum in the Punjab. The Mongols reached the Indus in 1220 in pursuit of the fugitive Prince Mangbarni. Iltutmish politely refused shelter to Mangbarni for he knew pretty well that the assylum would invite the danger of the devastation of the Mongols. The Mongols withdrew from the North-Western region without penetrating into the interior of India. Thus, Iltutmish had saved the infant Sultanate from the perilous Mongol invasions and attacks of Mangbarni.

Capture of Sind and Multan

While Jalaluddin Mangbarni took shelter in Punjab, he defeated Nasiruddin Qabachah of Multan with the aid of the local Khokhars. But when he left India Qabachah recovered Multan and Sind. Taking stock of the situation, Iltutmish attacked Qabachah from two directions and captured Lahore, Multan and Uch from him in 1228. This victory had raised the prestige of Iltutmish.

Recovery of Bengal and Bihar

Alimardan Khan was succeeded by Hisam-ud-din Ewaz in 1212. He too issued coins in his own name and collected tributes from the neighbouring provinces and thus, maintained his independence. After bringing North-West India into his control, Iltutmish now found time to devote upon Bengal's insubordination. He deputed his son Nasiruddin Muhammad to March against Bengal. Ewaz was defeated and killed in 1226. Bengal remained a vassal province till the death of Nasiruddin in 1229. After his death, another chief Balka Khilji, asserted his independence in Bengal. Iltutmish now led a second expedition to Bengal and killed the rebel Balka Khilji. Bengal and Bihar were recovered to the Delhi Sultanate.

War with Rajputs

Immediately after the death of Aibak, the Rajputs regained their independence. In order to re-establish the supremacy of Delhi over Rajasthan, Iltutmish launched a campaign in 1226. He laid seige over Ranthambhor and captured it. He defeated Udai Singh of Jalor, subdued Malayavarmadeva of Gwalior. Mandor, Ajmer and Jodhpur fell one after the other.

In Central India the Turkish armies fought unsuccessful wars against Trilokyavarma of Kalinjar and Kshetra Singh of Nagada. Anyhow Iltutmish entered Malwa and pillaged Bhilsa and Ujjain.

Reoccupation of the Doab

The Hindus living in the Doab region between Ganga and Yamuna declared their independence from Delhi. This was failed in Badaun, Kanauj and Benares also. Iltutmish reconquered those territories and reannexed Oudh also.

Administrative Services of Iltutmish

Iltutmish wanted to consolidate his kingdom by introducing a constitution to his administration. He invited Fakir-ul-Mulk, a Minister of the Caliph of Baghdad in order to streamline in administration. He divided his kingdom into provinces known as Igtas and every province was given to the charge of Igtadars. He established a corps of forty slaves in order to prevent the domination of Turkish nobles from occupying all the key positions of the Sultanate. Later on the slaves began to occupy important ranks of the administration. He was very keen on dispensing justice to the people. He installed a Bell of Justice in order to listen to the grievances of the citizens. He had equally devoted himself to the reforms in Royal finance. He introduced a purely Arabic coinage. This silver coin was 175 grains in weight with an Arabic inscription on it. He had displayed his interest in art and letters. He built the Qutub Minar in honour of the Muslim Saint Khwaja Qutub-ud-din Bakhtyar Kaki. He patronised men of letters like Minhaj-us-Siraj, the author of the Tabakati Nasiri and also Malik Tajuddin. Iltutmish was an orthodox Musalman. He was tolerant towards the Shia Sect of Islam but his intolerance towards Hindus was evident from the destruction of the temples at Bilsa and Ujjain. His political sovereignty was recognised and approved by the Caliph of Baghdad in 1229 who had offered him titles and insignia.

Estimate

The greatest achievement of Iltutmish was that he started a dynastic monarchy. In the task of empire building, Mohammad Ghori supplied the skeleton, Aibak infused the flesh and it was the task of Iltutmish to supply the blood and make it live. In short his accomplishments could be classified in three main elements :

1. He saved the infant Sultanate from the possible extinction.
2. He gave stability to the empire by an efficient administration.
3. He gave a legal status by obtaining an approval from the Caliph of Baghdad.

Contemporary historian Minhaj-us-Siraj praises his virtues in the following words, "Never was a sovereign of such exemplary faith, of such kindness and reverence towards recluses, devotees, divines and doctors of religion and law."

(IV) THE SUCCESSORS OF ILTUTMISH — RUKN-UD-DIN FIROZ (1236 A.D.)

Rukn-ud-din Firoz was the eldest surviving son of Iltutmish. Having known the incompetence of Firoz, Iltutmish nominated his daughter Raziyya to be his successor. But after the death of Iltutmish, the proud Turkish nobles violated his will because they hated to serve under a woman. Hence, they placed Rukn-ud-din Firoz on the throne of Delhi. Very soon they realised how accurate Iltutmish was in judging his son's capacities. Incompetent Firoz had immersed in sensuous pleasure and thereby earned unpopularity and hatred of the people. He left the administration to the hands of his ambitious mother Shah Turkan. She started taking revenge of her erstwhile enemies while she was a servant maid. Her headstrong temperament landed the country in troubles. She murdered Qutub-ud-din the younger son of Iltutmish and also conspired to kill Princess Raziyya. Her atrocities caused confusion in the country. Rebellions started everywhere. Ghiasuddin, the brother of the Sultan and Governor of Oudh raised a rebellion which was followed suit by the Governors of Budaun, Multan Hansi and Lahore. Saif-ud-din Hasan Qarlugh, the ruler of Ghazni invaded Sind and Uch. The discontentment of the public was exploited suitably by Raziyya who instigated the citizens of Delhi against Firoz by pointing out the atrocities of Shah Turkan and incompetence of Firoz and infuriated the mob. Shah Turkan and Firoz were imprisoned and put to death in 1236 A.D. Raziyya ascended on the throne of Delhi.

RAZIYYA (A.D. 1236-1240)

Raziyya, the first queen of Delhi Sultanate was not approved of her accession by all sections of the people of the country. The Governors of Badaun, Multan, Hansi and Lahore openly opposed her. Muhammad Junaidi, the Wazir of Rukn-ud-din also defied her authority. But very soon, through her wisdom, administrative efficiency, uprightness, and indomitable courage she was able to attract people to her side and thus was able to restore peace in the country. She had acquired sufficient training in the art of administration from the hands of her father. In spite of the weaknesses of her sex she dressed herself in the attire of men and transacted the business of the Government and went to the battlefield with the helmet and armour.

Rebellions that erupted against Raziyya

(1) The Mulahids and Kramids fanatics of Islam refused to accept the suzerainty of a female and fomented rebellions which were suppressed with an iron hand.

(2) The Governors of Multan, Badaun, Hansi, and Lahore openly defied the authority of Raziyya because they considered it to be a disgrace to submit to a lady on the throne.

(3) The opposition of Turkish nobles was very cleverly and easily tackled by Raziyya by means of sowing seeds of dissension among them and thereby she foiled their attempts of dethrowing her.

(4) She showed undue favours to an Abssinian slave named Jamaluddin Yaqut. This roused jealousy and indignation of "the forty" Turkish nobles. The elevation of Yaqut to the rank of the Master of Stables provoked them to murder him.

(5) A revolt raised by Kabir Khan Ayaz, the Governor of Punjab was easily put down. But another revolt staged by Altuniya, the Governor of Bhatinda caused her decline. She was taken a captive in the Altuniya when she marched against him. In the meanwhile the conspirators in Delhi placed Muizz-ud-din Bahran, a younger son of Iltutmish on the throne in 1240.

(6) Frustrated with the meagre reward from the conspirators, Altuniya married Raziyya and began to work for her claims of crown. The couple marched to Delhi where they were defeated. Both of them were murdered by Hindu robbers while they returned to Bhatinda.

Minhaj-us-Siraj, the contemporary historian explains the cause of her decline in the following words —

> "Was endowed with all the admirable attributes and qualifications necessary for a King but as she did not attain the destiny in her creation, of computed among

men, of what advantage were all these excellent qualifications to her?"

THE SUCCESSORS OF RAZIYYA

Muizz-ud-din Bahram Shah (1240-1242 A.D.)

Bahram Shah who was placed on the throne of Delhi by the mighty Turkish nobles was designed to act as a puppet in their hands. A new office named Naibi Mamlikat was instituted in order to bring the administration on efficient lines and Iktiyar-ud-din Itagin a powerful Turkish noble was placed incharge of that office. No cordial relationship existed between the Sultan and Itagin. Infuriated by the growing influence of Itagin, the Sultan got him murdered. Hence an alliance of conspiracy was formed by the Turkish nobles and was joined by the Muslim Ulemas. Internal dissension was added with external threat from Mongols. They ravaged the Indus Valley and captured Lahore. The imperial army sent to repulse the Mongols returned to the capital city being instigated by the intriguing Wazir Nizam-ul-Mulk against the Sultan. The Sutlan was imprisoned and murdered by the army in 1242 A.D.

Ala-ud-din Masud Shah (1242-1246 A.D.)

He was the grandson of Iltutmish and son of Rukn-ud-din Firoz. He too had become a puppet in the hands of the forty who were the king makers of the Delhi Sultanate. Among them Balban was the most influential figure. He dominated in the imperial affairs and also helped to establish tranquillity in the country. The provinces which were situated in far off places like Bengal, Uch and Mutlan began to severe their connections with Delhi. The Mongols once again appeared and occupied Multan and Uch. Masud Shah became a tyrant and drunkard at the end of his reign period. The confusion caused as a result of the Mongol avalanche created mutual jealousy among "The Forty". Balban played a leading role in the conspiracy of dethroning Masud Shah in 1246 and placed Nasir-ud-din the younger son of Iltutmish on the throne.

Nasir-ud-din Muhammad (1246-1265)

Nasir-ud-din Muhammad the fourth son of Iltutmish came to

power in 1246. He was a pious, simple and charitable man. Having seen the fate of the Sultans who preceded him, he had handed over the charge of the administration to the hands of "The Forty", which was dominated by Balban. Balban got his daughter married to the Sultan and thereby enhanced his prestige. He appointed his own men in the important key posts of the administration. He exercised complete royal authority, suppressed the rebellions, foiled the conspiracies and repulsed the Mongol attacks. His ascendancy had roused the jealousy of a section of the nobles and they plotted for the removal of Balban from his enviable position by poisoning the mind of the Sultan. The Sultan Nasir-ud-din Muhammad fell a prey to the traps of the conspirators. Hence, Balban was deposed from his office. But very soon the Sultan realised the might of Balban and reinstated him. Balban routed the Mongol invasions and subdued the Rajput Chieftains of Ranthambhor, Kalinjar, and Gawalior. Nasir-ud-din Muhammad had nominated Balban to be his successor since he had no male heir. Thus Balban who was so far exercising the legal powers as a *de facto* ruler now had become the *de jure* ruler also in 1266 A.D.

(V) GHIYAS-UD-DIN BALBAN (1256-1287 A.D.)

Early Career

The greatest Sultan of the Slave Dynasty was Ghiyas-ud-din Balban. He was born of an Ilbari Turkish family. His original name was Baharuddin. While young he was taken captive by Mongols and was sold to Khwaja Jamaluddin of Basra who in turn sold him to Iltutmish in Delhi. Iltutmish appointed Balban as his deputy for his keen intelligence, talents and loyalty. He was enlisted in the corps of forty slaves. Sultana Raziyya made him her chief huntsman Amir-i-Shikar. Her successor Bahram Shah rewarded him with the Jagir of Rewari. Masud Shah rewarded him with the district of Hansi. In 1245 he inflicted a crushing defeat upon the Mongols who had besieged Uch and recovered Uch from them. This achieved him the title of Ulugh Khan. He deposed Masud Shah and enthroned Nasir-ud-din Muhammad in 1246 as the Sultan of Delhi.

Balban the *De facto* Ruler

Balban administered the Sultanate for forty years, first as deputy of Sultan Nasiruddin and then himself as Sultan. During the reign of Nasiruddin, Balban acted as the *de facto* ruler. Since he was responsible for the enthronement of Nasiruddin, the Sultan gave him all powers of administration. Balban appointed his own men in all the vital posts of the Government. Further in 1249 he strengthened his position by giving his daughter in marriage to the Sultan. The Sultan remained contented with the life of a dervish copying the Koran.

Ramoval of Balban from the office

The ascendancy of Balban roused the jealousy of a section of the nobles and they plotted for the removal of Balban from the enviable position he was occupying in the palace. The Sultan fell a prey to the conspirators and dismissed Balban from service. Pandemonium prevailed everywhere. The Turkish nobles supported the cause of Balban and hence, the Sultan had to reinstate Balban in the office in 1254 A.D.

Balban's formidable tasks as the deputy of the Sultan

Balban took all possible steps to consolidate the authority of the Sultan. Bengal was once again brought under the control of Delhi in 1257. Balban subjugated the rebellious Hindu chiefs of the Doab. The rebellious tribes of Mewat were suppressed. He conquered Ranthambhor and launched an expedition against that of the Chandella chief of Kalinjar. The north-western territory became a perpetual place of problems because of the Mongol menace. Under these circumstances Nasiruddin died in 1266 and Balban assumed the reins of the Government.

Balban as *De Jure* Ruler of the Sultanate

Exaltation of the prestige of the Monarchy. Balban had faith in the divine right theory of kingship. He considered that the absolute authority alone could struck terror in the hearts of people and that would result in the obedience of the people to the monarch. He introduced the following measures in order to enhance the prestige and strengthen the authority of the crown :

(a) He claimed that he was a descendant of Afrasiyab, a hero in Turkish mythology. This feature gave him much desired respect.

(b) The Persian customs of the court were introduced in Delhi. Every one was ordered to lay prostrate before the king and kiss his feet as a mark of respect to the Sultan.

(c) Balban developed the habit of appearing always in regal robes. As familiarity breeds contempt, he cultivated dignified reserve and treated the nobles with neglect. He stopped talks with ordinary people. He disallowed the practice of drinking wine by the nobles and officials. He himself gave up wine and disassociated himself from all jovial parties. Even laughter was prohibited in the court.

(d) The Persian Nauroz festival was introduced. It added to the splendour of the court. Thus, Balban enhanced the status of the King from the debris into which it had fallen to the divine altitudes.

Emasculation of the Turkish Nobles

"The Forty" nobles of Turkish aristocracy who came into existence during the time of Iltutmish gained ground during the rule of his successors. They reduced the Sultan to a magnificent cipher. Balban lowered the prestige of "The Forty", and enhanced the dignity of the crown in the following ways :

(a) He elevated the Junior Turks to higher positions and brought them on a par with the forty nobles.

(b) Brutal punishments were meted out to the members of the forty even for simple crimes. Malik Baqbaq, the Governor of Badaun was publicly whipped because he had ordered one of his servants to be beaten to death.

(c) Haibat Khan, the Governor of Oudh was lashed 500 times for he was alleged to be a murderer.

(d) Amin Khan, another Governor of Oudh was ordered by Balban to march to Bengal in order to suppress the rebel leaders Tughril Khan. Since he failed in his mission, Balban ordered him to be executed.

(e) His own cousin Sherkhan, the Governor of Bhatinda was leading the Forty nobles and hence Balban get rid of him by administering poison to him.

Effective Espionage System

Balban had organised a very efficient spy system. It furnished him with exact and prompt information of the occurrences in the country. They were paid enormously and at the same time were taken to task for their failures in their duties. This espionage system served as a strong pillar for the preservation of the despotism of Balban.

Reforms in the Army

Balban realised that a very strong and well organised army was essential for the efficient administration of the country. He recruited more and better soldiers for the reorganisation of the army. Liberal promotions were given to those who had performed marvellous services in the battlefields. He changed the practice of granting lands to the soldiers in return for their military services because the successors of such soldiers were ill-suited for the discharge of military service. The lands were reallotted to the able-bodied soldiers. He appointed Imad-ul-Mulk as his army minister. The army minister enforced discipline and efficiency in the army.

Suppression of Rebellions in the Doab

Balban put an end to all the rebellions and disorders in the country with a firm hand. Doab and Oudh had become centres of rebellions. The dense jungles of Doab had offered sheltering grounds for the robbers and marauders. Delhi was exposed to the raids of the robbers every day. Balban provided security to the people of Delhi by hanging the robbers and rebels. He built four forts around Delhi and garrisoned them with Afghan troops.

Suppression of Rohilkhand rebellion

The rebellion roused in Rohilkhand was not able to be controlled by the Governor of Badaun. Hence, Balban marched towards Rohilkhand and slaughtered the rebels, seized their treasures and fetched them to Delhi. Balban also suppressed the Hindu rebels at Katchar with utmost cruelty. The entire male population of Katchar was put to death. Similar rebellions were suppressed in Mewar also.

Expeditions against Bengal

Tughril Khan, the Governor of Bengal raised the flag of insurrection in A.D. 1280, issued coins and made Khutba to be read in his name. Balban deputed Amin Khan Governor of Oudh to suppress the rebellion. But Tughril Khan routed him and sent him back. Balban sent two more expeditions and both of them ended in disastrous failures. Ultimately Balabn himself marched against Bengal at the head of an army of two lakhs. On hearing the impending disaster, Tughril Khan fled away from Lakhnauti. Balban chased him and got him executed. Balban inflicted in human barbarities against the followers of Tughril Khan by hanging them on the gillets erected on both sides of the bazaar of Lakhnauti. He appointed his second son Bughrakhan, as the Governor of Bengal. The revenging attitude of Balban could be clearly inferred from the words of warning to his son. "If ever designing and evil minded persons incite you to waver in your allegiance to Delhi and to throw off its authority, then remember the vengeance which you have seen exacted in the bazaar."

Mongol invasions

The incessant inroads of Mongols into Punjab caused continuous worries to Balban. Lahore, Multan and Uch were easy prey to their onslaughts. In order to arrest the penetration of the Mongols Balban erected a line of forts in the north-west frontier and garrisoned them with Afghan troops. He divided the north-west into two parts. The provinces of Multan, Sind and Lahore were put under the control of his eldest son Muhammad Khan and the provinces of Sunam and Samana under the charge of his second son Bughrakhan. At one time the two princes defeated and drove away the Mongols in 1279 A.D. But in 1286 A.D., Muhammad Khan lost his life in another encounter with the Mongols. The Mongols had their sway of authority extended up to the river Ravi in the Punjab.

Loss of the Prince Muhammad

The death of Prince Muhammad had left a rude shock on

Balban. The Prince was not only a great soldier and an excellent administrator but also a patron of art and letters. Balban had a great affection on the noble son and actually wanted to transfer the crown to him. It was an irreparable loss for him and it had a deleterious effect upon his health. After nominating Kal Khusrau, the son of Muhammad, as his heir-apparent, Balban went to the land of eternal rest in 1287 A.D. after a serious illness.

Estimate

Balban had patronised art and architecture. The Persian poet Amir Khusru, who was called as the Parrot of India adorned his court. Another poet Amir Hasan was also patronised by Balban. The services of Balban could be very well assessed in the words of Dr. Iswari Prasad, "All things considered, Balban was a most remarkable ruler who saved the infant Muslim State in India from the Mongol peril, and by establishing social order, paved the way for the military and administrative reforms of Alauddin Khilji. In the words of Lane-Poole, "Balban, the slave, water carrier, huntsman, general, statesman and Sultan is one of the most striking figures among many notable men in the long line of the Kings of Delhi."

KAIQUBAD (A.D.1287-1290)

Balban nominated Kai Khusrau, the son of Muhamad as his heir-apparent before his death. But the nobles set aside the nominee of the Sultan and enthrowned Kaiqubad the son of Bughrakhan. He ascended the throne with the title of Muiz-ud-din Kaiqubad while he was only 17 years old. Before his coronation he was a lad of discipline, virtues, and a teetotaller. But when he was placed on the throne, he found to his surprise all channels of pleasure open to him. He began to indulge in all sensuous pleasures and became a debauchee. Very soon the nobles realised that Kaiqubad was a wrong choice because during his reign period, the decline of the slave dynasty was quickened. Kaiqubad had become a puppet in the hands of one Nizam-ud-din who had all the powers invested in him. Kai Khusrau was murdered at the instance of the Sultan. Law and order situation in the country worsened. Hence, Bughrakhan came to Delhi at the head of an army to correct his son and to save him from the conspiracies of Nizam-ud-din. Bughrakhan advised his son to give up his vices and to drive out Nizm-ud-din from the position he was enjoying. Kaiqubad killed Nizam-ud-din by poisoning. The counsels of Bughrakhan had its impact upon Kaiqubad only for a brief period. Soon he resorted to his vices. Jalal-ud-din Firoz Khilji had now become the Commander of the army. Kaiqubad was afflicted with paralysis. Hence, the nobles enthroned Kaiqubad's infant son under the title of Shams-ud-din Kayumars. The nobles were hatching plots in order to get rid of Jalal-ud-din Firoz Khilji. But before the plots began to work Jalal-ud-din took the offence, murdered Kaiqubad and declared to be the regent of the infant Sultan in 1290 A.D. Soon the infant Sultan too was murdered and Jalal-ud-din ascended the throne of Delhi in the very same year. With the murder of Kayumars, the Slave dynasty lost its last ruler.

2

The Khilji Dynasty

(I) JALAL-UD-DIN FIRUZ KHILJI (A.D. 1290-1296)

Introduction

Jalaluddin Firuz Khilji, the founder of the Khilji dynasty was originally known as Malik Firuz. He hailed from the family of Khilji tribe of Turkey who had settled in Afghanistan. Jalaluddin entered into India and got recruited in the service of Balban. He was given the charge of the royal security force. Later on he was appointed the Governor of Samana in Punjab. He became the minister of the army during the period of Kaiqubad. The Turkish nobles hatched out a conspiracy against Jalaluddin who was mistaken to be an Afghan. In the conflict, Jalaluddin became victorious. Egged on by the excessive ambitions, Jalaluddin murdered the disabled Sultan Kaiqubad and then the infant Sultan Kayumars. Ultimately he occupied the throne of Delhi and thus, founded the rule of a new dynasty in 1290 A.D.

Oppositions for the accession of Jalaluddin

(1) Jalaluddin was 70 years old when he ascended on the throne of Delhi. The Ilbari Turks hated the sudden exaltation of Khilji Turks to the throne and opposed Jalaluddin's accession. Hence, he temporarily shifted his headquarters from Delhi to a suburban area called Kilokhri and there he celebrated his Coronation ceremony. He provided dwelling facilities for the nobles, Amirs and traders too in Kilokhri. Naturally Jalaluddin had an aversion for bloodshed and war. He displayed extreme sympathy and generosity even to his enemies.

(2) Rebellion of Malik Chajju

The new Balban and the Governor of Kara-Manikpur, Malik Chajju raised the standard of revolt against Jalaluddin. He was assisted by Hatim Khan, the Governor of Oudh. But the allied forced were rented out by the Royal forces at Badaun. Instead of punishing the rebel governors, they were released, pardoned and were offered a wine party. Such a type of treatment to the rebels was opposed by the supporters of the Sultan. Hence, the Jagir of Kara-Manikpur was assigned to his nephew and son-in-law, Alauddin.

(3) Once a thousand robbers who were disturbing law and order in the neighbourhood of Delhi were brought before him. Out of his extreme compassion he set them free and despatched them to Bengal. This only emboldened them to further their activities.

(4) Jalaluddin had deviated from this lenient policy in only one case. The followers of Sidi Maula, a Muslim Saint, conspired to murder Jalaluddin and enthrone the Saint. Having come to know this plot, Jalaluddin ordered the Saint to be trampled to death under the feet of an elephant.

Wars fought by Jalaluddin

(1) Jalaluddin launched an expedition against Ranthambhor in 1290 in order to recover it from the Chauhan Rajputs. Since there was a fierce resistance he returned to Delhi without besieging the fort. He did so because he did not want to shed the blood of Muslims for the sake of a fort. On his way back to Delhi, he captured Thain.

(2) He recaptured Mandawar from the Rajputs and conducted a second raid into Thain in 1292 A.D.

(3) In the very same year, Jalaluddin defeated a large army of one lakh and fifty thousand Mongols who threatened the city of Delhi. But they were permitted to retreat Ulugh, a descendant of Chingiz Khan, embraced Islam along with 4000 followers and settled down in Delhi. They were later on called as new Muslims who created disorder during the times of Alauddin.

(4) His nephew Alauddin invaded Malwa and captured Bhilsa in 1292 and hence was given Oudh also as token of his victory.

(5) In 1296, Alauddin led an another expedition against Devagiri and seized the enormous treasures from its King Ramachandradev. With the Deccan gold Alauddin triumphantly returned to Kara.

Murder of Jalaluddin 1296 A.D.

After his victory at Devagiri, Alauddin became ambitious of capturing power at Delhi. The officers at Delhi smelt and warned Jalaluddin not to trust too much his nephew. All these warnings vanished by the sweet coated words of Ulugh Khan, the brother of Alauddin. He said that Alauddin was afraid of Sultan's reprimand because of his expedition without the knowledge of the Sultan. Further he said that Alauddin had invited the Sultan to Kara in order to surrender the Deccan gold seized from Devagiri. In spite of the red signals from the officers, Jalaluddin proceeded to Kara where he displayed his immense love for his nephew. But the treacherous Alauddin ordered for the murder of the Sultan. Jalaluddin was beheaded and the head was brought in a procession in the capital city. While the blood was spilling from the head, Alauddin was declared to be the Sultan of Delhi in 1296 A.D.

Estimate

Jalaluddin was a benevolent ruler who had a deep love for peace in the country. He avoided wars and bloodshed as far as possible. But when he took military expeditions they were very severe which could be seen in the case of his conquest over the Mongols. According to A.L. Srivastava, "Jalaluddin was the first Turkish Sultan of Delhi who placed before him the ideal of benevolent Despotism."

(II) ALAUDDIN KHILJI (A.D. 1296-1316)

Introduction

Alauddin was the first Muslim imperialist and the first great Muslim administrator of India. The history of Muslim empire and Muslim administration in India really began with him. Alauddin,

Sher Shah, and Akbar — each marks a distinctive step in the evolution of Indo-Muslim history. Alauddin was the nephew and son-in-law of Jalaluddin Khilji. He was given the Governorship of Kara in 1292. His ambitions knew no bounds. He wished to become a world conqueror like Alexander the great. Hence, he murdered the Sultan Jalaluddin in 1296 in the most treacherous and cold blooded manner and ascended the throne of Delhi on 3rd October 1296.

Alauddin as Governor

(1) Alauddin raided Malwa and looted the city of Bhilsa in 1292, after obtaining the permission of the Sultan. The Sultan was much pleased with his victory and offered him with the charge of another Governorship of Oudh also.

(2) Alauddin was much allured by the enormous treasures of southern kingdoms. Fired by the excessive ambition, Alauddin marched against the Yadava Kingdom of Devagiri in 1294 even without the knowledge of the Sultan. The King Ramachandradev was defeated at Lasura. Ramachandradev came to terms with Alauddin, by ceding him the province of Ellichpur and paying large treasure.

Difficulties of Alauddin as Sultan

The Deccan victory of Alauddin made him to murder his uncle Jalaluddin treacherously who came to Kara Manikpur in 1296. He proceeded to Delhi and was duly crowned. He won over the nobles and the supporters of the former Sultan to his side by sprinkling gold and silver. The widowed queen Malikha Jahan put up the claims of her sons Arkali Khan and Qadr Khan to the throne. Alauddin defeated them quite easily and also imprisoned them. The Hindu vassals also started creating troubles in order to carve out their own independent Kingdom. Mongol invasions also added fuel to the fire of political confusion in the country. Alauddin ordered for the massacre of the New Muslims, the former Mongols who were pardoned and allowed to settle in the outskirts of Delhi.

Conquests of Sultan Alauddin

Alauddin was intoxicated by the easy, initial, incessant victories and hence, decided to become a world conqueror and also desired to become the founder of a New Religion in the world. But Malik-Ala-ul-Mulk, his friend brought him to senses not to entertain the idea of starting a religion but asked him to conquer the world first. For accomplishing this task, he had four most trusted generals namely Ulugh Khan, Zafar Khan, Nasrat Khan and Alap Khan.

North Indian Conquests

Gujarat (A.D. 1298)

Alauddin wanted to conquer almost all Hindu States and most of his conquests were unprovoked. Gujarat was the first victim of Allauddin's ambitious scheme of conquests. He deputed Ulugh Khan and Nasrat Khan the two generals to invade Gujarat. Rain Karan Dev II the King of Gujarat was defeated and his capital city Anhilwara was also captured. His beautiful queen Kamala Devi was taken to Delhi where she was married to Alauddin. Karan Dev and his daughter Deval Devi found asylum in the Court of Ramachandra of Devagiri. Further Nasrat Khan extended his ravages up to the port of Cambay. It was here that he found the young handsome Hindu slave Eunuch who had later on emerged as Malik Kafur the hero of Deccan expeditions of Alauddin. While the imperial army was marching back, a struggle was started on the war spoils by the new Muslims. But it was at once crushed.

Rajasthan

Ranthambhor (A.D. 1299-1301)

The next target of attack of Alauddin was the impregnable fortress of Ranthambhor, the capital of Chuhan ruler Hamir Dev. He provoked Alauddin by sheltering the new Muslims who had plotted against the Sultan. Hence, Alauddin sent a strong force under the command of Ulugh Khan and Nasrat Khan. The resistance of the Rajputs was strong enough and Nasrat Khan had lost his life in the siege. Infuriated by this shocking news, Alauddin himself had marched to the battle ground and won the war by seducing Ranamal, the Prime Minister of Hamir Dev. Hamir Dev, his followers and Ranamal too were punished to death. Ulugh Khan was entrusted with the administration of Ranthambhor.

Chittor (A.D. 1301)

Mewar became the next victim of Alauddin's expedition. Legends say that this expendition was conducted just to secure Padmini, a creation of peerless beauty wife of Rana Ratan Singh, the King of Chittor. The siege over Chittor prolonged for five months and ultimately the fortress fell. Hence, it was said that more than 10,000 Rajput ladies including Padmini performed Jauhar for they preferred death to disgrace. The episode of Padmini is considered to be simply a myth. But Alauddin renamed Chittor as Khizrabad and entrusted the administration with his son Khizrkhan. But the Rajputs drove away Khizr Khan and recaptured their Fort in 1311.

Malwa (A.D. 1305)

Another expedition was conducted at the head of Ain-ul-mulk the Governor of Multan over Malwa. Raja Mahlok Dev the King of Malwa was defeated and Malwa was annexed to Delhi. Soon the forts of Ujjain, Mandu, Dhar and Chanderi and Jalor also were captured in this campaign.

The Mongols

The Mongol raids proved to be a serious menace to the Delhi Sultanate. Between 1296 and 1308 a series of invasions were made by Mongols in Punjab, Multan, Sindh, Delhi and the Doab. Alauddin successfully repelled more than a dozen attacks of the Mongols. In one of the encounters Zafar Khan the military general of Alauddin realised the necessity of frontier defence and ordered for the erection of a chain of forts on the frontier and stationed garrisons there. Ghazi Malik was made the Governor of Punjab. Besides, the new Muslims of Mongol race who plotted to assassinate the Sultan were ordered to be massacred to the extent of 30 thousand by Allauddin.

Southern Campaigns

The immense wealth of Southern Kingdoms had snared and tempted Alauddin to invade them. Four powerful rulers dominated the South and they were always at logger heads and this rivalry among themselves provided an encouraging climate to Alauddin. They were Yadavas of Devagiri, Kakatyas of Warangal, Hoysalas of Dwarasamudra and the Pandyas of Madura. In addition to these four there were some minor rulers like Bhanudeva of Kalinga and Ravivarman of Kollam.

Devagiri (A.D. 1307)

Ramachandradev ceased to pay tributes for three years. Besides he was arranging the marriage of his daughter Deval Devi with Shankar Dev. Hence an expedition was ordered under the Generalship of Malik Kafur to subjucate Ramachandradev and to fetch Deval Devi to Delhi. Malik Kafur won a decisive victory and made Ramachandradev to pay huge indemnity. Deval Devi was taken to Delhi and married to Khizr Khan, the eldest son of Alauddin. Ramachandradev visited Delhi personally and accepted the suzerainty of the Sultan.

Warrangal (A.D. 1309-1310)

Alauddin sent an expedition under Malik Chajju in 1303 to conquer Warangal. But the imperial forces were inflicted a crushing defeat by Prataparudra II of Warangal. Hence, Alauddin despatched another expedition to wipe out the disgrace this time under the command of Malik Kafur. After a stiff resistance, Prataparudra II yielded to pay annual tribute to the Sultan. Besides Malik Kafur extracted an immense booty of 7000 horses, 300 elephants and a huge treasure from the King.

Dwarasamudra (A.D. 1310-1311)

Allauddin despatched an expedition against Hoysalas of Dwarasamudra in 1310 under Malik Kafur and Khwaja Haji. The troops crossed the Yadav Kingdom and got all possible help from the Yadava ruler. Vira Ballala III of Dwarasamudra was defeated and had given a huge amount of indemnity as a mark of his recognition of the overlordship of Allauddin.

Madura (A.D. 1311)

The Pandya King Maravarman Kulasekhara of Madura died and a war of succession followed between his two sons Sundara Pandya and Vira Pandya. Sundara Pandya appealed for rescue. Malik Kafur entered the Pandya Kingdom and plundered the city only on the plea of Sundara Pandya. Hearing the impending attack of Malik Kafur, Vira Pandya fled away from the capital and Kafur went up to Rameswaram to capture the fugitive Prince. The Madura campaign resulted in a huge booty of 2750 pounds of gold and 20,000 horses.

Last Expedition (A.D. 1313)

Shankardev, the son of Ramachandradev failed to pay annual tributes to Alauddin. He was defeated and killed by Malik Kafur in A.D. 1313. Kafur further proceeded Southwards and invaded the Hoysala Kingdom for a second time. All the four southern kingdoms accepted the overlordship of the Sultan. But they were not annexed to the Delhi Sultanate.

Conclusion

Alauddin was a successful conqueror who knew no failures. Alauddin Khilji can be considered to be the first Muslim emperor of India. During his period of reign for the first time the crescent dominated over the whole country from the Himalayas to the Cape Comorin.

Administration of Alauddin Khilji

Introduction

Alauddin Khilji was the first Muslim ruler who introduced a systematic administration for the Delhi Sultanate. The previous slave dynasty rulers based their state simply on force. But Alauddin made a bold experiment in innovating administrative methods. This administrative machinery was successfully utilised by the later Muslim rulers in India.

Alauddin's Views on Religion

Alauddin believed in the divine right theory of kingship and also that the monarch is endowed with superior wisdom. He firmly believed that his will should become law of the land and did not tolerate any force that hindered his powers. He had precluded himself from the controls of the nobility and the Ulemas. Moreover he diminished the status of the nobles merely as servants who could be appointed and dismissed at the will and pleasure of the Sultan. It was Alauddin who had brought the

Ulemas also under the control of the sovereign for the first time. He did not even seek for the approval of the Khalifa and yet he appeared to be a devout Mussalman.

Persecution of the Hindus

With regard to the Hindus, Alauddin followed the traditional Muslim policy of persecution and plunder. The land revenue was raised to one-half of the gross produce. Alauddin imposed new taxes like the grazing tax and the house tax long with other taxes on Hindus. Moreover the collection of the revenue was made very strict. The Hindus were reduced to such abject misery that the Hindu wives were forced to seek service in Muslim houses. The people were so much preoccupied with the means of winning their bread that the very name rebellion was never mentioned.

Suppression of Rebellions

The beginning of Alauddin's reign period was marred by a number of rebellions. In 1298, the "new Muslims" revolted against Alauddin because of their discontentment over the spoils of the expedition against Gujarat. The next rebellion was staged by Alauddin's own nephew Akat Khan. The third rebellion was raised by his two other nephews at Badaun and Oudh. The fourth one was caused by Haji Maula a disaffected officer who had murdered the Kotwal of Delhi. Alauddin had crushed all of them severely with brutal punishments. Such frequent rebellions forced Alauddin to conduct an enquiry over the causes of rebellions and came to certain conclusions. They were (1) inefficiency of the espionage system (2) the use of liquor by the people (3) the inter-marriage among the nobles and (4) the excessive wealth in the hands of certain people. Alauddin promulgated four ordinances to prevent the recurrence of rebellions.

The Four Ordinances

1. He aimed at the confiscation of property held by private people. The inams and religious endowments were confiscated. The revenue officials were asked to extract as much money as possible from the privilege class. This ordinance was so sweeping that according

to Barani gold was not to be seen except in the houses of nobles.

2. Secondly he reorganised the spy system on efficient lines. They were stationed in all important places including the houses of nobles. The spies had to inform even the most trivial matters to the Sultan so much so even the gossip of nobles and officers had to be reported.
3. Alauddin ordered for the prohibition of liquors and he himself had given up that habit. But later on the ordinance was relaxed to nobles alone.
4. The last ordinance had forbidden the nobles to organise social parties and settle marriages without the prior permission of the Sultan.

Reorganisation of the Army

Alauddin realised the necessity of a standing army, recruited, equipped and paid by the Sultan himself, and he did so. The former Sultan depended upon the irregular forces supplied by the nobles. Hence, Alaudin reorganised the army under the control of a minister for army namely Ariz-i-mamalik. The nobles were prohibited from maintaining order to avoid fraud by proxy. The system of branding horses to prevent false musters was introduced. According to Ferishta, Alauddin's army consisted of 4,75,000 cavalry. The strength of the infantry must have definitely far exceeded the number of cavalry. Above all these things, Alauddin had bestowed his personal attention over the reforms in the army.

Control of the Market

The maintenance of a large standing army necessitated the cheapening of the necessaries of life. Alauddin appointed two officers known as Diwan-i-Riyasat and Shahana-i-Mandi to control the market. The prices of all essential commodities were fixed. Hoarders, speculators and black-marketeers were punished severely. Grains were stored in the State Grannaries for the times of drought. Here we can find out the foresighted Sultan Alauddin. Barani testifies to the fact that scarcity of grain was not felt even during the times of drought. With regard to the fixation of prices, it is generally believed that it must have been confined only to Delhi and its suburbs.

Revenue Policy of Alauddin

1. It was Alauddin who had devoted attention for the first time over the formulation of a good policy of taxation. He took various steps for augmenting the revenue of the state. He collected one-half of the gross produce from the Hindus and one-fourth from the Muslims as land revenue. In addition to the land revenue, house tax, grazing tax and import, export duties were also imposed. Besides these taxes, the Hindus had to pay the Jizya tax too.
2. Alauddin had confiscated the lands enjoyed by Muslims as inams, pensions and endowments.
3. All the privileges enjoyed by the Hindu revenue officials were abolished.
4. He introduced a new system for measuring the lands on the basis of standard yields. Thus, the State's exchequer was greatly enriched.

Alauddin's patronage of Arts and Crafts

The Royal Court was adorned by a large number of poets and scholars. Amir Khusru was the most popular among them. He wrote a book named Tarikh-i-Alai, in which the conquests of Alauddin were described. Another of his book deals with the love story of Khizr Khan and Deval Devi. He was also a musician called by the popular name Parrot of India. Amir Hasan was another scholar who enjoyed the patronage of Alauddin. Kabiruddin and Amir Assalan Koti were the eminent historians patronised by Alauddin.

Alauddin was also an enthusiastic builder of forts and mosques. He was the builder of new city called Siri adjoining the old City of Delhi. He was the builder also of the Alai Darwaza, "the most beautiful and perfect specimens of early Turkish architecture."

Defects of his system

Dr. Iswari Prasad points out the following defects in the administration of Alauddin's political system. It was based on unsound foundations. A lot of discontentment amongst the various sections of society was created by his policy. The Hindu rulers wanted to recover their lost territories. The nobles hated the restrictions imposed upon them. The merchants opposed the market regulations The Hindu people felt aggrieved over their humiliation. Overcentralisation, repression and espionage undermined the authority of the Sultan. The paramount mistake of Alauddin was that he allowed Malik Kafur to become all powerful.

Estimate

Alauddin's reign has three features of permanent interest. In the first place he was the first Muslim ruler of Delhi to create an empire embracing the larger portion of India. Secondly, he had some sort of administrative cohesion to the Turkish empire in which the creation of a standing army was a creditable achievement. Thirdly, despite his ruthless measures for the suppression of the Hindus, he was a bold innovator in respect of the relation between the State and the Islamic Law.

(III) THE SUCCESSORS OF ALAUDDIN

Conditions immediately after the death of Alauddin

The mantle of administration was caught in the hands of Malik Kafur, the indomitable military general of Alauddin. To retain all the powers in his hand, he had arranged for the nomination of Shihabuddin Umar, a six years old son of Alauddin. Kafur put the minor son on the throne and became the *de facto* ruler of the empire. Kafur married the wife of Alauddin and acquired precious treasures. He had blinded Khizr Khan and Shadi Khan the sons of the late Sultan also. Another son Mubarak Shah and his queen mother were imprisoned. Kafur ordered for blinding Mubarak too, but the soldiers turned sides and murdered Kafur himself. Hence, Mubarak, after escaping from the conspiracy of Kafur, acted as the regent of Shihabuddin. Then Mubarak usurped the throne by blinding Shihabuddin in A.D. 1316.

Qutb-ud-din Mubarak Shah (A.D. 1316 to 1320)

Mubarak began his reign well. He released many prisoners and relaxed Alauddin's despotic rule. He restored the confiscated lands to their owners, and repealed his father's economic regulations. The sudden liberalisation of the administration encouraged lawlessness and the Sultan's licentiousness provided chances for rebellions to erupt. Soon Mubarak became a puppet in the hands of a vile favourite named Khusrau, originally a Hindu belonging to a military caste "Baradu." Two rebellions had broken out, one in Gujarat and another in Devagiri. The rebellion in Gujarat was quelled and Harapala, the ruler of Devagiri was flayed alive.

Mubarak's infatuation for Khusrau had the most tragic result. In July 1320, the Sultan was murdered by Khusrau's men, the Baradus.

Nasir-ud-din Khusrau Shah (A.D. 1320)

Khusrau had ascended the throne under the title of Nasir-ud-din Khusrau Shah. No scion of the Khilji dynasty was left alive. Deval Devi the widow of Khizr Khan was dragged into Khusrau's harem. Originally a Hindu and later on converted to Islamic faith, the Sultan Khusrau had wounded the feelings of the orthodox Muslims by desecrating the Koran.

Ghazi Malik, Governor of Depalpur, took upon himself the task of punishing the infidel traitor. In September 1320 he defeated Khusrau near Delhi. The adventurer was captured and beheaded. The successful conqueror was hailed as Sultan of Delhi by the assembled nobles and came to be known as Ghiyas-ud-din Tughluq Shah. Barani says, "Islam was rejuvenated and a new life came to it. Men's minds were satisfied and their hearts contented."

3

The Tughluq Dynasty

(I) GHIYAS-UD-DIN TUGHLUQ (A.D. 1320-1325)

Ghiyas-ud-din Tughlug the founder of the new dynasty "Tughluq" was probably a Qarauna Turk of humble origin. Ferishta fixes that his father was a Turkish slave of Balban and his mother to be a Jat woman of Punjab. His accomplishments against the Mongol raids raised him to a prominent place in Alauddin's reign. At the time of his accession he was fairly an aged and experienced warrior. He ruled the Sultanate only for a period of five years and in that short span he proved his worth to be an able and emergetic administrator.

Ghiyas-ud-din Tughluq's administrative measures

At the outset he set himself to the task of replenishing the depleted treasury due to the lavish extravagance of Mubarak and Khusrau. He recovered all the lands taken by fraudulent methods. He saved the peasants from excessive taxation by reducing the State's demand to one-tenth of the gross produce and also giving remission of taxes during times of famine. Ghiyas-ud-din Tughluq was an efficient administrator. Agriculture was encouraged; Canals were excavated for irrigation purpose. Taxation system also underwent reforms. Proper arrangements were made for the collection of revenue and the auditing of accounts. The departments of justice and police were also reformed. Excellent postal arrangements were made. Corruption was stamped out from the country by appointing upright governors and by recruiting people with better salaries to public offices on the basis of merit.

Fall of Kakatiya dynasty (A.D. 1321)

In the Deccan Prataparudra, the Kakatiya ruler of Warangal refused to acknowledge the suzerainty of the new dynasty. Ghiyas-ud-din sent an expedition against Warangal under the Crown Prince Juna Khan. On his arrival at Warangal Juna Khan besieged the fort. Epidemics broke out in the camp. Besides a rumour that the Sultan was dead in Delhi was also spread. Believing the story, Juna Khan raised the siege and returned to Delhi. Two years later, he led another expedition to Warangal and compelled Prataparudra to surrender. Then he was sent to Delhi. Barani tells us that Warangal was renamed as Sultanpur and Telingana was put under the control of Muslim officers. But epigraphic evidence refers to Prataparudra as the king reigning even in 1326.

Ma'abar and Jajnagar

After the subjucation of Warangal, Juna Khan led an expedition to Gutti and Madura (1323). It was followed by a raid into Jajnagar (Orissa) where Juna Khan captured 40 elephants. Juna Khan was given a hero's welcome by the jubilant Sultan. But the merriment was marred by the sudden raids of Mongols over Samana after crossing the Indus. But the Mongols were beaten back.

Rebellion in Bengal (A.D. 1324)

Bengal was ruled independently by the scions of Balban. Till 1322 it was ruled by Shamsuddin Firuz Shah. After his death a war of succession arose between his sons Shihabuddin, Nasiruddin and Ghiyas-ud-din. Ghiyas-ud-din, who had been enjoying practical independence for some years as Governor of Sonargaon now occupied Lakhnauti from Shihabuddin. The disturbed condition in Bengal attracted the attention of the Sultan. He marched towards Bengal in A.D. 1324. Nasiruddin who in the meantime occupied Lakhnauti, joined with Sultan at Tirhut, Ghiyasuddin Bahadur was defeated, captured and sent as a prisoner to Delhi. Nasiruddin was recognised as the vassal ruler of North Bengal with his capital at Lakhnauti. Eastern and Southern Bengal's with their capitals respectively at Sonargaon, Satgaon were incorporated with the Sultanate and Baharam Khan was deputed to govern them. The Sultan returned with a large booty, defeating the Hindu ruler of Tirhut on the way.

Death of Ghiyas-ud-din Tughluq (A.D. 1325)

While the Sultan was returning from Bengal, he was received at Afghanpur near Delhi by Juna Khan in a specially constructed pavilion, which was "so designed as to fall when touched in a certain part by the elephants." At his son's request the Sultan allowed the elephants brought from Bengal to be paraded around the pavilion. When the elephants came into contact with the weaker part of the structure, the pavilion gave way and the Sultan was crushed to death in 1325. Historians hold different views on the question whether Juna Khan was a parricide.

According to the contemporary chronicle of Ibn-Batuta, an African Muslim, whose travel diary is well-known for its authenticity, the collapse of the pavilion was due to a premeditated plot of Juna, who got the pavilion so constructed that it would collapse, when trodden by elephants.

(II) MUHAMMAD-BIN-TUGHLUQ (A.D. 1325-1351)

Introduction

After the death of the Sultan, Ghiyas-ud-din Tughluq, the Prince Juna Khan, ascended the throne of Delhi. The murder that was committed by Alauddin was open and bold. But the murder that was executed by Muhammad-bin-Tughluq was most tactful so that even historians like Saxani are made to believe that pavilion accident was only casual incident. Like Alauddin, Muhammad-bi-Tughluq too scattered gold and silver to the people of Delhi in order to hide the blood tinge. Anyhow Muhammad-bin-Tughluq occupies a unique place in the history of the Delhi Sultanate.

His Administrative Measures

1. Diwan-i-Kohi

The Sultan realised the importance of agriculture and created a separate department known as Diwan-i-Kohi in order to promote agriculture. The Sultan provided financial aid to the farmers so that more lands could be brought under cultivation.

Landless people were allotted lands. All these schemes did not bear desired results because the funds were misappropriated by the officers.

Oppressive taxation in the Doab (A.D. 1325-1327)

Another of the Sultan's earliest measure was the enhancement of the rate of taxation of the Doab. The purpose of this measure was varied according to various scholars. To some it was just to replenish the treasury of the depleted coffers, to some it was just to execute his plans of conquest while some others say that the object was to punish the Hindus of the Doab. In any case, the people who were already heavily taxed under the Khiljis suffered untold miseries and sought solace in emigration particularly as the new taxation coincided with the outbreak of famine. The peasants who were fleeing their villages were surrounded by the imperial forces to coerce them to pay the taxes. The peasants who could not pay were hunted down like animals. After teaching a lesson to his people, the Sultan arranged for the ameliorative measures like agricultural loans, sinking of wells, free feeding of the destitute. But these measures came too late and the Doab did not recover its prosperity.

Gurshasp's rebellion (A.D. 1326)

In 1326, Baha-ud-din Gurshasp, a cousin of the Sultan and Governor of Sagar claimed the throne and revolted. The Sultan at once marched against the rebel, and defeated him. But he escaped to the Court of Hoysala Ballala III, who, however, handed him over to the Sultan. Gurshasp was flaged alive, his cooked flesh was sent to his wife and children. Besides the stuffed skin of Gurshasp was taken in rounds through the important cities as a token of warning against the recalcitrants.

Transfer and Retransfer of Capital (A.D. 1326-1327)

Gurshasp's rebellion probably suggested to the Sultan that Delhi was far north and that a more central capital would help prevent rebellions. He decided to shift the capital to Devagiri. The motive behind this move might have been to ward off the frequent Mongol invasions or to secure the proximity of the newly acquired southern kingdoms. It was not a novel experiment in those days. What Muhammad wanted was only to have a second capital. But the follow up measures which he undertook were ill-considered and irrational. He renamed Devagiri as Daulatabad and ordered his officers and courtiers to move into the new capital and build new houses for themselves. He himself beautified and enlarged the city. He ordered the whole population of Delhi to migrate to Devagiri, a distance of 700 miles.

The people had undergone untold sufferings during the exodus. The people not only had to forego their belongings but also their pleasant memories of their long association with Delhi. Many people perished on the way. Not even a cat or dog was allowed to remain at Delhi. It is said that even a blind man was forcibly dragged to Daulatabad. The City of Delhi which ranked with Cairo and Baghdad was almost deserted. The north-western frontier was exposed to the Mongol invasions. After seventeen years the fickle minded Sultan realising his folly ordered the retransfer of the capital of Delhi (1344). As Lanepoole observes, "Daulatabad was a monument of misdirected energy." The Sultan's mistake was that he had unnecessarily ordered for the entire population to move from Delhi.

Introduction of Token Currency (A.D. 1329-1330)

Muhammad has been described by a modern numismatist as a 'Prince of Moneyers'. He reformed the coinage and attempted the issue of token currency. Faced with an acute shortage of money caused by his lavish gifts and the necessity of meeting the ever increasing military expenditure, he was forced to try this new experiment. Token currency was in use in China and Persia in the thirteenth century. Muhammad had probably heard of it and wanted to introduce the change in his own currency.

Without consulting his ministers, the Sultan ordered bronze or copper coins to be issued and allowed them to circulate on par with gold and silver like legal tender. The experiment ended in a colossal failure. The Sultan took no step to prevent the circulation of counterfeit coins. Barani says that the house of every Hindu was turned into a mint. Gold and silver were hoarded, and taxes were paid in forged coins. Trade came to a state of flux. Commerce was paralysed. The foreign merchant refused to accept the token currency. When the confusion became worse confounded, the Sultan withdrew the token currency. He paid for every copper coin brought to the treasury at its face value in gold and silver. The people made enormous profits at the cost of the treasury which suffered a very heavy drain. The scheme failed on account of lack of proper safeguards than on account of any inherent defect. It was a daring and costly experiment.

Muhammad's religious attitude

Muhammad followed the model of assertion of the supremacy of sovereign over the religious leaders. He did not seek for the recognition of the Khalifa. He simply ignored the canon law and followed the dictates of his own reason to pronounce political judgments. He did not admit the Muslim theologians to interfere in the judicial administration and the Ulemas in the State affairs. On the other hand Muhammad appointed even non-religious persons also as judges. He showed respect for Hinduism and appointed Hindus to prominent positions. The net effect of all those measures was that he incurred the displeasure of the Ulemas and orthodox Muslims.

Like Balban he believed that the Sultan was the shadow of God on earth. He stood for absolute monarchy. But in the late years of his reign, because of his growing unpopularity, he tried to re-establish his position among the Ulemas by paying his homage to the Khalifa and requesting the Khalifa to confirm him as the Sultan of Delhi. All coins bore the name Caliph and all royal orders were executed in his name. But all these measures only augmented his worries and did not save him from imminent fall.

Conquests of Muhammad-bin-Tughluq

Central Asian Expedition

Like Alauddin Khilji, Muhammad entertained wild schemes of external conquests, but while the former gave up his wild plans on the advice of the Gazi the latter would not take advice. He first planned to conquer Khurasan (East Persia) which was in a disorderly condition being ruled by a dissolute prince Abu Said. He also thought of conquering Transoxiana and Iran. Not minding the difficulties of transport across the Hindu-Kush mountains he galleried a big cavalry force of 3,70,000. The army was paid for one full year and could not be paid for the second year. The scheme was finally abandoned. This was an example of his unpracticable plans.

Conquest of Nagarkot (A.D. 1337)

Nagarkot was a fort in the Kangra district of the Punjab ruled by an independent Hindu king. Muhammad led an expedition against the fort in 1337 and captured it. But he gave the fort back to the Hindu king on condition of paying tribute. This was his only victory after ascending the throne.

Expedition against Qarajal (A.D. 1337-1338)

Ziauddin Barani and Ibn Batuta clearly describe Muhammad's expedition against Qarajal, a Hindu kingdom situated at the foot of the Himalayas. But some writers like Ferishta have attributed this expedition to the Sultan's visionary scheme of the conquest of Tibet and China. This expedition against Qarajal was perhaps directed against some refractory Himalayan Chieftains. A force of 1,00,000 horse was sent but the campaign ended in great disaster. The Delhi soldiers who were accustomed to fight in the warm plains against weak princes, failed in the cold terrain and against hardy mountaineers. The entire army was destroyed except ten horsemen who returned to tell the tale. The angry Sultan immediately ordered their execution.

Relations with China (A.D. 1341)

The Chinese emperor Toghan Timur, sent an ambassador to the Court of Muhammud in 1341. He requested Muhammad's permission to rebuild the Buddhist temples which were destroyed during the Sultan's expedition to Qarajal. Muhammad deputed Ibn Batuta to China replying the emperor that the canons of Islam forbid the reconstruction of temples if the Jizya tax was not paid.

Mongol Menace (A.D. 1328-1329)

The transfer of the capital from Delhi to Daulatabad was an advantage to the Mongols. Tamashirin, the Mongol ruler of Transoxiana played havoc in the region extending from Lahore to Multan in the neighbourhood of Delhi. According to Ferishta, instead of fighting, Muhammad purchased peace by offering the Mongols gold and silver. This unwise policy had greatly undermined the military prestige of the Sultanate.

Rebellions

The ill-timed and absurd projects of the Sultan made him unpopular. The sufferings of the people were aggravated by the natural disaster like famine and plague. The pent up feelings of the people found expression in a number of rebellions. There were about 22 rebellions in the country. In 1337 Fakruddin Mubarak Shah asserted independence in East Bengal and struck coins in his own name. In 1339, West Bengal declared independence under Ali Shah.

In South India, Kapaya Nayaka recaptured Warangal and founded his kingdom. Hari Hara and Bukka founded the Vijayanagar empire in the South. The Amirs of Daulatabad rose in revolt and founded the Bahmani Kingdom in 1347. Sayyed Ahsan Shah, the Kotwal of Ma'bar proclaimed his independence in A.D. 1334-35. There were revolts in Sindh, Malwa and Gujarat also. He described his helpless condition in the following words : "So in my kingdom disorders have broken out, if I suppress them in one place, they appear in another."

The Sultan passed away in 1351. Badauni remarks, "The king was freed from his people and they, from their king."

Character and Estimate of Muhammad

The character of Muhammad is a matter of disputed discussion. Muhammad was undoubtedly a versatile genius. He was a scholar in a number of subjects like logic, mathematics, philosophy, astronomy and so on. He composed verses in Persian. He was a "veritable wonder of creation" with an unfalling memory and unrivalled eloquence. He generously gave alms to innumerable beggers. He adhered to the sacred tenents of Islamic faith in his private life.

In spite of all these accomplishments, he also possessed a number of vices. He inflicted barbarous punishments even for petty offences. He was narrow minded and cruel. Ziauddin Barani and Ibn Batuta remark that some dead bodies were hung always at the gates of the Sultan's palace. He presented thus, "an amazing compound of contradiction." Elphinstone suspects whether Muhammad had some mental derangement.

A balanced view would hold him neither a lunatic nor a monster but a mixture of opposites." He lacked practical judgement and sense of proportion with the best of intentions, he undertook many projects. But he failed miserably because he was not a practical minded man.

According to Lanepoole, "With the best intentions, excellent ideas, but no balance or patience, no sense of proportion, Muhammad-bin-Tughluq was a transcendent failure."

(III) FIRUZ TUGHLUQ (A.D. 1351-1388)

Early Life

Firuz was the son of Rajab, Ghiyas-ud-din Tughluq's younger brother. His mother was a Bhatti Rajput lady. Muhammad treated Firuz with affection and confidence since Muhammad had no male heir, he nominated Firuz as his successor.

The accession of Firuz (A.D. 1351)

When Muhammad-bin-Tughluq died suddenly at Thatta his army became leaderless and was thrown into utter confusion. The rebels of Sind began to harass the army and plunder the camp. Under these circumstances, Firuz was crowned by the generals in 1351. This at once resulted in the restoration of some order in the army. In the meantime, Khwaja Jahan, the Governor of Delhi had set up in the interest of peace a boy on the throne of Delhi, a "suppostitious child" of the late Sultan. When Firuz returned to Delhi, the aged Governor gave up the pretender and submitted to him. The new Sultan pardoned Khwaja Jahan and granted him the fief of Samana. Later on he was murdered by the jealous nobles.

Character of Firuz

Firuz Shah was a mild and peace loving king. He was a bigoted Muslim, who regarded the Quran as his only guide in all matters. Generally he avoided war and bloodshed but he would never shed Muslim on any account. He loved ease and pleasure as much as he loved peace and Quran. He entrusted his administrative responsibility to his able Wazir Khan-i-Jahan Makbul and led comparatively a quite life.

Services of Malik Maqbul

The sympathetic, generous and good nature of the Sultan was well reflected in his administration. Though he failed as a general he won 'Victories of Peace' and his reign provided the much-needed peace and calm after the storm of the previous reign. A large part of the credit of his Government goes to his minister Khan-i-Jahan Makbul, a Hindu covert, who was Governor in Telengana. As Prime Minister, he shaped the administrative system of Firuz Tughluq.

Relief Measures

People were fed up with the chaotic rule of Muhammad Firuz Tughluq at first tried to win over the people by writing off all the pending debts due to the State from the people. He paid them compensation for their losses during the reign of his predecessors. His reign was marked by a high degree of economic progress coupled with comparative prevalence of peace and prosperity.

Revenue Policy

Firuz proudly claims credit for abolishing many unlawful taxes levied during the previous regime, in his autobiography. As a matter of fact, the system of taxation was placed on the Quranic basis, and the work was entrusted to Khwaja Husan-ud-din, to fix up the land revenue for the whole kingdom. Four main taxes were levied; Kharaj (land tax). It was 1/10 of the produce. Khams was 1/5 of the war booty acquired during the war. Jizya was poll tax payable by non-Muslims and Zakat was 2½% of the property collected from the Muslim to be spent for religious purposes. Later on, a fifth tax was added; an irrigation tax payable by cultivators who used water from the State canals. By this liberal taxation policy people were encouraged to produce more and become prosperous.

Works on Irrigation

Agriculture was promoted by means of excavation of five

important canals dug from the rivers Sutlej and Yamuna. One of them was 150 miles long carrying waters from the Yamuna to the city of Hissar in the Punjab. 150 wells were dug for irrigation purposes as well as for the use of travellers. Consequently new lands were brought under cultivation and these works increased the fertility of the Doab and the Delhi region. About 1200 orchards were laid out around Delhi.

Works of Public Utility

Firuz was a zealous builder of towns and mosques. He was the founder of towns like, Jaunpur, Firuzabad, Fatehabad and Hissar Firuza. He built 4 Mosques, 30 Palaces, 200 Caravan Sarais, 5 Hospitals, 5 Reservoirs and 100 Bridges. Two monoliths of Asoka were brought to Delhi, one from a village near Khizrabad on the Jumna, the other from Meerut. Firuz had 36 Karkhanas under State management, divided into two groups, those providing daily food for men and animals, and those dealing with commodities produced by human labour.

Judicial Reforms

In the Judicial department Muslim law reigned supreme. Firuz rendered a great service to the people by abolishing torture and inhuman forms of punishment. He imposed mild punishments on criminals. For some of these reforms the Sultan was probably indebted to his competent Wazir Khan-i-Jahan Makbul, a converted Hindu of Telengana. His philonthropical measures included the setting up of an employment bureau, a free hospital which supplied both medicines and food to the patients, and "a charity bureau" which paid dowries to Muslim brides belonging to middle-class families.

Promotion of Learning

An orthodox Sunni, Firuz was naturally interested in the spread of Islamic learning. He built many madrasas which were liberally endowed. Many learned divines and scholars enjoyed his patronage. The celebrated historical works of Barani and Sham-i-Siraj Afif, both bearing the name of Firuz were written during his reign. He himself was the author of Fatuhat-i-Firuz Shahi. After the conquest of Nagarkot a large library fell into the hands of the Sultan. Under his orders 300 such Sanskrit works were translated into Persian. He maintained magnificent Court of Delhi.

Religious Policy

Firuz was a bigot Sunni Mussalman. He respected the Ulemas very much and got their counsels in all vital matters. Firuz proved his orthodoxy by an ostentation display of loyalty to the Caliph, whose deputy he claimed to be in India. On his coins, his name was printed side by side with that of the Caliph. Twice he received patents and robes from the Caliph. He enticed people to embrace Islam by exempting them from Jizya tax.

Firuz appeared to be devil inernate in the eyes of Hindus. He was delighted in persecuting not only the Hindus but also the Shias and other Muslim heretics. He had proudly claimed that he killed the leaders of infidelity who seduced others into error, destroyed Hindu temples like Jwalamukhi temple of Nagarkot and Jagannath temple of Puri and built mosques in their places.

A Brahmin was burnt alive for the crime of preaching his religion. At Katchar, he came to know that two Sayyids were put to death. Immediately he ordered for the general massacre of all Hindus of that place. Thousands of them were enslaved and converted to Islam.

Slave System

Firuz ordered his officers to capture prisoners at the time of war and make them slaves. The total number of royal slaves were estimated at 1,80,000 of whom 40,000 were employed in the Sultan's palace. They developed a strong *espirit de corps* without any loyalty to the head of the State. A separate department was established for the proper management of the slaves. There was a separate treasury for payment of their salaries. Slavery had become a potential source of danger to the decadent Sultanate.

The Revival of the Jagir System

In spite of the inherent defects in the Jagir system Firuz unwisely and foolishly consented for the system. Jagirs were granted to military officers. It greatly undermined the authority of the Sultan.

Reforms in the Army

Firuz introduced certain changes in the army which led to the dissolution of the empire very soon. He weakened the military organisation by his misplaced generosity. The regular soldiers were sanctioned lands which yielded sufficient income for their livelihood. The others were paid a share of the war booty. Afif says that Firuz promulgated an order to the effect, "when a soldier grows old and incapable, his son shall succeed him as his deputy; if he has no son, his son-in-law, and failing any son in law, his slave shall represent him." Thus, military service became hereditary and merit was overlooked. It led to corruption and inefficiency in the army. The annual inspection of the cavalry horses was rendered ineffective by the prevalent corruption, which was sometimes even encouraged by the Sultan.

Defects of his administration

Firuz Tughluq's chief weakness was his mildness. He ruled the country during the period which required a strong Central Government and military despotism of the type of Alauddin Khilji and not a mild Government.

Secondly, the Jagir system which was abolished by Alauddin Khilji, was revived by Firuz Shah. All military and civil officers became landholders of the feudal type. The revival of the hereditary feudal nobility undermined the strength of the Sultan.

Thirdly the slave system had a demoralising effect on society and Government. The slave system brought loss to the Central exchequer. Besides the slaves indulged in plots and intrigues and when the opportune time came, they shook up the Delhi Sultanate.

Fourthly, his anti-Hindu policy severely affected the interests of the State.

Lastly the Sultan failed miserably to reconquer the territories which assumed independence during the later years of Muhammad-bin-Tughluq reign. He also failed to destroy the newly established Bahmani Kingdom.

Estimate

Firuz is eulogised for his just merciful and benevolent rule. His far-reaching reforms contributed to the material prosperity of the people. His benevolent reforms like writing off the taqavi loans, abolition of unjust taxes, his constructions, the steps taken by him for the promotion of learning, the employment bureau and the setting up of departments like Diwan-i-Khairat speak volumes of his munificence.

In spite of all these good traits, he was not without vices too. His bigotry, revival of Jagir system, failure to recover the lost territories, institution of slave system and administrative measures contributed to a large extent to the downfall of the Delhi Sultanate.

Firuz Tughluq's Foreign Policy

Introduction

Firuz Tughluq was a pious and passive type of Muslim. He did not have the required boldness and spirit for conducting wars which are the essential qualities of an efficient king in those days. He was a man of indecisive nature and hated wars and bloodshed. He met with failure during the times of rebellions caused by various vassals like Bengal. He had no inclination to recover Deccan. When his officers advised him to reconquer the Bahmani kingdom, he shed tears and said that he decided not to wage wars against Muslims.

Expedition to Bengal (A.D. 1353-1354, 1359-1360)

Firuz led two expeditions to Bengal which ultimately failed to achieve their purpose. Shams-ud-din Iliyas had brought both Lakhnauti and Sonargaon under his independent rule. He also marched against Tirhut to annex the kingdom in 1353. The Sultan marched against Iliyas at the head of an army of 70,000 strong against Bengal. On the Sultan's approach Iliyas left his capital and took shelter in the strong fort of Ekdala. After a long drawn battle, Iliyas was defeated without capturing the fort, the Sultan returned to Delhi in September, 1354.

Sikandar Shah, the son of Shamsuddin Iliyas was ruling over Bengal. Firuz Tughluq undertook another expedition against Bengal in 1359 on the plea of helping Zafar Khan, a son-in-law of a previous Sultan of Eastern Bengal. Sikandar Shah, the son and successor of Iliyas like his father took shelter in the fort of

Ekdala and ably defended himself. Since it was rainy season, the area was flooded and hence, the Sultan was forced to come to terms with Sikandar Shah. Bengal remained independent.

Expedition to Orissa (A.D. 1360)

After his expedition to Bengal, Firuz led an expedition to Jajnagar (present day Orissa). The Hindu King of Jajnagar fled from his capital city. Firuz occupied Puri and desecrated the great temple; the idol of Jagannath was either thrown into the sea or taken to Delhi to be trodden under foot by the Muslims. The Hindu King promised to send Delhi 20 elephants every year as tribute.

Conquest of Nagarkot (A.D. 1365)

The City of Nagarkot, with its fort called Kangra was captured by Muhammad-bin-Tughluq but soon it became independent. In 1365, Firuz led an expedition against Nagarkot. After a siege of six months, Firuz compelled the Hindu chief to submit, although the fort could not be seized.

Expedition to Sind (A.D. 1365-1367)

Firuz fitted out an expedition against Jhatta, the capital of Tam Babaniya of Sind, for his disloyalty to Muhammad-bin-Tughluq. Firuz left Delhi in 1365 at the head of an army of 90,000 horses and 480 elephants. The ruler of Jhatta strongly defended his fort. The imperial army was severely affected by famine and pestilence. Firuz gave the siege and led his army to Gujarat. On his way, the Sultan got stranded in the Rann of Cutch along with his army. No news of the army reached Delhi for six months. In the meanwhile, Khani-i-Jahan Maqbul the minister sent fresh reinforcements to the successor of the Sultan. With the help of his additional army the Sultan attacked Jhatta for the second time. Tam Babaniya submitted and promised to pay tribute.

Failure of reconquer Deccan

After his return to Delhi, Firuz declared that he would never again wage war but for the suppression of rebellion. He kept up this promise. The Bahmani kingdom was founded in 1346 by Hasan Gangu Bahman and later on an invitation to interfere into the affairs of the Bahmani kingdom was given to him. The Sultan refused to act during these periods and failed to recover Deccan. Moreover Vijayanagar kingdom was established in 1336, and Warangal became independent in course of time. The Sultan simply ignored the disintegration of his empire.

The policies of Firuz which caused the break up of the empire

The contribution of Firuz Tughluq towards the disintegration of Delhi Sultanate was great.

(1) The Jagir system which was abolished by Alauddin and Muhammad bin Tughluq was revived by Firuz. By this large areas were assigned to important persons instead of paying them their salaries. Jaunpur, Gujarat and Bihar were given to the charge of people who later on became recalcitrant and severed from the control of Delhi. They became independent. Jaunpur became independent under Khwaja Jahan. This was followed by Gujarat, Malwa and Khandesh too. Gwalior became an independent Hindu state. The Doab region became a hot bed of intrigues and rebellions of Hindus. All these disintegrations were caused by the revival of Jagir system.

(2) Firuz Tughluq developed a huge system of slavery. He had a collection of 1,80,000 slaves out of which 40,000 were deputed for royal palace service. The maintenance of this corps incurred heavy drain on the exchequer and so they all became a liability. Moreover they indulged in secret plots and conspiracies against the Sultan himself.

(3) The principle of the organisation of army was based on unsound footings. The payment of the army personnel was made by transferrable assignments of the royal revenue. In turn they sold those assignments to others. This caused a fall in the standards of the army. Moreover the military service was made hereditary by Firuz and this also led to corruption and inefficiency in the army. With this inefficient army supplied by his nobles, the Sultan could not accomplish anything tangible.

(4) Firuz's bigotry and his delight in persecuting Hindus created unrest in the country. At Katchar alone, he massacred thousands of Hindus and demolished their homes. He himself

proudly claimed that he killed the leaders of infidelity, demolished Hindu temples and built mosques in their places. Hindus were converted to Islam in large numbers by the bait of exemption of Jizya tax.

(5) Firuz's failure to annex Bengal, his retreat from Sind and Gujarat, his unwillingness to reconquer Deccan, his reluctance to shed the blood of recalcitrant Muslims and all other military failures of the Sultan had led to the decay and downfall of his empire.

Sir Wolsely Haig remarks that military might and alertness in military expeditions, the indispensable qualities of a military despot were not found in the person of Firuz and hence he proved to be a dismal failure in consolidating and maintaining the army intact.

(IV) TIMUR'S INVASION OF INDIA (A.D. 1398)

Early Career

Timur-i-Lang was born in 1336 at Ketch near Samarkhand in Transoxiana. At the age of 33, he was able to assume the leadership of the Chaghai Turks through his skill and tact. Before invading India, Timur had established a vast empire comprising of Transoxiana, Persia, Iraq and Afghanistan. He did not like to expand his empire in India. But his prime motive behind the Indian invasion was to plunder and destroy the infields and idol worshippers. He himself had declared his purpose of Indian invasion "My object in the invasion of Hindustan is to lead an expedition against the infields... to convert to the true faith the people of that country, and purify the land itself from the filth of infidelity and polytheism."

Conditions that prevailed in India on the eve of Timur's invasion

After the death of Firuz Shah, in 1388 Ghiyas-ud-din Tughluq II, succeeded. He was killed and succeeded by Abu Baker in 1389. Soon he was forced to abdicate the throne in 1390 by Muhammad who assumed the Sultanate under the title of Nasir-ud-din Muhammad. He died in 1394 and was succeeded by his son Alauddin Sikandar Shah who also died of illness within six months. He was succeeded by his younger brother Nasiruddin Mohammad Shah in 1394. A war of succession took place between Nasiruddin Mohammad and Nasrat Khan a son of Fateh Khan and grandson of Firuz Khan. The civil war continued for three years. There was anarchy and disorder in the kingdom. For some time, there were two rival Sultans — one at Delhi and the other at Firuzabad.

Timur's Invasion

Under such circumstances, Timur invaded India in 1398 and gave a stunning blow to the tottering empire. Timur's expedition started by means of an advance guard sent at the head of his grandson Pir Muhammad. Pir Muhammad crossed the Indus in September 1398, and entered the Punjab. He captured strategic places like Uch, Multan, Dipalpur and Pakpatan. Then he reached the banks of Sutlej and stayed there. An immense booty fell into his hands.

Timur started his personal expedition in April 1398. He passed through the Khyber Pass, entered the Punjab, and plundered the people of Dipalpur and Pakpatan. Then Timur joined with Pir Muhammad near Sutlej. They crossed the river and attacked the fort of Bhatnir. Its King Rai Dulchand put up a stiff resistance but had surrendered ultimately. Timur ordered a general massacre of its citizens. The entire city was burnt and demolished.

Then he proceeded to Delhi. On the way he ravaged the cities of Sirsa, Fatehabad, Aharwan and Tohana. On the eve of the occupation of Delhi, Timur ordered a general massacre of all Hindu prisoners in his camp 100,000 in number, for he was afraid that on the day of battle they might "break their bonds, plunder out tents, and join the enemy." At Tohana alone 2,000 Jats were massacred.

Capture of Delhi (17th December 1398)

The Sultan of Delhi Nasiruddin Mahmud and his Prime Minister Mallu Iqbal were informed of the impending catastrophe. They put up a feeble resistance to the invader. Timur was assisted by able commanders namely Pir Muhammad, Amir Yadgar Barlas and others. The great battle was fought on the outskirts of Delhi. The resistance became futile, the invaders entered the city triumphantly. On 18th December 1398 Timur defeated and occupied Delhi. Mallu fled to Baran and the Sultan to Gujarat. The catastrophe caused by the Timur's invasion was beyond all imagination. The whole country was bled white. Plundering and devastation went on for several days. The huge number of people who were put to swords were commented by a Muslim chronicler in the following way; "High towers were built with the heads of Hindus and their bodies became the food for ravenous beasts and birds.... Much of the inhabitants as had escaped alive were made prisoners."

Return Journey of Timur

At Delhi, Timur was joined by Sayyid Khizr Khan, who had been expelled by a rival from the Governorship of Multan in 1395-1396. He accompanied Timur as far as the borders of Kashmir. Timur left Delhi in January 1399, and marched to the north-east, occupying Meerut, Kangra and Jammu. Khizr Khan was appointed Governor of Multan, Lahore and Dispalpur. Timur crossed the Indus in March 1399, "after inflicting on India more misery than had ever before been inflicted by any conqueror in a single invasion."

Results of his Invasion

(1) Timur's invasion left Delhi a desolate City. Badauni says that "the City was utterly ruined, and those of the inhabitants who were left died, while for two whole months not a bird moved a wing in Delhi."

(2) Chaos and confusion prevailed throughout the length and breadth of the country. To add to the misery of the people, famine and pestilential diseases also broke out.

(3) The Tughluq empire was shattered into pieces. The Sultanate existed only in name. It became a provincial kingdom and lost any pretence to an all-India character. The provincial Governors and the fief holders of Northern India, became independent. The Sultan's authority remained confined to Delhi. Khwaja Jahan of Jaunpur, Muzafar Shah of Gujarat, Dilawar Khan of Malwa and Ghalib Khan of Samana severed their connections with Delhi and asserted their independence.

(4) Khizr Khan who was appointed as the Viceroy of Timur ruled the territories of Multan, Lahore and Dipalpur. These regions also severed from the Delhi empire.

(5) North-West India and the Punjab were plundered and devastated by Timur. The whole country was bled white. Especially great cities like Dipalpur, Pakpatan, Bhatnir, Meerut and Kangra were deprived of their wealth and beauty.

(6) Massacre of Hindus in large scales, building of towers with their skulls, demolition and desecration of Hindu temples by the invaders widened the gulf between the Hindus and Muslims in India. The Hindus considered Muslims as devils incarnate and coexistence was impossible for the people of these two religions.

(7) Timur carried off not only immense wealth from India but also a large number of captives, to Samarkand. Among the captives were many skilled artisans, including some masons who were sent to Samarkand for the construction of a great Mosque there. Indian art and architecture found its entrance into Transoxiana.

(8) Babur the founder of the Mughal dynasty claimed descent from Timur and on this basis he claimed throne of Delhi also. Thus, Timur's invasion paved the way for the establishment of the Mughal empire by Babur in A.D. 1526.

Hence, it can be concluded that the invasion of Timur gave a stunning blow to the Sultanate and in particular it hastened the decline of the Tughluq dynasty.

4

The Sayyid Dynasty (A.D. 1414-1451)

Khizr Khan (A.D. 1414-1421)

After the death of Nasir-ud-din Mahmud, the last ruler of the Tughluq dynasty, in 1413, the nobles chose an Afghan noble Daulat Khan Lodi by name for the throne of Delhi. In 1414, Daulat Khan Lodi was defeated by his more ambitious rival Khizr Khan. He was the founder of the Sayyid dynasty. He did not assume any royal title. He professed to rule as the Viceroy of Timur's son and successor Shah Rukh. His dynasty has been called the Sayyid dynasty because it was believed that he was a descendant of Prophet Muhammad.

With his accession, Punjab, Dipalpur, and parts of Sind came under the control of the Sultanate. Bengal and Deccan were lost to the Sultanate even in the middle of the 14th century. Jaunpur, Malwa, Gujarat and Khandesh became independent. His reign of seven years was an unending story of fighting the rebels at one place or the other. Most of his expeditions were unsuccessful and in return he obtained only "small payments and large promises" which were not kept up. He sent frequent expeditions to suppress the turbulent Hindus of the Doab, but no attempt was made to subjugate the provinces which had seceded from the Sultanate. Khizr Khan's authority was confined to Delhi, the Doab and the Punjab.

Mubarak Shah (A.D. 1421-1434)

Khizr Khan was succeeded by his son Mubarak Shah. He assumed the royal title of Shah, while his father called himself, till his death, the Governor of Timur's dominions. Mubarak fared no better than his father in re-establishing the old kingdom. He occupied the throne for about 13 years but a few expeditions against the Khokars of the Punjab and the Hindus of Katehar, Mewat, and the Doab exhaust the pages of the history of his reign. Mubarak Shah fell a victim to the conspiracy hatched by Sarwar-ul-Mulk his own Prime Minister and lost his life.

Muhammad Shah (A.D. 1434-1445)

Mubarak was succeeded by his nephew Muhammad Shah. He was elevated to the throne by the nobles of Delhi and with their help he succeeded in killing the ambitious Sarwar-ul-Mulk. The independent ruler of Malwa advanced as far as Delhi with a view to capture in haste to save his own capital from a threatened attack by Ahmad Shah of Gujarat. Bahlul Lodi, the Afghan Governor of Sirhind, helped the Sultan against the ruler of Malwa. As a mark of appreciation for his help, Muhammad Shah rewarded him with the title of Khan-i-Khanan and publicly addressed him as his son. Pretending to be loyal, Bahlul Lodi, occupied the major part of the Punjab. The ambitious Lodi was also instigated by the Khokars to seize the throne of Delhi. His abortive attempt on Delhi in 1443 failed. Hence, Lodi retreated. The Sultan's authority was defied everywhere. Even the Amirs who were at the distance of 20 miles from Delhi began to withdraw their allegiance. Multan severed its connections with Delhi. Muhammad Shah passed away in 1445 after nominating his son Alauddin as his successor.

Alauddin Alam Shah (A.D. 1445-1451)

Muhammad Shah was succeeded by his son Alam Shah, the weakest of the Sayyid princes. Bahlul Lodi occupied Delhi in 1451 with assistance of Hamid Khan, the Wazir of Alauddin. Alam Shah who had already established his residence at Badaun, resigned his crown without opposition. He continued to live at Badaun and rule over a tiny principality till his death in 1478. The traitor Hamid Khan was later on arrested with the resignation of Alauddin, the Sayyid dynasty came to an end in A.D. 1451 and Bahlul Lodi ushered in the Lodi dynasty.

5

The Lodi Dynasty (A.D. 1451-1526)

Introduction

The Lodis, the successors of the Sayyids, belonged to a tribe of Afghans. The succession of Bahlul Lodi marked the commencement of the first Afghan kingdom in India, while the preceding dynasties were all Turkish. The Lodis were better fighters than their predecessors. They succeeded in re-establishing the prestige of the Delhi kingdom to a great extent.

Bahlul Lodi (A.D. 1451-1489)

Bahlul Lodi the Governor of Sirhind overthrew the tottering Sayyid dynasty and founded the Lodi dynasty in 1451. He was a capable and ambitious man but he had the wisdom to realise that the Sultanate could no longer be restored to its former power and prestige. He got rid of the able but treacherous Wazir Hamid Khan who had helped him for elevation to the throne.

Soon after his accession he led an expedition against Multan' but during Multan absence from Delhi, the capital was attacked by Sultan Mahmud Sharqi of Jaunpur Mahmud Sharqi was the son-in-law of Alam Shah the last ruler of the Sayyid dynasty. Hence, he marched against Delhi for seven times in order to wipe out the disgrace caused to his father-in-law Bahlul Lodi hurried back to Delhi and forced Mahmud Sharqi to retreat. The defeat of Mahmud enhanced the prestige and power of Bahlul. Bahlul began a long drawn war against Jaunpur which resulted in the defeat of Hussain Shah Sharqi and the incorporation of his kingdom in the Sultanate (1479). The Governorship of Jaunpur was entrusted to his eldest son Barbak Shah. This success of the Sultan forced the nobles of Kalpi, Dholpur, Basi and Alipur to acknowledge the overlordship of the Sultan. He also undertook a successful expedition against Gwalior.

Though Bahlul Lodi raised the prestige of the Delhi empire which had gone down during the regimes of the later Tughluqs, Bahlul Lodi was not successful enough to revive the past glory of the Sultanate.

Sikandar Lodi (A.D. 1489-1517)

Nizam Khan the third son of Bahlul Lodi, ascended the throne with the title of Sikandar Lodi. His assumption of the charge of the sovereign was disputed by his eldest brother Barbak Shah of Jaunpur. Sikandar Shah suppressed the rebellion with an iron hand. However, he reinstated his brother to power after appointing his own Afghan men in the important posts of the administration. But the Zamindars of Jaunpur defied Barbak Shah because of his incompetence and invited Hussain Shah of Jaunpur to occupy the throne. Hussain Shah came at the head of a large army, but he was defeated and forced to take asylum in the territory of Alauddin Hussain Shah of Bengal. Sikandar Lodi completely annexed Jaunpur and Bihar. The Sultan invaded Bengal, but a treaty of non-aggression followed and confrontation were avoided. He also made successful expeditions against Chanderi and Nagpur. Sikandar Lodi is specially remembered for founding the City of Agra in 1504.

Sikandar Lodi was no doubt the greatest of three Lodi Sovereigns. He exalted the prestige and power of the Sultan. His administration was noted for its efficiency. He made arrangements for audit of the Afghan nobles and misappropriation of public accounts were severely punished. Roads were made safe and irrigational facilities provided for the benefit of the peasantry. He had knowledge of Persian poetry and he patronised learned men.

But he was a bigoted Mussalman. He destroyed many Hindu temples including those at Mathura. He imposed several social disabilities on the Hindus like prohibition of Hindus from bathing in Yamuna. In this respect he anticipated Aurangazeb.

Ibrahim Lodhi (A.D. 1517-1526)

He was the eldest son of Sikandar Lodi. He was proud and wanted to establish some forms of royalty. He decided to crush the power of the nobles who were the source of the intrigues and conspiracies in the past. He wanted to humble them by all means. He gave the same treatment to the highest Afghan nobles and his lowest subjects. He ordered them to stand before him withfolded arms. He gave severe punishment to some prominent nobles even under the trivial pretext. The nobles at first tied to curtain the power of the Sultan by placing his brother Jalal Lodi, on the throne of Jaunpur. Soon some of the experienced nobles realised their mistake and deserted him. Hence, Jalal had to seek shelter at Gwalior. Ibrahim captured Gwalior and Jalal was captured in Gondwana and murdered. Ibrahim Lodi dismissed Azam Humayun, the Governor of Gwalior on grounds of suspicion and also suppressed the rebellion ruthlessly which followed the dismissal. Azam Humayun and his son Islam Khan were defeated and killed. Many prominent nobles defied his authority and were in a rebellious mood.

The discontent of the nobles gradually reached its climax. Daulat Khan Lodi, the Governor of the Punjab and Alam Khan, the uncle of Ibrahim extended an invitation to Babur to invade Hindustan. Daulat Khan wanted to utilise Babur as an instrument to establish his authority in the Punjab and put Alam Khan on the throne of Delhi. In 1524 Babur invaded the Punjab and occupied Lahore. Because of differences with Daulat Khan, he could not proceed further. In 1526, Babur won the battle of Panipat and captured Delhi and Agra. In the words of Ishwari Prasad, "The battle of Panipat placed the empire of Delhi in Babur's hands. The power of the Lodi dynasty was shattered to pieces and the sovereignty of Hindustan passed to the Chaghtai Turks."

Thus, it is seen that there was instability and uncertainty throughout the period of the Lodis. Hence, it is not an exaggeration to describe them as phantom or unreal Sultans of Delhi.

6

Decline of the Sultanate

Introduction

The Delhi Sultanate was founded by Qutub-ud-din Aibak in A.D. 1206 and it reached its apex of glory during the period of Muhammad-bin-Tughluq. The Delhi Sultanate at that time included the whole of India excepting Orissa, Assam, Nepal and Tamilnadu. Such a vast and extensive empire reduced into a small principality around Delhi during the times of Nasir-ud-din Muhammad Tughluq, the grand nephew of Muhammad-bin-Tughluq. A sarcastic remark was passed commenting on the very limited area "The rule of the Lord of the world extends from Delhi to Palam." This pitiable plight went on for some more years and ultimately the kingdom passed into the hands of Babur who founded the Moghul empire in A.D. 1526. A number of causes had contributed towards the decline and downfall of the Delhi Sultanate. They are analysed one after the other.

Personal despotism

The Delhi Sultanate was at typical oriental despotism. This despotism required a strong personal ruler at the head of the State. Everything went on well so long as strong and capable rulers were at the helm of affairs. But once the strong hand was removed, the collapse of the Sultanate became inevitable. Rulers like Balban and Ala-ud-din Khilji were strong and powerful. But many other Sultans who loved ease and pleasure were too weak to suppress the recalcitrant provincial Governors.

Undue centralisation and unwieldy nature of the empire

Sultan was vested with all powers concentrated in himself.

In course of time, the extent of the empire exceeded the saturation point. Hence, the evils of centralisation began to operate. Excessive work brought senselessness at the centre and paralysis at the extremities. The unwieldy size of the empire caused provincial revolts and it haunted the emperor with the phantom of the domestic traitor. When the Sultan was not able to control the country's administration, the provincial Governors asserted their independence, *i.e.*, Malabar, Bengal, Vijayanagar, Bahmani. Finally the vast empire was reduced to ridiculous extent of spreading from Delhi to Palam.

The Reign of Muhammad

The decline of the empire had its origin — in the miscalculated policies of Muhammad-bin-Tughluq. The repressive taxation of the Doab, the transfer of capital from Delhi to Devagiri, the issue of token currency, the disastrous failure of his grand expedition to conquer Khurasan, all these depleted the State treasury. They created popular discontent which caused the outbreak of nearly twenty rebellions. Vijayanagar was established in 1336. Bahmani kingdom was founded in 1347 at Gulburga. Bengal, Sindh, Malwa, Gujarat and Malabar carved out their own independence. The repressive measures of Muhammad-bin-Tughluq sowed the seeds of disintegration of the empire.

The Role of Firuz Tughluq

Firuz Shah's policy of peace did not arrest the decline of the empire. The fortunes of empire might have been revived if Firoz had been a strong and able ruler, but he was a weak minded bigot who was afraid of war and carried generosity beyond its logical limit. He revived the much despised Jagir system and encouraged the slave system. He made no serious attempt to recover the lost provinces of the Deccan, Bengal, Sind and Rajasthan. On the other hand he acknowledged the independence of those principalities which had broken away.

The Power of the Nobles

The Delhi Sultans could not built up an absolute Government largely due to the power of the amirs. These nobles of the Court could not be easily cowed down as the Sultan himself required their help both in civil and military matters. They received payment by means of Jagirs. They were aiming at augmenting their power and prestige in the Royal Court for which they indulged in intrigues, conspiracies and civil war to the detriment of the stability of the Sultanate. Thus, the Jagir system was the bane of the Muslim Kingdom.

The Anti-Hindu Policies of the Sultans

Most of the Sultans of Delhi were religious bigots. They were intolerant towards the Hindus. They considered it their primary duty to demolish and desecrate the temples, build mosques in their places and convert Hindus to Islam on a large scale. Alauddin Khilji reduced the Hindus to the position of hewers of wood and drawers of water. Firuz Tughluq demolished the sacred Jagannath temple of Puri and threw the idol into the sea. He imposed Jizya on the Brahmins also. Sikandar Lodi, an other fanatic destroyed the Hindu temples like Mathura, Utgir and Mandrel. He prohibited Hindus from bathing in the river Yamuna. All these repressive measures had wounded their feelings and this pent up feelings of the Hindus found expression in a number of revolts against the authority of the Sultan.

Timur's Invasion of India (A.D. 1398)

The invasion of Timur and the inhuman atrocities committed by him had given a death blow to the already tottering Delhi Sultanate. He massacred over a lakh of Hindus in Delhi. Famous cities like Dipalpur Pakpattan, Meerut, Haridwar and Bhatnir were plundered and razed to the ground. There was no sovereign on the throne of Delhi for three months. He left India in 1399 "after inflicted by any conqueror in a single invasion." The Delhi Kingdom lost all its glory and power. The kingdom was confined only to a few districts around Delhi.

Responsibility of Ibrahim Lodi

The last Sultan Ibrahim Lodi also contributed his share for the downfall of the empire. He was proud and insisted on some forms of royalty. He forced the nobles of his court to adhere to certain forms of obeisance. He harassed and humiliated the nobles in many ways. When the treatment became highly unbearable a group of discontented party invited Babur to invade Hindustan. Babur seized this opportunity. He defeated and killed Ibrahim Lodi in the first battle of Panipat (1526). So, Ibrahim Lodi, by means of his unstatesman-like policies and acts drove the last nail into the coffin of the Delhi Sultanate.

The Disintegration of the Empire

The power and authority of the Delhi Sultans gradually disappeared from a number of regions from the time of Muhammad bin Tughluq. A number of independent states rose up and thereby they caused decline of the Sultanate :

(a) Jalal-ud-din Hassan the Governor of Madura proclaimed his independence in 1335.

(b) In 1336 A.D. Hari Hara and Bukka founded the Vijayanagar empire and in the same year Kapaya Nayaka recaptured Warangal.

(c) In 1347 A.D., the Amirs of Daulatabad rose in revolt against Muhammad-bin-Tughluq and contributed to the establishment of the Bahmani kingdom under Allauddin Hasan at Gulbarga.

(d) In 1345 A.D. Bengal became free from the control of Delhi under the leadership of Haji Iliyas. He also collected tributes from the kings of Orissa and Tirhut.

(e) Khwaja Jahan rose to power at Jaunpur and established an independent State for himself in 1391 A.D. Jaunpur challenged the authority of the Delhi Sultans and created lot of hardships to the Lodi Kings.

(f) In 1401 A.D. Gujarat and Malwa became independent.

(g) The Rajputs of Mewar carried on a long-drawn battle against the Sultans and they had determined to recover their lost glory and prestige by any means.

The Immediate Cause

It was the defeat of Ibrahim Lodi at the hands of Babur in the first battle of Panipat in 1526 A.D. which led to the Mughal conquest of India. While Babur's troops were hardy mountaineers, Ibrahim's men were only accustomed to fighting in the plains in a warm climate. Their attack was weak and half-hearted. Babur was well versed in tactics like ambush. The Afghan forces were not attached to their king because of his proud, uncompromising attitude towards them. Within half a day the Afghan forces were "laid in the dust."

7

The Administrative System of the Delhi Sultans

Kingship, A Theocracy

The Delhi Sultanate was basically a theocracy in which the Sultan was endowed with both the powers, *i.e.*, Religious and Temporal. Their avowed object was to rule the country as per the tenets of the Quran and to propagate Islam. Most of the Sultans considered themselves to be the deputies of the Caliph of Baghdad and received investitures from them. Besides they acknowledged the nominal sovereignty of the Caliph. But for all practical purposes, the Sultans enjoyed and exercised absolute power without any curbs whatsoever from the Caliph. The extent of proselytisation also depended upon the personal convictions and ability of the Sultans.

The Sultan

The Sultan was a despot, exercising all kinds of powers. He was the supreme executive, legislative and judicial authority. Besides he was the chief commander of the army and appointed the military generals as well as the high officers of the civil departments. The real source of his strength and authority was his army. He kept up a magnificent court and enforced an elaborate court etiquette like kissing the ground in the presence of the king.

There was no definite law of succession. Both hereditary succession and election were in vogue. The nobles and the Ulemas played a decisive role in recognising a succession or undoing it. According to Islamic law, females had no right to ascend the throne. That is why the ascendancy of Sultan Razia created a furore and resentment.

The Sultan had to ever alert against the scheming nobles who wanted to assume upperhand over the Sultan. Whenever there was an incompetent ruler, the nobles conspired and replaced the Sultan with their own men. The Sultan should ever be ready to face the external threat, revolts of the Provincial Governors and the resistance of the Hindu Princes who were never thoroughly conquered and who refused to accept Muslim sovereignty.

The Ministers

The Sultan was assisted by a council of six ministers in the day-to-day administration of the country. They were not his colleagues but subordinates who could be appointed and dismissed at his will. Some Sultans used to appoint Naib-ul-Mulk who acted as the deputy of the Sultan for all purposes. He was incharge of the military organisation. The following were the ministers :

(1) Wazir

He was the Prime Minister. His main concern was the finance. He acted as the head of the entire Governmental machinery. He received a handsome allowance and maintained his camp with great splendour. Under Wazir's control and supervision functioned the following departments :

(2) Diwan-i-Rasalat

He was incharge of foreign affairs and he maintained diplomatic relations with other countries.

(3) Diwan-i-Insha

This ministry was incharge of royal correspondence wherein all the orders of the Sultan were drafted and despatched by them.

(4) Diwan-i-Ariz

It was the ministry of war. The minister was called by the name Ariz-i-Mumalik. He was empowered to recruit, equip and maintain the necessary army. All matters connected with military campaigns were looked after by this minister.

(5) Diwani-i-Qaza

It was the department of judiciary under the control of the Chief Qazi.

(6) Sadr-us-Sudur

This minister looked after all religious matters and Muslim endowments and charities. It was his duty to see that the Muslim population followed Islamic doctrines.

Among the above six the first-four were full-fledged ministers of the first rate of the council of ministers.

In addition to these ministers there were also other departmental heads. Barid-i-Mamalik was the head of the Agriculture department. Mustafi-i-Mamalik was the Auditor-general. Amir-i-Bena was the Controller of Boats. Apart from all these ministers, the Sultan had a council of advisers known as Majlis-i-Khalwat and their counsels were not binding on him.

Revenue Policy

The Sultan have five main sources of revenue : They were as follows :

(1) Zakat

It was a tax collected only from the Muslims. 1/40 of their property was collected as Zakat from them. Such property should be possessed by them at least for a period of one year. The amount collected under this was used for the benefit of the Muslim community and for religious purposes like reconstruction and renovation of Mosques and tombs.

(2) Jizya

It was a poll tax imposed on non-Muslims. Non-Muslims were considered to be Zimmis or people living at the mercy of the Sultan. Non-Muslims were given the option of either conversion to Ialam or paying Jizya for exemption from conversion. Three grades of Jizya taxes were levied upon Hindus namely 48,24 and 12 Dirhams. However, women, children, monks, beggars, the blind and the crippled were exempted from this tax.

(3) Kharaj

Kharaj was another tax collected from non-Muslims. It varied from one-ten to one-half of the total produce of the lands.

(4) Ushr

This was also a land tax but collected from the Muslims. It was 1/10 of the produce of the lands irrigated by natural means.

(5) Khams

It was 1/5 of the spoils of war confiscated from the infields. The remaining 4/5 of the booty went to the soldiers.

Besides these taxes sanctioned by Quran, there were also other taxes such as customs duties, excise duties, tax on income from mines, taxes on heirless properties, house tax, grazing tax and water tax.

Land Revenue

Agricultural lands were classified for the purpose of collecting land revenue and the revenue collection was entrusted to tax farmers and jagirdars. There were four kinds of lands divided for the purpose of collection of land tax. They were :

(1) Khalisa lands which were directly administered by the Sultan.

(2) Lands divided into Iqtas which were held by Muqtis either for a certain number of years or for life time.

(3) The Hindu principalities who have acknowledged the suzerainty of the Sultan.

(4) Inam lands awarded to Muslim scholars and saints.

Collection of Land Revenue

Officers like Chaudharis were appointed to collect land revenue from farmers cultivating Khalisa lands. The officers in the upper ranks were Amil who used to collect revenue from the Chaudharis and remit it to the Government.

In the case of Iqtas, the collection of revenue was made by Muqtis who used to remit to the Government after deducting the required share for themselves. An officer called Khwaja was appointed to supervise the revenue collection made by Muqti.

The Hindu chiefs paid their annual tributes to the Sultan, whereas the Inam land-holders were exempt from taxation.

The Army

The Delhi Sultans designed their country into Military State which was not liked by the indigenous Hindus. Hence, the Sultans needed a huge army. Moreover, such a big and efficient army was necessitated because of the Mongol inroads and innumerable rebellions fomented by local chieftains and kings. The army consisted of four varieties of soldiers :

(1) Permanent soldiers recruited by the Sultan.
(2) Soldiers offered by the Provincial Governors and nobles.
(3) Soldiers recruited during the times of war.
(4) Muslim volunteers enlisted for fighting Jihad or Holy War.

Alauddin Khilji was the first Sultan to introduce the principle of Standing Army for the Sultan. That army was recruited, equipped and paid by the Sultan. There were about 4,75,000 soldiers in his standing army. Cavalry men were paid 234 Tankas for every month.

The army was composed of cavalry, infantry and elephants. Among these cavalry formed the backbone of the army. Army was under the control of Diwan-i-Ariz. All the reforms introduced by Alauddin were reversed by Firuz Shah Tughlug because he followed the Jagir system. Hence, the army became very weak and lost all its strength and glory.

Justice

The Sultan was the fountain-head of Justice of the land. A separate department known as Diwan-i-Qaza was functioning to dispense Justice. Sultan was the highest court of appeal. Capital punishments were meted out only after obtaining the sovereigns' consent. The Sultan held his court twice a week and dispensed justice as per the advices given by the Chief Qazi in the temporal affairs and by the Sadr-us-Sudur on religious affairs. Chief Qazi was the highest judicial officer. The cases were decided in accordance with the Islamic law. Qazis were appointed in provinces, districts and towns for rendering justice to the people. City Magistrates like Amir-i-dad were appointed for apprehending the criminals and trying the cases. Kotwals were also appointed for city administration. The Criminal Code was very severe. But Firuz Tughlug had relaxed the severity of the rules and abandoned many brutal punishments.

Provincial Administration

The empire was divided into three varieties of provinces. The first category consisted of the Iqtar which were under the command of Muqti. The second category was composed of newly conquered provinces under military Governors known as Walis. The last variety comprised of the suppressed and subdued Hindu kingdoms. The Delhi Sultanate had 23 provinces during the apex of its glory under Muhammad bin Tughluq. The provincial administration was similar to that of the Central Government.

The provinces were divided into Shiqs and each Shiq was placed under the control of Shiqdar. The next unit was Pargana which was under the control of Amil. The last unit was the Village and it was administered by a Panchayat. Chowkidar and Patwari were the officers working in villages.

8

Social and Economic Conditions under the Delhi Sultanate

SOCIAL CONDITIONS

Hindus

All the 320 years rule of the Delhi Sultans was a period of humiliation and disgrace for the Hindus in India who formed the majority of the population. The Sultans indulged in destruction and desecration of Hindu temples, raids and robberies of the cities and the violent conversions of the people to Islam. The Hindus lost their political and religious freedom. They were massacred in lakhs. The Hindu ladies were outraged and hence lost their security.

Most of the Hindus were agriculturists and traders. They were employed in the lower cadres of the administration like Chaudharis and Muqaddams. They were imposed a poll tax called Jizya besides other disabilities. The most important impact of the invasions and the supremacy of the Muslims on Hindus was that it made the Hindus to crystalise their way of life and also to have a secluded orthodox way of life from the others. In order to avoid the beautiful Hindu girls from being abducted by the Turkish Lords to their harems, the Hindu womenfolk began to adopt ways of seclusion like, "Purdha system," "Child marriages," denial of remarriage for widows, rejection of education to womenfolk. However, women of aristocratic Hindu families were exempted from all these disabilities. Chastity was considered to be the most important ornament of a woman and hence at times of war ladies performed "Jauhar" and escaped from molestation at the hands of Muslims.

Muslims

The Muslims occupied an enviable position in the Indian society. The Muslim population comprised of Muslims from Central Asia, Turks, Persians, Arabs, Abysinians. Among them the Turks were the ruling class. The Indian Muslims were not treated on par with other Muslims and were treated with contempt and hatred in the beginning. The conquest of Central Asia by the Mongols, stopped the inflow of Turks into India. Hence, Indian Muslims began to be associated with administration. Alauddin appointed Malik Kafur as one of his commanders. Firuz Tughluq appointed Malik Maqbul, a Brahmin convert to Islam to the post of the Wazir.

The Muslim ruling class had five categories : (1) Khan (2) Malik (3) Amir (4) Sipah Salar (5) Sar-i-Khail. The Muslim theologians called Ulemas had great influence both in society and in the administration. They dominated the judiciary as well as education. The Ulemas also were engaged in missionary activities. Literature was under their control. No Sultan was powerful enough to free himself from the control of Ulemas except Alauddin Khilji.

Economic Conditions

India was traditionally popular for its economic prosperity and this can be testified by the innumerable list of war spoils and booties siezed by Muslim invaders like Ghazni, Ghori and Timur. Agriculture was the main occupation of the people. Firuz Tughluq had undertaken many agrarian projects. In the towns Guild system of trade flourished. There were separate Guilds for each handicraft. It was able to thrive because it was based on the caste system. The Sultan founded Karkhanas or factories in Delhi for the manufacture of silk, cotton, cloth, silver and gold articles and so on. India exported, grains, cotton and silk clothes. Opium, indigo and horses occupied an important place in the items of import. During the period of Sultans, India had a favourable balance of trade. This fact is testified by the evidences of the accounts of Marco Polo and Ibn Batuta.

In spite of its riches, there was no equitable distribution of wealth among the people. While the Muslim nobles rolled in luxury, the common people led a miserable life even without basic necessities. These common people had to bear the burden of heavy taxation. Besides the vicissitudes of monsoon combined with famine also affected the people very much. Price level was not maintained uniformly because of inadequate transport facilities.

Literature and Art

Persian language was patronised by the Delhi Sultans and their court was adorned by learned scholars and historians. Hence, Amir Khusru compared the Delhi City to that of Bukhara a city known for its eminence in learning in the Central Asia. An imperial library was founded under the care of Amir Khusru. He was the greatest of the poets of the Delhi court. He entered the Delhi court during the reign of Balban and continued there till Alauddin Khilji. Amir Hasan was another reputed poet. He was in the court of Muhammad-bin-Tughluq.

Many historical literatures were also produced. Zia-ud-din Barani wrote Tarikh-i-Firuz Shah.

Hasan Nizami wrote Tajul-Masir. Minhaj-us-Siraj wrote Tabakat-i-Nasiri. Sham-i-Siraj Afif was another eminent historian during the times of Firuz Tughluq.

Besides the above Muslim scholars, some Hindu scholars and poets were also patronised by the provincial chiefs.

Kabir was an inspiring poet who wrote his "dohas" and "Sakhis" in Hindi.

Krittivasa translated the Valmiki Ramayana into Bengali.

Ramanuja wrote commentaries on the Brahma Sutras.

Parthsaradhi Misra wrote a number of books on Karma Mimamsa.

Mirabai, composed devotional songs; Guru Nanak produced verses in Punjabi; Namadev, a saint of Maharashtra, composed poetry in Marathi language.

During the period of Sultans, Urdu as a language got evolved. Amir Khusru was the first Urdu poet.

Architecture

In the field of architecture an amalgamation of Indian as well as Islamic art took place. It was due to the following reasons :

The Delhi Sultans initially employed only Indian sculptors and architects to build mosques and palaces. The technicians had their own method of construction. The construction materials were brought from the demolished Hindu temples and hence, the Sultans were forced to change their style of architecture. In some cases, the Hindu temples were converted into Muslim Mosques. Hence, they retained the Hindu features of architecture. The famous architectural centres of the Delhi Sultans are as follows :

The construction of Qutb-Minar at Delhi was commenced by Qutb-ud-din by using the materials collected from the demolition of 27 Hindu temples. This was completed by Iltutmish. It was a height of 234 feet. He also built Quwat-ul-Islam Mosque at Delhi in 1311 to commemorate his victory at Delhi. Alauddin constructed a number of buildings like the city "Siri" near Delhi, Jamaat Khana Masjid and Ali Darwaja at Delhi. During the Tughluq's period, the finer architectural features were not seen. They were simple and without architectural ornamentation which could be seen in the Tughluq Shah Tomb, Ferozabad City of Firuz Tughluq.

The Hindu art has dominated the buildings of Sharqi of Jaunpur. Atheena Mosque of Bandwa of Bengal is known for its beauty and majesty.

Mosques were constructed with the materials collected from the Hindu temples in Gujarat and Malwa. Among them Jami Mosque is important.

Hence, there was a harmonious blending of both the Hindu and Muslim arts in the architectural field even though they were at logger heads in politics and social relations.

9

The Bhakti Movement

The Hindu society had absorbed into its fold a number of foreign invaders like the Greeks, the Sakas, the Huns and the Kushanas. But with regard to Muslims it was not possible to do so because, the Muslims had a well established religion of their own. Besides they aimed at the conversion of Hindu infidels into Islam by forcible means and imposed a number of restrictions and disabilities on the Hindus. Hence, the Hindus began to love their religion and in order to protect themselves from the onslaughts of Muslims, they lightened the caste distinctions, intensified the rituals and emphasised the exclusive Hindu ways of life. However, the democratic and equalitarian features of Islam, combined with their monotheism had slowly permeated the Hindu religious society and thereby caused the emergence of a new movement called Bhakti Movement. It is a mistake to attribute Islam alone as the cause for this movement. For, Bhakti (devotion) was advocated as one of the three means of attainment of salvation in the scriptures like Bhagavadgita.

The Bhakti movement advocated the following principles : All religions are equally great; Almighty is one; All are equal before him. Greatness lies not in the birth but in noble actions. All can attain salvation for which devotion towards the Almighty is essential. The chief exponents of this movement were Ramanuja, Ramananda, Vallabhacharya, Chitanya, Kabir and Nanak.

Ramanuja

The earliest exponent of Bhakti way was Ramanuja the great Vaishnavite leader of the 12th Century A.D. Born at Conjeevaram, studied under Yadava Prakash and sought asylum at the Court of the Hoysala Kingdom of Vishnu Vardhana in order to escape the persecution of the Chola king who wanted to convert him from Vaishnavism to Saivism. He advocated the wordship of Saguna Iswara or personal God. One of his important followers was Ramananda.

Ramananda

He belonged to a Brahmin family of Allahabad. He preached Rama Bhakti to the people of all castes and both sexes. He abandoned the principle of casteism and drew disciples from all castes. This was his unique contribution. Kabir was his important disciple who was a Muslim weaver formerly.

Vallabhacharya

He was an exponent of Krishna cult. He was a Telugu Brahmin by birth. He advocated Suddha Advaita which meant that Individual soul itself is a Brahman and it should attain salvation by uniting with Brahman. Later on his teachings were misinterpreted as the pursuit of worldly pleasures and hence was called "Epicureanism of the East" by Monier-Williams.

Chaitanya

He was the contemporary of Vallabhacharya and the greatest exponent of the Bhakti cult. He was born in 1485 A.D. in a Bengal Brahmin family. Becoming tired of this material life, he became a Sannyasi at the age of twenty-four. He propagated the Krishna cult. His faith was that through love and devotion one can realise the personal presence of God. He ignored the casteism and ceremonial rituals of Hinduism.

Mirabai

She was a Rajput Princess of the 15th century. She gave up the royal life for the sake of divine bliss. She immersed herself in Krishna Bhakti and composed beautiful devotional songs. Her bhajans in Hindi and Gujarati had become extremely popular. She was a disciple of Ramananda.

Namadev

He belonged to Maharashtra and advocated Bhakti cult there. He was a cloth dyer by profession. He was opposed to priestly ritualism and also idolatry. He declared that salvation could be attained only through love of God.

Kabir

He was one of the twelve disciples of Ramananda. His unique contribution was his preaching of Hindu-Muslim unity. He was nominally a Muslim and his thoughts were more of a Hindu. He said that Ram and Rahim were the same. He condemned idol worship. His was a religion of love and devotion to God. He denounced caste and all forms of ritualism both in Hinduism and Islam. His followers were from both Hinduism and Islam.

Nanak

The spiritual successor of Kabir was Nanak and he organised the Sikhs or disciples into a sect called Sikhism. He was born in 1469 at Talwani in West Punjab. He had a deep religious bent of mind right from his early days. He started preaching goodwill and co-operation among Hindus and Muslims during the age of religious fervour prevailing then. He reconciled the ritualistic Brahmanism and authoritative Muhammedanism by means of Sikhism. He preached among the people principle of one invisible God. He exhorted his people to lead a virtuous life and display toleration to other creeds. He discouraged asceticism and preached a crusade against blind orthodox. He said, "Religion consists not in mere words. He who looks on all men as equal is religious." He also taught : "Abide pure amidst the impurities of the world, thus, shall you find the way to religion."

Guru Nanak nominated Angad, as his successor and died in 1538 A.D. His religion came to be known as Sikhism.

Conclusion

Through the emergence of Bhakti cult, Hinduism got a new lease of life and vigour. It gave sufficient strength to Hinduism to withstand the onslaughts of Hinduism and survive with fresh outlook. Moreover a reconciliation was attempted between Hinduism and Islam by the prophets like Kabir and Nanak. Besides this the vernacular literatures flourished as the preachers of Bhakti cult preached in their mother tongue. Anyhow Hinduism had its revival.

10

The Sultans of Madurai

After the demise of Maravarman Kulasekara Pandiyan of Madurai, his two sons entered into a war of succession. Sundara Pandian was the elder and Vira Pandian was the younger of the two. Defeated by Vira Pandyan, Sundara Pandian sought the help of Malik Kafur, the military general of Alauddin Khilji. Taking this opportunity Malik Kafur proceeded to Madurai with a large army in 1311 A.D. Vira Pandyan fled from the capital in terror. Kafur plundered Madurai and obtained 2,750 pounds of gold and 20,000 horses. The invasion of Malik Kafur did not result in any long lasting effect in the country. In the same way, Khusrau Khan, the Chief adviser of Qutb-ud-din Mubarak Shah also attacked Madurai in 1314 A.D. But in 1327, Muhammad-bin-Tughluq invaded Madurai, annexed it with his empire and handed it over to a Governor Jalaluddin Asan Shah. Tamilagam which was called by the name of "Mapar" formed the 23rd province of Tughluq's empire.

Since Madurai was far away from the capital city and the Sultan was engaged in suppressing the rebellions in other regions, the Governor of Madurai was tempted to carve out separate kingdom. Hence, he declared himself to be an independent Sultan in A.D. 1333. Thus, it seceded from the far fetched control of Delhi.

Muhammad-bin-Tughlaq marched against Asan Shah, the insubordinate Governor. Since his forces were afflicted with epidemics, the Sultan had to drop his expedition. However, he took revenge upon Asan Shah by torturing his brother Ibrahim in Delhi.

Asan Shah's position was strengthened. He issued coins in his name. But the period of Madurai Sultan was a period of torture and tyranny in which a number of political murders took place. Ibn Batuta married the daughter of the first Sultan of Madurai. Asan Shah was murdered by Alauddin Uddauji in 1340. Alauddin Uddauji too could not rule the Sultanate for more than a year. While Alauddin Uddauji was engaged in a war with a Hindu ruler an arrow which came from unknown direction struct him and he died. Then he was succeeded by his nephew Qutbuddin who ruled the Sultanate only for a brief period of forty days. Then he too succumbed to the conspiracy of his enemies.

He was succeeded by Ghiyathuddin Thamagani, the nephew of the first Sultan Asan Shah. Ibn Batuta, the historian had stayed at Madurai for a brief period. Of all the Sultans of Madurai, Ghiayathuddin was the worst tyrant. But he had a number of conquests to his credit. Hoysala king Virsa Ballala III marched against Madurai in order to overcome it. He proceeded at the head of a large army of one lakh soldiers and sieged the Kannanur Koppam. Ghiyathuddin managed to repulse the enemy with a sheer force of 6000 soldiers. Ultimately he feigned to start peace talks and suddenly pounced upon the Hoysala troops. This sudden and unexpected attack made the soldiers run helter skelter. Vira Ballala became a captive in the hands of Ghiyathuddin. After collecting all the treasures of Vira Ballala treacherously, he was murdered. His body was stuffed with hay and suspended at the entrance of the Madurai Fort. Ghiyathuddin died a few days after this ghastly murder.

He was then succeeded by Nasiruddin. Nasiruddin prevented all the possible claimants for the throne by means of butchery. Then he was succeeded by Adil Shah and then by Fakruddin Mubarak Shah.

Sikandar Shah who ascended the throne after Fakruddin had witnessed the downfall of the Madurai Sultanate. Kumara Kampanna, the military general of Vijayanagar empire marched against Madurai and sounded the death-knell of the Madurai Sultanate. This expedition is narrated in the "Madura Vijayam" a Sanskrit epic.

This was written by Gangadevi, the wife of Kumarakampanna. The causes for the expedition are analysed. The suppression of Hinduism and the unleashing of tyrannical rule of Muslims hastened this expedition. Kumarakampanna seized Kannanur, Koppam and killed the Sultan Sikkandar Shah. Then Madurai was brought under the Vijayanagar empire.

11
Vijayanagar Empire

Origin

The emergence of Vijayanagar empire is a remarkable event in the medieval Indian History. Vijayanagar was considered to have the key for understanding the political conditions of that period. After the great deluge of Muslim supremacy, the Hindu culture got revived in the forum of Vijayanagar empire. It dominated the political and cultural conditions for the period of two and a half centuries. The empire was established for two main purposes.

1. The establishment of the new kingdom of Vijayanagar was an attempt by the surviving Hindu powers to stop the Hindu rot and re-establish the freedom and glory of the old Hindu Kingdom.

2. To preserve the Hindu culture from the onslaughts of Muslim Sultans. The Vijayanagar empire had to face a number of battles in order to accomplish those two goals. Hence, the rise of Vijayanagar is considered to be a renaissance of Hindu political and religious movements.

There are differing opinions with regard to the origin of Vijayanagar. According to Father Heras, Vijayanagar was founded by the Hoysala King Vira Ballala III and his officer named Hari Hara. Others advocate that Vira Ballala himself would have founded the city. However, all the historians unanimously accept the fact that it was founded by Hari Hara and Bukka with the blessings of Vidhyaranya, a Hindu sage.

Establishment of the City Vijayanagar

Hari Hara and Bukka the two brothers were serving the Treasury of Prataparudra II, the Kakatiya ruler of Warrangal.

When Warrangal became a prey for the depredations of Mohammedans, they fled to Karnataka and were finally arrested and sent to Delhi in 1332 where they were coerced to embrace Islam. Later on they were deputed to Karnataka to take up the administration of the region since the Governors there became recalcitrant.

When they returned to their motherland, their religious fervour was kindled by the prevalent rebellous conditions among the Hindus. Under the influence of a Hindu sage Vidhyaranya, they reverted to their mother religion Hinduism. According to his advice, they established their stronghold at Anegundi on the northern banks of the Tungabhadra and laid the foundation of Vijayanagar empire in 1336 A.D.

SANGAMA DYNASTY

Hari Hara I (1336-1356)

The dynasty of Hari Hara was named after his father Sangama. Hari Hara did not wear any Royal insignia but called himself to be the representative of Virupaksha his deity. He appointed his brother Bukka as Yuvaraja and co-regent. he introduced internal reforms by re-organising the kingdom into various divisions such as Sthalas, Nadus and Simas. He also appointed officers for the collection of taxes. He built forts and Anegundi, Badami and Udayagiri on the border lines of the empire. When the Hoysala ruler Vira Ballala III was treacherously murdered by the Sultan of Madurai, Hari Hara annexed the Hoysala kingdom with his empire. Kadambas of Banavasi were also defeated and their Konkan coastal region was annexed. In 1352, Alauddin Hasan Bahman Shah, the founder of Bahmani kingdom attacked Vijayanagar and demanded tribute from Hari Hara. Hari Hara in turn surrendered Raichur-Doab to him. This region became a bone of contention for both Vijayanagar and Bahmani kingdom perennially.

Bukka I (1356-1377)

Bukka succeeded his elder brother. Conquest of Madurai was the greatest achievement of his reign. This is vividly narrated in the "Madura Vijayam", written by Gangadevi, the wife of

Kampana, who was a son of Bukka I. He also repulsed the three attacks of the Bahmani Sultans like Muhammad Shah I and Muzahid Shah.

Bukka patronised the Telugu Poet Nachana Sama. He brought about reconciliation between the Jains and Vaishnavas at Sravana Belagola over the damage of Jain temple caused by Vaishnavites. After consolidating his position, Bukka I died in 1377 A.D. He can be considered as the real architect of Vijayanagar empire.

Hari Hara II (1377-1404 A.D.)

He assumed the title of Maharajadhiraja. He lavishly endowed the Hindu Temples. His empire extended over the whole of South India including Mysore, Kanchi, Chingleput, Malabar and Madurai. His minister Madhava conquered Goa. Hari Hara also conquered places like Panagal, Kurnool, Nellore, Chaul and Thapol. Hari Hara II was succeeded by his son Virupaksha. But Bukka II usurped the throne from his brother and ruled Vijayanagar for a period of two years. Bukka II too was deposed from the throne by Devaraya.

Devaraya I (1406-1422 A.D.)

During the reign of 16 years, Devaraya carried on incessant wars with the Bahmani Sultan and Reddis of Kondavidu. He captured the forts of Kondavidu, and Udayagiri from the hands of the Reddis of Kondavidu. During his period, "Vijayanagar became the city of learning and the abode of the goddess Saraswathi." Nikolo Conti, an Italian traveller visited the kingdom in 1420.

Vijaya Raya I (1422-1426 A.D.)

Devaraya was succeeded by his son Vijaya Raya I who is assigned a reign period varying from six months to four years. During the short reign of Vijaya Raya, Ahmad Shah Bahmani undertook a terrible war of revenge. The country was laid waste, temples destroyed, cows butchered and people were killed in thousands. He returned to his capital carrying much booty and many prisoners. Vijaya Raya narrowly escaped capture by the enemy.

Devaraya II (1426-1446 A.D.)

He was the greatest of kings of Sangama dynasty. He conquered Kondavidu and Rajamundry of Reddis. Epigraphic evidences show that he defeated Ahmad Shah Bahmani, and also had two other victories against the ruler of Andhra and Orissa. Alauddin Ahmad succeeded Ahmad Shah in Bahmani kingdom and undertook two expeditions against Vijayanagar. Ferishta writes that the Sultan had defeated on both occasions. But Abdur Razack, a Persian envoy at the court of Vijayanagar wrote that Devaraya II went up to Gulbarga and had taken a large number of prisoners. Probably the wars did not yield definite results.

According to Portuguese accounts Devaraya II undertook an expedition against the Ceylonese and conquered Jaffna. Hence, the King of Ceylon accepted to pay tribute. Along with him other kings of Pegu and Tennasarim of Burma also sent presents to him.

Devaraya strengthened his army by appointing Muslims for giving the necessary training to his soldiers. Ferishta says that he had a huge army. He also undertook to improve the finances of the State.

In the midst of his war-like activities, Devaraya found time to construct temples and promote fine arts. He beautified the city of Vijayanagar and built the Vittalaswamy temple. He also built a mosque for the use of Muslims in his capital. He himself was a Sanskrit scholar. He patronised Dindima Bhat his court poet. Abdul Razack had paid glowing tributes to the peace and prosperity of the country during Devaraya II's reign.

Mallikarjuna (1446-1465 A.D.)

Devaraya II was succeeded by his son Mallikharjuna. He was an incompetent king. His period of reign witnessed the decline of the Sangama dynasty. In a war with the Gajapathi of Orissa, Mallikharjuna lost the two of his important forts Kondavidu and Udayagiri. Mallikharjuna was said to have been assassinated by his cousin Virupaksha II.

Virupaksha II (1465-1485 A.D.)

In his period chaos and confusion prevailed because of his

inefficiency. In a war with Muhammad Shah II of Bahmani kingdom he lost Northern Konkan and Northern Karnataka regions. While the decline was fast, Saluva Narasimha, a chief of Vijayanagar, became the deliverer of the day and usurped throne in 1485 A.D. He laid the foundation for the Saluva dynasty.

(I) KRISHNA DEVARAYA (1509-1529 A.D.)

Krishnadevaraya, the greatest king of the Vijayanagar Empire succeeded his brother Vira Narasimha to the throne in 1509. Under him the empire enjoyed the zenith of its glory and prestige. He was born in 1487 A.D. to his parents Tuluva Narasanayaka and Nagamba. He was very well brought up by Timmarusu who had also served as his minister.

Military Expeditions

Krishnadevaraya very soon realised that the throne was not a bed of roses. He was surrounded by difficulties on all sides. Hence, he undertook a number of expeditions to consolidate his position.

War with Bahmani Sultan

Immediately after the accession of Krishnadevaraya the Bahmani Sultans Muhammad Shah and Yusuf Adil Shah had declared Jihad against the infidels of Vijayanagar and attacked it. Krishnadevaraya defeated them at Diwani and Golkonda respectively and captured the forts of Raichur and Mudgal. This was his first victory.

Southern Campaigns

Subjugation of Ummathur

Ummathur was the next target of attack of Krishnadevaraya. He wanted to avenge the crimes committed by the Palaigars of the South by defying his authority. He led an expedition against them. It was a great military feat for him. He captured Penugonda at first. Then he conquered the rebel leader Gangaraja of Ummattur and captured Srirangapatam and Sivasamudram from him.

Krishnadevaraya proceeded further south and entrusted the

work of conquering the Tamil Kingdom to his generals Vijayappa and others. He himself personally annexed Coorg and Malabar. A portion of Ceylon was also annexed. Hence, he assumed the title of "Dakshina Samudradhiswara." or Lord of the Southern Seas.

Eastern Campaign

Gajapati was hatching a plot in alliance with the Bahmani Sultans against the Vijayanagar. Hence, Krishnadevaraya launched his campaigns against Orissa in 1513. He captured Udayagiri and Kondavidu. He seiged the fort of Kandapalli and imprisoned the son of Gajapati. The war which lasted from 1513 to 1518 came to an end by a treaty signed in 1518. According to the treaty, Gajapati gave his daughter Annapurnadevi in marriage to Krishnadevaraya and the latter surrendered all the territories north of the Krishna conquered from Gajapati.

Battle of Raichur

When Krishnadevaraya was engaged in his campaign against Orissa, Ismail Adil Khan, the Sultan of Bijapur, captured Raichur. Krishnadevaraya started an expedition with a huge army and defeated the Bijapur Sultan. Saluva Timma assisted him in this campaign. The Muslim camp was sacked and a large booty fell into the hands of Krishnadevaraya. Raichur was recaptured.

War with Golkonda

At the time of Krishnadevaraya's eastern campaigns, Quli Qutb Shah, the ruler of Telengana invaded Vijayanagar and captured some places there. In order to avenge this act, Krishnadevaraya despatched an army under Saluva Timma to Kondavidu to expel the invader from there. Saluva Timma was successful in his endeavour.

Relations with the Portuguese

Krishnadevaraya did not try to reconquer Goa from the hands of Portuguese. But he maintained cordial relations with the Portuguese in order to get good horses, generals and soldiers to his army. Their assistance was mainly responsible for some of his striking victories against Muslims.

Rebellion in Madurai

The Governor Nagama Nayaka of Madurai became headstrong and behaved like an independent ruler. But he was brought to his senses by his own son Visvanatha Nayaka. He replaced his father and remained faithful till his life.

Krishnadevaraya as a patron of art and letters

He was a great builder. He built a new city Nagalapur by name in memory of his mother near Vijayanagar. He was a very devout Vaishnavite and built a number of temples in Tirupati and Tiruvannamalai. He built the Krishnaswami Temple and made ornamental works to the Vittalaswami temple.

Krishnadevaraya was also an accomplished scholar and wrote several works in Sanskrit and Telugu. He was also a generous patron of learning. His court was adorned by eight literary giants known as "Asta-dig-gajas." The most celebrated of them were Allasami Peddana, Timmanna and Tenali Ramakrishna. He wrote two Sanskrit plays Jambavati Kalyanam and Usha Parinayam and a Telugu poem Amuktamalyada. His munificence to scholars earned for him the title "Andhra Bhoja".

A great general and administrator

He was pre-eminent as a general, led his armies in person, displayed exemplary boldness in moment of danger and paid great attention to the well being of his soldiers. He was also a great administrator and statesman. He exercised full control over the provinces and maintained strict supervision over even the local administration. He maintained friendly relations with Orissa and Goa.

Estimate

Krishnadevaraya occupies a unique place in the medieval history of South India. He had a number of marvellous military victories. His attempt to unite the whole of South India was a grand success. Sewell writes in his book "A Forgotten Empire" that Krishnadevaraya was physically strong in his last days and maintained his strength to the highest pitch by hard bodily exercise. Peas, the Portuguese traveller praises him in the following words "he is the most feared and perfect king that could possibly be... He is a great ruler and a man of much justice, but subject to sudden fits of rage...." Krishna Shastri calls him the greatest of the South Indian monarchs who sheds a lustre on the pages of history.

(II) BATTLE OF TALIKOTTA (A.D. 1565)

The actual decline had started right from the times of the demise of Devaraya II of the Sangama Dynasty. He was succeeded by the incompetent rulers like Mallikharjuna and Virupaksha II. They indulged in sensuous pleasures and hence neglected administration. This led to the decline of the Vijayanagar empire. But it was avoided by Saluva Narasimha who occupied the throne and founded the Saluva Dynasty in 1485. This first usurpation adjourned the Talikotta war for a period of 80 years. Saluva Narasimha was succeeded by his minor son Immadi Narasimha whose throne was usurped by Tuluva Narasanayaka. Tuluva Narasanayaka founded the Tuluva dynasty. This second usurpation also averted the catastrophe of the decline of the empire. But the third ruler of this dynasty Krishnadevaraya made his empire a powerful one.

The successors of Krishnadevaraya

After the death of Krishnadevaraya, his brother Achyutadevaraya succeeded him in 1539. But his accession was challenged by Ramaraya, the son-in-law of Krishnadevaraya. Anyhow Achyuta came to terms with Ramaraya and ruled the empire till his death in 1552.

Sadasivaraya the nephew of Achyuta succeeded him. But the *de facto* ruler was his famous minister Ramaraya. The civil wars that followed Krishnadevaraya's death, also largely contributed to the decline of the empire.

Ramaraya's Provocation towards the war of Talikotta (1565)

Ramaraya the son-in-law of Krishnadevaraya wanted to restore the former glory and prestige of the empire. He was an able commander and capable administrator. He was successful to a great extent in restoring fame and name of the empire. He suppressed the rebellious Nayaks of Madura, Jinji and Tanjore. He was mad after power. He interfered in the quarrels of the

Muslim Sultans by putting one against the other. He wanted to exploit the rivalries between the Sultans. But this very policy proved to be detrimental to the Vijayanagar empire itself.

(1) He formed an alliance with Nizam Shah of Ahmadnagar and Qutb Shah of Golkonda against Bijapur. Bijapur was ruled by Ibrahim Adil Shah and he was defeated in the war that ensued in 1543.

(2) Then Ramaraya joined with Ali Adil Shah of Bijapur and Ibrahim Qutb Shah of Golkonda against Ahmadnagar. The territory of Ahmadnagar was ravaged and the trimphant army of Vijayanagar "destroyed the mosques and did not even respect the sacred Quran."

(3) The arrogant behaviour of the Hindus enraged the Muslim rulers. They forgot their former rivalries and united themselves against Ramaraya. Chand Bibi daughter of Hussain Shah of Ahmadnagar was married to Ali Adil Shah of Bijapur. Except Berar the other four Sultans of Bijapur, Golkonda, Bidar and Ahmadnagar allied together against Vijayanagar.

Battle of Talikotta (1565)

The armies of the four Muslim States met at Bijapur, crossed the river Krishna and encamped at Talikotta at the end of 1564. Then they proceeded further South of thirty miles and Vijayanagar army stationed on a plain between two villages ten miles apart Rakshaji and Tanagadi. Ramaraya was confident of success. The battle was fought on 23rd January 1565. In the preliminary engagement the Hindus were successful. Hence, the Muslims resorted to a strategem of conspiracy by which they were able to make two Muslim generals of Vijayanagar army to defect against their king. These traitors caused chaos and confusion in the army. The aged Ramaraya, who was directing the campaign from a litter, fell into the hands of Hussain Nizam Shah, who decapitated him with his own hand and raised his head on a spear for the Hindus to see. In the pursuit that followed more than 100,000 were killed. On the third day, the Muslims reached the great city of Vijayanagar. Robert Sewell in his book "A Forgotten Empire" gives a vivid account of the destruction wrought on Vijayanagar in the following way : "The enemy had come to destroy and they carried out their objects relentlessly... Nothing seemed to escape them. They set fire to shops and houses and smashed the exquisite stone sculptures in the temples. With fire and sword, with crowbars and axes, they carried on day after day their work of destruction. Never perhaps in the history of the world has such havoc been wrought, and wrought so suddenly, on so splendid a city; teeming with a wealthy and industrious in the full plenitude of prosperity one day, and on the next seized, pillaged and reduced to ruins, amid scenes of savage massacre and horrors beggaring description."

The battle of Talikotta was not a decisive one. After hearing the terrible news of defeat, Tirumalaraya, brother of Ramaraya along with the king Sadasivaraya, fled away to Penugonda, leaving the capital unprotected. The battle of Talikotta closed a brilliant chapter in the history of South India.

Effects

1. Tirumalaraya, brother of Ramaraya crowned himself at Penugonda and founded the Aravidu dynasty in 1570. The successors ruled over a diminishing empire which finally disappeared through a process of attrition and disintegration.
2. The Muslims did not gain any territory as a result of victory. All their old jealousies and recriminations were revived and soon they were engulfed in Mughal imperialism.
3. The Nayak kingdoms of Madura and Tanjore got themselves separated from Vijayanagar after the battle of Talikotta.
4. Portuguese had well established their power on the west coastal regions because of the rapport that existed between them. But with the disappearance of the Vijayanagar empire, they too began to lose their strength and influence.
5. In 1612 Raja Odayar founded the kingdom of Mysore.

12

Administration and Social Life of the Vijayanagar Empire

THE CENTRAL GOVERNMENT

(a) King

King was considered to be the pivot of the administrative machinery. He was the supreme authority in civil, military and judicial matters and was indeed the most powerful man in the State. The prime duty of the king was to protect the life and property of his citizens and redress their grievances. He was always keen on securing the goodwill of the people. He ruled the country with an eye towards Dharma. Agriculture, Trade and Commerce had developed under the Vijayanagar rulers. They dispensed equal justice to his people.

(b) Imperial Council

This was comprised of ministers, provincial governors, military commanders, priests and poets. The king was assisted in the task of administration by a council of ministers appointed by him. It had a Prime Minister who was noted for his age and wisdom, the heads of the departments and a few members of the royal blood. There was no hard and fast rule governing the selection of a minister or his term of office.

(c) The Secretariat

There was a Secretariat to carry out the orders of the minister and officers. There were officers like Chief Treasurer, Custodian of Jewels, the Perfect of the police, the Chief Master of the house, etc. in order to assist the ministers. They were called by the following designations : Sarvanayaka, Tirumandira Olainayagam, Mudra Karta, Rayasam, Karanikan, etc.

Divisions of the Empire

The empire was divided into provinces like Kottams or Ventis. They were further divided into "Nadus" or "Seemas," "Sthala" was constituted by a number of villages and village was the lowest unit of administration. The great degree of independence enjoyed by the Provincial Governments greatly undermined the stability of the Central Government.

Revenue administration

The State derived its main revenue from the land tax which was based upon the fertility of the soil. Besides the land tax ryots had to pay the house tax, grazing tax marriage tax, etc. Other sources of revenue were customs duties, tolls, property tax, commercial tax, tax on industries and so on. The income from the prostitutes alone was sufficient to pay the Police department of Vijayanagar. All taxes were payable only in cash. An office called "Adhvani" was incharge of collecting the taxes. The chief sources of expenditure were the palace establishment, ministers and officers, army, religious endowments, and presents to scholars and savants.

Justice

The king was the supreme judge and the final court of appeal. The law was based on customs and was evolved out of Hindu Dharma. Besides the King's court, there was a court at the centre presided over by a judge or a panel of judges. The provinces and the villages had also their own courts. Severe punishments were inflicted on the gualty, *e.g.*, death or mutilation for theft, adultery and treason. Punishments like torture, impaling, trampling by the elephants and confiscation of property were given for other crimes varying in accordance with the gravity of the crime.

The Army

The king had his own standing army of a million troops. He was supplied another million troops by the feudal lords like Nayaks. There was a separate department for military affairs called Kandachara with several officials under the Dandanayaka. The infantry comprised of various sections of the population. The cavalry had sturdy horses imported from Persia through Portuguese. A corps of elephants, were given sufficient training for fighting in the battlefield. The expeditions to Ceylon make us to infer that there must have been some navy. Fortresses also played their role significantly. The Hindu soldiers though strong and brave, lacked in manoeuvring and tactics when compared to the Muslims.

Local Administration

The village was the lowest unit of administration and the Central Government had stricter control and supervision over them. The village assembly was in charge of the administration with executive and judicial powers. The village officers were paid grants of land. The Chief Officer of the Central Government who supervised the village administration was called Mahanayakacharya.

Society

The kings considered the preservation of the social solidarity as their duty. The Brahmins enjoyed a dominant status in the society. They distinguished themselves in different fields. Kaikkolas were also highly influential who were entitled with temple administration.

Infant marriages were in vogue. Sati was common. Polygamy was permitted. Women were honoured in the society. The tax collected from the prostitutes was utilised for the payment of police personnel. Bribery was also prevalent. The rich people led a luxurious life. Wrestling, hunting, horse-riding, and chess were the favourite pastimes of the people. Nicolo Conti describes three popular festivals of Vijayanagar, one of which was Dassarah. It was conducted for nine days. He refers to another festival like Holi in which colour water was sprinkled on the people.

Women were given place of honour in political, social and literary fields. They were employed in carrying litters, and in astrology and music. Their deep interest in literature could be borne out from their master pieces like Gangadevi's "Mathura Vijayam" and Thirumalamba's "Naradhambigai Parinayanam."

Some Social Customs

Nunis says that Brahmins and Lingayats alone had vegetarian food habits and all the others were omnivarous. Since cow and ox were considered to be sacred, they were not slaughtered for their meat. Abdur Razack points out that all people from ordinary to elite level had the habit of wearing ornaments.

Religious Conditions

Hinduism was followed in its various sects like Saivism, Advaitha, Pasupatha, Veera Saiva, Vaishnavism. Basava founded the sect of Veera Saivism in the Karnataka region. They opposed the domination of Brahmins and the Vedas. People who offered special veneration to the Phallus were called as Lingayats. The Vaishnava Bakthi cult was advocated by Vallabhacharya who propagated special devotion to Lord Krishna. The rulers of Vijayanagar had constructed big and beautiful Hindu temples and endowed them with large tracts of land. Their religious toleration is clearly vindicated by Portuguese traveller Barbosa's remark on it. "The king allows such freedom that every man may come and go and live according to his own creed without suffering any annoyance and without any enquiry whether he is a Christian, a Jew, a Moor, or a Hindu."

Literature

The Vijayanagar kings patronised Sanskrit, Telugu, Tamil and Kannada languages. Devaraya I constructed Pearl Pavilion in order to honour literary laureates and poured golden coins on them. The Vijayanagar empire's period was considered to be the renaissance of Telugu language and Krishnadevaraya's period was called as the golden age of Telugu language. His court was adorned by the eight great scholars called by the name of "Ashta dig gajas" chief among them was Allasani Peddanna who was offered the title of "Andhra Kavitha Pithamahar." His masterpiece was Manucharitha. Nandi Timmanna wrote Parijatha Parinayanam. Krishna Devaraya himself was the author of "Amukthamalyada".

In the court of Ramaraya also there were a number of savants. Ramaraja Bhushana wrote Vasu charitara and Pingali Surana wrote Prabhavati Pradyumnam and Kala purnodayam. Purandharada wrote devotional songs and Lord Vaishnu.

Art and Architecture

Painting and sculpture flourished in the Vijayanagar empire. Painting on the walls of Praharams and on the inner roofings were the special features of Vijayanagar empire. The life of Rama is depicted in the Hazara Ramaswamy temple. Monolithic sculptures like Narasimha incarnation and the Rama Statue of Malaya Vantha temple are remarkable.

The temple architecture of the Vijayanagar reached a high degree of excellence. The Vittalswamy temple and Hazara Ramaswamy temples are the typical specimens of the Vijayanagar temple architecture. Pillared Mandapas could be seen in Parvathi temple, Chidambaram, Varadaraja Perumal temple, Kanjeevaram. The remnants of the ruined Vijayanagar like Lotus Mahal, Elephant Madap depict the reflection of the Islamic elements of architecture.

Economic Affluence

The economic prosperity of the Vijayanagar empire is amply borne out by the accounts given by foreign travellers. Abdur Razack says that the king's treasury was filled with molten gold forming one mass. All people, whether high or low, wore jewels and gilt ornaments in their ears and around their necks, arms, wrists and fingers. The cost of living was cheap and things were available in abundance. Agriculture, trade and industry flourished under the fostering care of the kings. Vijayanagar had maritime trade with China, Pegu and Alexandria for which a number of prominent ports like Calicut, Mangalore, Nagapatam, Masulipatam were maintained.

13

The Bahmani Kingdom

Origin

The Delhi Sultanate had its boundary extended all over the Southern India during Muhammad-bin-Tughluq's reign. But he was incompetent to rule such an extensive empire. Hence, he resorted to repressive measures. This resulted in the outbreak of a number of rebellions. The Muslim nobles of Daulatabad raised the flag of insurrection and proclaimed Ismail Malik as the Sultan of the Deccan. But he resigned in favour of an intrepid soldier named Hasan, who assumed the royalty under the title of Alauddin Bahman Shah. He established Bahamni kingdom in 1347. Hasan claimed descent from the royal house of Persia and the title of "Bahman Shah" assumed by him was merely a formal assertion of that claim. He established his capital at Gulbarga.

Alauddin Bahman Shah (1347-1358 A.D.)

Hasan devoted himself in the task of expansion and consolidation. He attacked Kapayanayaka of Warangal and acquired Bhongir. He conquered Goa, Dabhol, Kolhapur and Telengana. He divided his kingdom into four provinces with their headquarters at Daulatabad, Bidar, Berar and Gulbarga. The kingdom spread between Bhongir, the Wainganga, the Arabian sea and the Krishna. An expedition against some Hindu chieftains in Karnataka captured an immense booty.

Muhammad Shah I (1358-1377 A.D.)

Muhammad Shah, the eldest son of Alauddin succeeded him. He conquered the Hindu kings of Warangal and Vijayanagar. Bukkaraya of Vijayanagar captured the Mudgal fort and plundered the territory between the Krishna and Thungabhadra. In order to avenge this, Muhammad Shah attacked Vijayanagar, defeated Bukkaraya and murdered a number of Hindu women and children. Muhammad Shah also conquered Warangal from Kapaya Nayaka.

Mujahid Shah (1377-1378 A.D.)

Muhammad Shah was succeeded by his son Mujahid Shah. He undertook two expeditions against the Vijayanagar and faced a disastrous defeat at the hands of Bukkaraya; but he threw the blame on his uncle Daud Khan. Daud Khan killed him and usurped the throne. Within a month, however, Daud Khan was murdered in a mosque while offering prayers. Muhammad Shah, a grandson of Alauddin I, was raised to throne.

Muhammad Shah II (1378-1397 A.D.)

His reign was peaceful and benevolent to the people. He built mosques and schools and invited savants from all parts of Asia. For his deep erudition, he earned the nick-name Aristotle. For eight years there was a severe famine (1387-1395 A.D.) and the Sultan took speedy arrangements for relief measures. He set up a number of orphanages. He passed away in 1397.

Firuz Shah (1397-1422 A.D.)

Firuz Shah was the son-in-law of Muhammad II. He undertook three expeditions against Vijayanagar and was successful in the first two expeditions. He murdered the son of Hari Hara II of Vijayanagar by ensnaring him in a music concert. Hence, Hari Hara concluded a peace treaty with him. The second war against Vijayanagar was over the cause of a beautiful girl of Mudgal. Firuz Shah defeated Devaraya I of Vijayanagar. But in the third encounter he was defeated and it was followed by successful invasion of the Vijayanagar troops and loss of the Southern and Eastern districts of the Bahmani kingdom. Firuz was deeply affected by the defeat both in mind and body. Hence, he retired from the political affairs by handing over the administration to his favourite slave. But his brother Ahmad murdered him and assumed the throne.

Firuz Shah is considered as an enlightened ruler. He founded the city of Firuzabad. He delighted himself in the company of learned men. He was learned in the Bible and employed Brahmins in positions of trust. Firuz freely indulged in drinking and debauchery. He had 800 women chosen from different nationalities in his harem and being an accomplished linguist he could boost of talking to each and every one in their own mother tongue. With his death the "Gulbarga Period" was over.

Ahmad Shah (1422-1435 A.D.)

He was the brother of Firuz Shah. He transferred the capital to Bidar and hence, commenced the "Bidar Period". The aggressive policy of his brother was continued against Vijayanagar. He waged a savage war to avenge the losses of the previous reign caused by Vijayanagar. He massacred 20,000 people, demolished temples and slaughtered cows. Devaraya II paid a vast treasure and made peace. He attacked Warangal, defeated and killed its ruler and annexed his kingdom. He defeated the Sultan of Malwa and extended the Bahmani's boundary up to Elichpur in the north. But he met with failure in a war with Gujarat. He appointed foreign Muslims in higher posts.

Alauddin II (1436-1458 A.D.)

He was the son and successor of Ahmad Shah. He reduced the Hindu kings of the Konkan and Sangameshwar. The latter gave his daughter in marriage to the Sultan. She was noted for her matchless and surpassing beauty. He undertook two expeditions against Devaraya II of Vijayanagar and inflicted heavy defeat on both occasions. The revolt of Jalal Khan the Governor of Telengana was at once suppressed by Alauddin's Persian Officer, Muhammad Gawan who was coming into prominence then.

Humayun (1458-1461 A.D.)

Alauddin's eldest son and successor was Humayun. He was notorious for his vices and cruelty which earned him the name of tyrant. His reign witnessed the outbreak of a number of rebellions in the country but Humayun put down all of them with an iron hand. He committed a number of atrocities and was murdered in one of his drunker orgies. The people hailed the event as "Delight of the World".

Nizam Shah (1461-1463 A.D.)

Humayun was succeeded by his minor son Nizam Shah of eight years old. His mother ruled the kingdom as a Regent with the assistance of Muhammad Gawan. The Sultan of Malwa invaded the Bahmani kingdom and besieged Bidar. But his invasion was routed with the help of Sultan of Gujarat. The second attempt of Malwa Sultan was also foiled.

Muhammad Shah III (1463-1482 A.D.)

He was the younger brother of Nizam Shah. The Regency continued till 1466. Muhammad Gawan became the Prime Minister because the Wazir Khwaja Jahan had misappropriated public fund and was executed in the open court. He ably served his master and under his guidance the Bahamni kingdom flourished in several ways. In spite of his unquestioned authority, Muhammad Gawan served his master with the utmost sense of fidelity.

SERVICES OF MUHAMMAD GAWAN

War with Malwa

In 1468 the fortress of Khelna was captued from Mohmud Khilji, the Sultan of Malwa. By a treaty, Khelna was returned to Malwa and Berar was retained.

Western Campaigns

Bagalkot and Hubli were reduced. An immense booty was taken from the local chiefs. In 1470, Gawan, undertook an expedition to Konkan and it was annexed. Goa was conquered. Belgaum also fell into the hands of the Bahmani kingdom. Gawan also conquered the forts of Rajamundry, Kondapalli, and Kondavidu from Purushottama Gajapati of Orissa.

Southern Campaign

In 1481, the Sultan invaded Kanchi and demolished the Hindu temples. Masulipatnam was also captured. The kingdom had a vast stretch of territory between Tungabhadra and Tapati.

Other Campaigns

A rebellion staged by Hamir Rai a vassal of the Bahmani in Telengana was suppressed. Orissa too was subjugated.

Administrative Reforms

Gawan improved the administration and expanded the kingdom. He divided the kingdom into eight provinces. He introduced a revenue system which took the area of the land into consideration for the assessment of revenue. The same system was later on adopted by Todar Mal and Malik Ambar of Ahmadnagar. A college was founded at Bidar by Gawan.

Military Reforms

Gawan took pains in reorganising the military administration. The provincial governors called tarafdars were reduced of their hold over the military affairs. Muhammad Gawan thoroughly overhauled the Mansabdari system. He fixed the salary of the Mansabdars and stipulated the number of soldiers to be kept by them. If the mansabdars kept a less number of troops, they were asked to refund the amount in proportion to that number to the State exchequer.

Murder of Muhammad Gawan

Ever since the Bahmani kingdom came into existence the "foreingers" like Afghans and Mughal Amirs wielded great pomp and power in the Government. This policy of entertaining foreign elements in the country roused the jealousy of the "Deccan" Muslims. This resulted in a feud between these two groups. In course of time the feud assumed grave dimensions. The foreigners were at the height of their power towards the close of the 14th century. This state of affairs provoked the rancour of the "Deccan" Muslims and they began to follow vile conspiracies in order to gain upperhand. Muhammad Gawan was a foreigner belonging to Persia and hence naturally his ascendancy was not tolerated by the "Deccans". All the discontented Deccani nobles hatched a plot to bring about the downfall of Gawan. They forged a letter purporting to have been written by him to the Raja of Orissa inviting him to invade the Bahmani kingdom and promising him his own assistance. Gawan's seal was obtained by foul means and affixed to it. They brought this letter to the notice of the Sultan Muhammad Shah III while he was in a drunken mood. Without any enquiry the Sultan ordered for the immediate execution in his presence of Muhammad Gawan. Thus, the innocent and loyal minister was murdered.

Muhammad Gawan was the greatest of the Muslim administrators of the Deccan. He was a shrewd politician and statesman. He was known for his fidelity towards his master. He had rendered remarkable services in the military strategy of the Bahmani kingdom. He was a lover of art and letters. He believed and practised the proverb of "Simple living and high thinking." In short "Muhammad Gawan excelled as a diplomat, as a soldier as an administrator and as a man of letters — in all the walks of life" (Sherwani).

Mahmud Shah (1482-1518 A.D.)

Muhammad Shah III was succeeded by his son Mahmud Shah. During his reign, the Bahmani kingdom was dismembered into five independent states. Imad-ul-mulk declared independence of Berar with its capital at Elichpur in 1490. Kasim Barid proclaimed the freedom of Bidar in the year 1492.

Malik Ahmad established the Nizam Shahi dynasty at Ahmadnagar in 1490.

Quli Qutb Shah founded the Qutb Shahi dynasty in Golkonda in the year 1512.

Estimate of the Bahmani regime

Most of the Bahmani Sultans were cruel tyrants and fanatics who waged savage wars with Vijayanagar. They became victims to the vices like drunkenness and debauchery. The only bright chapter in their history is that of Muhammad Gawan. The Bahmanis did not disturb the local institutions. There was some encouragement of Muslim education and architecture.

PART II

MUGHAL EMPIRE

14

India on the Eve of Babur's Invasion

On the eve of Babur's invasion there was no strong power in the country. There were many warring states and a war for supremacy was going on among them. India was unable to show her united strength to any enemy who might possess the audacity and ambition to carve out an empire for himself. Dr. Ishwari Prasad said that India was a congeries of states on the eve of Babur's invasion. She would be the easy prey of an invader who had the strength and will to attempt her conquest. Let us see the positions of various kingdoms.

Kingdom of Delhi

Ibrahim Lodi, the last ruler of the Lodi dynasty was tactless. He did not consolidate his power and position. The kingdom had many independent principalities, jagirs and provinces ruled by Zamindars or Governors. They had abnormal powers. So the inhabitants looked more to their master rather than the king. Lanepoole said that the kingdom was depending upon the aristocracy of turbulent chiefs. The nobles acted to their whims and fancies. Ibrahim Lodi wanted to root out the strengthening powers of the nobles. For example, Mian Bhave and Azam Humayan were the victims to his anger against the nobles, which instigated them to start a rebellion against Ibrahim Lodi. Further the nobles could not tolerate the insult and decided to weaken the position of Delhi Sultan.

Kingdom of Mewar

Mewar was one of the important kingdoms on the eve of Babur's invasion. Rana Sanga was a powerful ruler of Mewar and he was the head of the Rajputs. He wanted to capture the throne of Delhi and Agra which were next to his territory. With this view in his mind he invited Babur to invade India. He thought that Babur would come to India, capture Delhi and plunder it. After accumulating the plundered wealth, he would go back to Kabul leaving Delhi in his hand. But his dream was true and after conquering Delhi, Babur established Mughal Empire in India.

Kingdom of Vijayanagar

It was a Hindu empire started in the 14th century with the object of checking the spread of Islam in South India. The important king of Vijayanagar was Krishnadeva Raya who embraced literature and science in his kingdom. The glory of Vijayanagar was peak during his reign. He was an outstanding and most brilliant ruler in the South Indian monarchs. The fabulous wealth that he conferred as endowments on temples and Brahmins mark him indeed as the greatest of the Indian ruler.

The rulers of Vijayanagar fought now and then against the Bahmani Kingdom which was vigorously spreading their religion Islam. Due to frequent fight between Bahmani Sultans and Vijayanagar rulers, the strength of Bahmani Sultans was broken and in the course of time, Bahmani Kingdom was broken into five independent kingdoms of Ahmednagar (1488-1633), Bijapur (1489-1688), Golkunda (1512-1687), Berar (1484-1527) and Bidar (1490-1574).

Kingdom of Kashmir

This kingdom was started by Shah Mirza in 1339. The important ruler of Kashmir was Zain-ul-Abidin. He adopted the policy of religious tolerance and patronage of Sanskrit. After his rule the successors were not effective and strong in consolidating their powers which resulted chaos and confusion in Kashmir.

Kingdom of Khandesh

This Kingdom was set up by Malik Raja Faruqi. It was an independent kingdom from the end of the 14th century. The rulers of Gujarat were against this kingdom and there were frequent wars between the two kingdoms. After 1508 there was a dispute over the question of succession to the throne in Khandesh. The rival claim was supported by Gujarat and Ahmedabad and in the war of succession Adil Khan III was succeeded. Thus, there was no peace in Khandesh also.

Kingdom of Malwa

It was independent Kingdom during the reign of Firoz Tughluq. In the beginning both Hindus and Mohammedans were happy and maintained a friendly intercourse with each other. After 1512 most of the key posts were filled up by Hindus and the power was captured by Rajputs which led the Mohammedans for bickering against the Rajputs.

Rana Sanga, the most powerful man of Rajputs helped to Medini Rao who defeated the forces of Malwa.

Kingdom of Bengal

During the reign of Firuz Tughlaq, Bengal attained the status of an independent nation. When Babur came to India, it was ruled by Nusrat Shah who restored peace and law and order in Bengal. He was a patron of Bengalee literature. There was prosperity in trade and commerce and people lived happily.

Kingdom of Orissa

It was an independent Hindu state which checked the aggression of Muslim ruler of Bengal to South India. As it was a small Hindu State, it did not have influence on the politics of Northern India.

Kingdom of Gujarat

The important ruler of Gujarat was Begarha. He defeated the Portuguese in 1508. However, later on the Portuguese recovered their places. After Begarha, the throne was given to Muzaffar

Shah II who had to fight with the enemies throughout his life time. Finally, he was defeated by Rana Sanga of Mewar. When Babur invaded India it was ruled by Bahadur Shah, the son of Muzaffar Shah II.

Babur's view

"The five kings who have been mentioned are great princes and all Mussalmans and possessed of formidable armies and rulers of vast territories. The most powerful of the pagan princes in point of territory and army is the Raja of Bijanagar. Another is the Rana Sanga who has attained his present high eminence, only in these later times, by his own valour and his sword. His original principality was Chittor."

Though there was no strong political power in India there was a cultural awakening. Bhakti movement was started under the leadership of Ramananda, Kabir, Chaitanya and others. Their teachings were against casteism, and groupism and both Muslims and Hindus must live as brothers and sisters. Many reformers came into existence in Muslim religion. They started propagating the important concepts of Musalmans which resulted there was progress in the cultural activities of India.

With regard to trade and commerce, India was prosperous. She had trade relations with Malaya, Tibet, China, Japan, Central Asia, etc. The agricultural production was surplus. In the field of military, India had good trained soldiers. But they did not know the latest know-how in the field of military science. Thus, when Babur invaded India, Indian soliders were unable to give strong resistance to Babur.

15

Babur

Babur, the founder of Mughal dynasty was born in 1483 and was connected with the families of Timur and Chingiz Khan. His mother Qutlugnigar Khanum was descendant of Chingiz Khan and his father Shaikh Mirza had the blood of Timur. His father the ruler of Farghana, died at the age of 12 and Babur became the King of Farghana. At the time of his accession he was surrounded by his enemies on all sides. Due to his inexperience he had to face many difficulties. His uncle Ahmed Mirza attacked Babur in 1495 but Babur fortunately succeeded with the help of his Amirs.

Conquest of Samarkand

His uncle, Ahmed Mirza, the ruler of Samarkand died in 1495. After his death there was confusion and chaos in Samarkand. Babur took full advantage of the chaos and led an expedition to Samarkand. The desire of capturing Samarkand was fulfilled in 1497.

Loss of Farghana

After capturing Samarkand Babur fell ill in Samarkand and his ministers declared that he was dead. So Jahangir, the younger brother of Babur was put on the throne of Farghana. When Babur recovered from his illness he found that he was not the King of any place. He led a life of wandering for more than a year. Babur himself writes, "For the sake of Farghana I have given Samarkand but now I find I had lost one without securing the other."

Babur—a wanderer

With great difficulties, Babur was able to recapture Samarkand in 1500 but after eight months, he was forced by Uzbegs to leave the country. The period from 1502 and 1504 was the period of ups and downs in his life. In 1502 he ran away from his native land and wandered here and there to try his luck.

Babur captured Kabul

During his wandering life, the political condition in Kabul was not conducive. Ulugh Beg, the ruler of Kabul died and the throne was given to his son Abdul Razack who was deposed by an usurper named Mukin Beg. The people of Kabul did not like the usurper as their king and they wanted a royal blood should be put on the throne of Kabul. Babur took this opportunity and won over the nobles to his side and thus he himself became the King of Kabul in 1504.

Capture and loss of Samarkand

Saibani was the ruler of Samarkand. His relations with Shah of Persia was not good. Considering this condition Babur concluded an alliance with Shah of Persia for the purpose of capturing Samarkand. "With the help of Shah, Babur captured Bokhara and Samarkand but he was not able to sit on the throne of Samarkand for long. Within a year Babur was again driven out from Samarkand and he returned to Kabul. So Babur made up his mind to divert his attention to East instead of invading the Western direction. It was only after his final failure in Samarkand that Babur paid his full attention to the conquest of India.

Circumstances leading to the battle of Panipat

(i) *Desire of Babur*

Babur desired to establish a dynasty. So he first tried to fulfil his ambition in Central Asia. He invaded Samarkand several times but all the times he could not succeed. So he made up his mind that the desire of establishing a dynasty in Central Asia could not be possible. So he changed his mind on India.

(ii) *Religious fanaticism*

Babur was a fanatic in religion. He was against the Hindu principles of idolatry and polytheism. He felt that the duty of every pious Muslim was to spread and penetrate Islam in various parts of Asia. To fulfil this desire and ambition, he selected India.

(iii) *Babur's Army*

His army was very strong and efficient. Many great leaders like Ustad Ali and Mustaffa were the great fighters. He learned military techniques from Afghans, Mongols and Persians and introduced the techniques in his army. His artillery worked wonderfully.

(iv) *Wealth of India*

Babur came to know that India was rich in her financial status. He was bankrupt and in case he captured India he could take away huge treasure from India to meet out his financial crisis.

(v) *Geographical knowledge of India*

Babur was the ruler of Kabul. As India was nearer to Kabul, he came to know the geographical position of India. Further he had been to Punjab in 1504 and knew the geographical situation of India. The knowledge of India made him boldly to invade India.

(vi) *Immediate cause*

When Babur had an idea of invading India, he was invited by Daulat Khan Lodi, Governor of Punjab who revolted against Ibrahim Lodi and declared himself independent. Further, Ibrahim Lodi, the Delhi Sultan was inefficient and weak monarch. This fact was also intimated to Babur. If Babur would like to invade Delhi, he would be helped by Daulat Khan Lodi. Further Rana Sangram Singh who was against Ibrahim, also assured his full support to Babur against Lodi Sultan. So Babur decided to march towards India from Kabul and reached Lahore.

Battle of Panipat, 1526

Babur made elaborate preparation for the war. First of all, he marched with huge forces to India. He took this action due to the conspiracies of Daulat Khan of Punjab and unfaithfulness of Alam Khan, uncle of Ibrahim Lodi. First he defeated Daulat Khan and pardoned him. Then Babur advanced his forces to Delhi. Ibrahim Lodi came out with his mighty forces and the two forces met at the historic plains of Panipat in 1526. Artillery wing of the Babur's army was in the central position. The right wing of his force was protected by the town Panipat and the left wing was protected by a ditch that had been dug. The artillery was functioning effectively. In spite of the superior numerical strength of Ibrahim Lodi's forces, he was defeated and killed in the battlefield itself. Babur captured Delhi and Agra. Dr. Ishwari Prasad said, "The Battle of Panipat placed the empire of Delhi in Babur's hands. The power of Lodi Dynasty was shattered to pieces and the sovereignty of Hindustan passed on to the Chaghtai Turks."

Reasons for the success of Babur at Panipat

(i) Babur himself was a great general and learnt military tactics and knowhow. Due to his efficient and quick decision in the battlefield he divided his army into three sections — the right, the centre and the left and he posted skilful generals on the extreme left and right ends. Babur's forces surrounded the Indians on all directions and slaughtered the Indian soldiers.

(ii) Babur had a powerful artillery rather than Ibrahim Lodi who did not have even guns. The conservative and traditional types of weapons could not play havoc in the war field. So Babur's artillery completely rooted out the Indian soldiers. It was one of the causes for Ibrahim's defeat at Panipat.

(iii) Ibrahim Lodi could not get support the local chiefs who declared themselves independent. Further Daulat Khan Lodi of Punjab and Alam Khan raised their banners of revolt against Delhi Sultan and extended their whole-hearted support to Babur in case he led an expedition against Ibrahim Lodi.

(iv) Ibrahim used a large number of elephants in his army. It proved fatal for the army.

(v) The inefficiency of Ibrahim was one of the reasons for the failure in the Panipat. He did not maintain a good trained army. He lacked the qualities of a good general. The espionage system adopted by Ibrahim Lodi was very poor and they could not give correct information to Ibrahim about the strategy of Babur.

Results of the War

(i) It was a turning point in the history of India. Just as Clive established British Empire in India after the battle of Plassey, Babur established Mughal Empire after the first battle of Panipat.

(ii) Babur crushed the mighty power of Ibrahim Lodi and the remaining Lodi chiefs were too weak to restore their strength in the country.

(iii) Artillery was first used in Panipat, Indians changed their age old conservative method of war technique. They began to use guns and modern weapons in the battlefield.

(iv) Mr. R.B. William said, "The defeat of Ibrahim's army was but the beginning of the huge task." Babur had to fight with Rajaputs and minor Afghan rivals.

(v) In the words of Lanepoole, "The people of India were definitely against the foreigners and as such, every city and every official, small or great had prepared himself for an opportunity of opposition to Babur."

(vi) Babur had to face troubles and discontentment of his soldiers who would like to return to their mother country. So, to satisfy them Babur had distributed much booty to the soldiers which resulted the treasury of Babur empty and he found extremely difficult to gear up the administrative machinery.

Battle of Kanwah 1527

(1) Before the battle of Panipat there was an agreement between Babur and Rana Sanga of Mewar. As per the agreement Rana Sanga should help Babur when he attacked Ibrahim Lodi of Delhi but Rana Sanga did not keep up his promise. So after the victory in the Panipat, Babur accused him of bad faith and refused to hand over Kalpi, Dholpur and Biyana to Rana Sanga as promised already.

(2) Rana Sanga was an ambitious man and decided to sit on the throne of Delhi. This was unliked by Babur and wanted to teach a lesson to Rana Sanga.

(3) Rana Sanga of Mewar attacked Nizam Khan, the ruler of Biyana who unable to meet him, sought the help of Babur. Babur readily sent his armed forces and Rana could not establish his rule in Biyana.

In 1527 Rana Sanga marched his forces to the plains of Kanwah. Babur also advanced his forces and the battle took place at Kanwah in 1526. The advance guard of Babur was defeated by Rajputs. Babur's oldiers learnt the bravery and valour of Rana Sanga of Mewar. So they lost the hope of winning in the battle. Further their thinking was precipitated by the news of the astrologers that Babur would be defeated in this battle. But he did not lose his heart. He gave a thundering, powerful and impressive appeals to his soldiers. To encourage and instigate the soldiers, he gave up wine and broke his costly vessels. The address given by him at that moment is given below :

> "Noblemen and soldiers! Every man who comes into the world is subject to dissolution. When we are passed away and gone God only survives and is unchangeable. Whoever comes to the feast of life must, before it is over, drink from the cup of death. He who arrives at the inn of mortality must one day inevitably take his departure from that house of sorrow — the world. How much better it is to die with honour than to live with infamy....If we fall in the battle we die the death of martyr; If we survive we rise victorious. Let us then with one accord swear on God's holiness that none of us will even think of turning his face from this warfare till his soul is separated from his body."

This appealing had a stirring, intense and deep effect on the soldiers. They got fresh vigour and strength and fought with the enemy with extra power. Babur adopted the same technique as he had adopted in the battle of Panipat. The army was divided into three parts — the right, the left and the central wings and each wing was put under an able Commander-in-Chief.

Babur himself attacked the enemy like a lion rushing from the lair. In the battle Rana Sanga was seriously wounded. The powerful confederacy of Rajputs was shattered into pieces. After the victory Babur ordered to erect a tower of skulls near the camp. He assumed the title of Ghazi or the champion of Faith.

Results of the War

Firstly, supremacy of Rajaputs was crushed. Secondly, Mughal empire was firmly established and recognised by the minor chiefs. Thirdly, before the battle Babur was the King of Kabul but after his victory in the battle of Kanwah he remained in India throughout his life. Fourthly, Rana Sanga took a vow not to enter his palace at Chittor and revenge Babur. When he heard of Babur's invasion of Chanderi, he started for that place. But he died in January 1528 before he could render any help.

Capture the Fort of Chanderi 1528

It was a strong and rock fort ruled by Medini Rao. After the battle of Kanwah, the powers of Rajputs were not completely destroyed. So they joined together under the leadership of Medini Rao and offered stiff resistance to Babur who crushed their mighty power. After this, there was no Rajput Chief to challenge the authority of Babur.

Battle of Ghagra 1529

After crushing the powers of Rajput, Babur had to face the resistance of Afghans who joined together under the leadership of Mahmood Lodi, the brother of Ibrahim Lodi. Babur sent his brother Askari to deal with them and himself followed his brother. On hearing the news many Afghans deserted Mahmood Lodi. Greatly disgusted by this act, he ran away from Bihar and sheltered with Nusrat Shah of Bengal. Babur went in hot pursuit of him and defeated Mahmood Lodi at Ghagra in 1529. After the battle there was an alliance between Nusrat Shah of Bengal and Babur in which Shah accepted not to give shelter to the enemy of Babur.

Death of Babur, 1530

The death of Babur was strange and curious. His son Humayun fell in sickness and doctors declared that he could not survive. At that time Babur did not like his son to die. So he walked three times round the bed of Humayun and prayed God that he should die instead of his beloved son. It is said that from that time onwards Humayun began to recover and the conditions of Babur had gone from bad to worse and died on 25th December, 1530. As requested by Babur his body was taken to

Kabul and laid in peace in his garden surrounded by those he loved, by the sweet smelling flowers of his choice and the cool running stream.

Estimate. Babur was deeply engaged in establishing Mughal empire, he carried out many administrative reforms. He replaced the weak confederal monarchy of the Afghans by a divine right of despotism. The powers of the king was unquestionable and supreme. He treated all his subordinate nobles as his slaves. Mir Nizam-ud-Din-Khalifa was appointed as Prime Minister who acted as a link between the king and nobles. He introduced Persian way of life in India. Many palaces, underground rooms and baths had been constructed during his reign. He was subjective neither to Hindus nor to Afghans. He treated all people equally with affection and tender heart. All the key posts were filled up by both Hindus and Afghans. In short he embraced the policy of religious toleration after becoming the ruler of Delhi.

Babur constructed Dak Chaukis at every 15 miles interval where the good horses were maintained. By means of Dak Chaukis, Babur was able to get latest and current information about the country from distant places. Babur did not have effective control over the local officers in the provinces. They enjoyed a lot of autonomy. Babur did not take steps for the promotion of agriculture. The economic condition was deplorable and squandered away the treasures of Delhi and Agra by distribution of prizes to the nobles after the victory of Delhi.. So he had to face financial difficulties.

As he followed the policy of religious toleration, he married the daughter of Medini Rao to Humayun and Kamran. The son of Rana Sanga was appointed as his Vassal.

Character of Babur

Babur was a brilliant man. He was the founder of Mughal Empire. V.A. Smith writes, "Babur was the most brilliant Asiatic Prince of his age and worthy of a high place among the sovereigns of India."

According to Rushbrook Williams, "Babur possessed eight fundamental qualities — lofty judgement, noble ambition, the art of victory, the art of Government, the art of conferring prosperity upon his people, the talent of ruling mildly the people of God, the ability to win the hearts of his soldiers and love of justice.

No doubt Babur was a founder of a new dynasty. He rooted out the resistance of his enemies. He was a great conqueror. In the battle of Panipat, Kanwah and Ghagra he showed his excellent talent in the military science. He introduced all his skill and tacts to win over the wars. Babur was very kind, pious and generous man. He sacrificed his life for the survival of his son Humayun.

He was patron of art and literature. He had immense love for nature. Babur did not leave behind him any decent public and philanthropic institutions and so could not win over the goodwill of the people.

Babur's Memoirs

Autobiography of Babur called Tuzuk-i-Babri is popularly known as Memoirs of Babur. This book was written in Turki language. It was translated in many languages. This book was the authentic and original source material. It gives a vivid description of his life in a frank and free manner. The shortcomings of Babur were also clearly mentioned. The nature and geographical location of his empire, the custom and tradition of people with whom he contacted, the boundaries of his dynasty, the wars that he undertook, the political, social and religious conditions of the people were stated in his book. It gives light on the history of other Central Asian countries like Farghana and Samarkand. This book is praised by various eminent historians.

According to Rushbrook Williams, "Babur's place in history rests upon his Indian conquests, but his place in biography and literature is determined by his delightful Memoirs."

16

Humayun (1530-1556)

Humayun, the eldest son of Babur was born in March, 1508. Humayun means "the fortunate." His mother's name was Mahim Begam who was probably a Shia. He had three brothers namely Kamran, Askari and Hindal.

Humayun's Early Education

Babur, the father of Humayun took very keen interest to give proper education to his beloved elder son. Humayun learnt Turki, Arabic, Persian in his early years and he was interested in Mathematics, Philosophy, Astronomy and Astrology. He learnt the art of administration with the help of his father. He was appointed as Governor of Badakshan at the age of 20. The district of Hissar Firoza and the Jagirs of Sambal were given to him for his training in the administration. Though he was given good education, he was noted for his carelessness.

He took part in the battle of Panipat in 1526, and Kanwah in 1527 and learnt the military secrets and the qualities of good generalship. In 1527 he was sent to Badakshan. In 1529 he returned to Agra and was ordered by his father to look after the management and administration of Jagirs of Sambhal. When he was in Sambhal and fell in sickness and was brought to Agra. Then his father prayed for his survival. His father died and he recovered.

Humayun's Accession

After the death of Babur there was difficult for Humayun to enthrone Delhi empire. The Prime Minister, Khalifa Nizam-ud-Din Ali, decided that the empire required a strong and best administrator who must serve to the will of the people and Din Ali liked Mahmud. Khwaja the brother-in-law of Babur to put on the throne of Delhi. He was a rich experienced and competent man. But Humayun lacked such qualities and a large section of the people was against him. So there was confusion over the question of succession. Finally Humayun was able to sit on the throne of Mughal empire after four days confusion on 30th December, 1530.

Early Difficulties of Humayun

The empire that he inherited was not a bed of roses. He had to face many challenges and ecounters. Babur did not consolidate his position and authority. Though the Rajput's powers were crushed, they wanted to revenge Humayun. The great provinces of Bengal, Malwa and Gujarat were against the rule of Humayun. Further administration was not sound and economic condition was deplorable. The Jagirdars were acting as independent rulers and they could not be controlled by Babur. So Humayun found extremely difficult to run the administration. The empire that he inherited was ill-organised and unconsolidated.

No Law of Primogeniture

There was no law of primogeniture among the Muslims. Every time, when the king died there was a dispute or war of succession among the sons of the dead kings. According to Erskine, "The sword was the grand arbiter of right, and every son was prepared to try his fortune against his brothers."

Mixed Body of Army

The army consisted of the Uzbegs, the Turks, the Mughals, the Afghans and the Persinas and it was undependable. Since the army was heterogenous nature, there was no uniformity in their ideas and customs. There was no national spirit and enthusiam among the soldiers. Further, unable to tolerate the excess heat in India, they wanted to go back to mother country.

Empty Treasury

Humayun got a depleted treasury from his father who lavishly spent the money by way of giving prizes to the nobles after the battle of Panipat. As he found the treasury was empty, he lost hope and interest to gear up the administration. So he had to face financial crisis right from the beginning.

Enmity of Afghan Nobles

Though the Afghans were crushed in the battle of Panipat (1526) and Ghagra (1527), they raised their revolt against Humayun. Alam Khan, the Bahadur Shah, Mohammad Lodi and Sher Khan were the notable Afghan rivals. All the Afghans supported the cause of Mohammed Lodi. Not only this, Sher Khan had already started his career of adventure and conquest in Bengal and Bihar.

Weakness of Humayun

He was very kind to his brothers and as requested by his father Babur, he gave the province of Sambhal to Askari and Alwar to Hindal. Kamaran, another brother was given Kabul and Kandhar. He was not satisfied and demanded Punjab. So Humayun gave Punjab to his brother and the cession of Punjab, Kabul and Kandhar to Kamran was a suicidal step. The revenue that he got from these provinces was lost. He was left only with the empire which was newly conquered and over which his hold was not secured.

"The worst enemy of Humayun was he himself." According to Lanepoole, "He lacked character and resolution. He was incapable of sustained effort after the moment of triumph and would busy himself in his harem and dream away the precious hours in the opium eaters paradise while his enemies were thundering at his gate."

Expedition of Kalinjar (1531)

Humayun led an expedition against the Raja of Kalinjar who was in favour of Afghans. The seige of this fort was lasted for many months and Humayun was forced to accept a huge indemnity from the Raja of Kalinjar. Humayun could not defeat the Raja due to his own weakness.

Defeat of Mahmood Lodi

The Afghans under the leadership of Mahmood Lodi marched to the province of Jaunpur to revenge Humayun. Humayun who was actually engaged in besieging Kalinjar had to give up his attempt and met the Afghans at Dourah (1532). In this battle the Afghans were defeated by Humayun.

Invasion of Chunar (1532)

After defeating Afghans at Dourah, Humayun besieged the fort of Chunar. It was a strong fort under the command of Sher Khan. Instead of defeating Sher Khan, Humayun accepted a purely perfunctory submission. It was a mistake done by Humayun and he did not punish Sher Khan, the rising star against him and he had to pay heavily for his mistake later on.

War with Bahadur Shah (1535-1536)

After the seige of Chunar, Humayun spent huge money in erecting Din Panah, a big citadel at Delhi. At that time Bahadur Shah was increasing his power in leaps and bounds. He acquired the territory of Malwa in 1531, captured the fort of Raisin in 1532 and defeated the Raja of Chittor in 1533. He gave shelter to Mohammad Zaman Mirza who had escapted from Humayun and when the latter requested Bahadur Shah to hand over him, Shah refused to do so. So a war was inevitable with Bahadur Shah.

Bahadur Shah besieged the fort of Chittor. The mother of the Raja appealed help from Humayun. The request was accepted and Humayun sent his forces to Chittor. But he changed his decision later on the basis of principles of Koran that he could not attack Bahadur Shah when he was engaged in war with non-Muslim. If Humayun might have attacked him he would be victorious to revenge his enemy. Then after the fall of Chittor, Humayun led an expedition against Bahadur Shah who took shelter in the fort of Mandu. Humayun advanced to the fort of Mandu and captured. When Mandu fort was captured, Bahadur Shah ran away to Champanir and then to Cambay. Here Humayun made a mistake by not consolidating his position at Mandu and Champanir. He wasted much time in merry making and squandered away the treasure that had fallen into their hands at Champanir. The administration of Champanir was rotten and considering the situation in the province of Champanir, Bahadur Shah attacked Gujarat and got back a large number of towns. The local chief also helped Bahadur Shah and he was able to capture the whole of Gujarat in 1536. "One year had seen the rapid conquest of the two great provinces, the next saw them is quickly lost."

War with Sher Khan (1537-1539)

After the defeat at Gujarat, Humayun stayed at Agra. At that time, Sher Khan was increasing his power by capturing Bengal and Bihar in 1536. He was the real master of Bihar, Humayun made up him mind to fight with Sher Khan only in 1537 and he invaded the fort of Chunar and captured it only by means of a trick. After capturing the fort he did not consolidate his position and wasted six months in Chunar for nothing. Then Humayun proceeded towards Banaras and stayed there for some time. In 1538 he reached Gaur and wasted eight months in merry making, Sher Khan cut off the roads leading to Delhi from Bengal and strengthened his position. He captured the whole of the country between Kosi and Ganga. When Humayun realised his follies, he decided to return to Agra and he did it immediately in March 1539.

Siege of Chausa (1539)

As the roads leading to Agra from Bengal was completely cut off, Humayun decided to fight with Sher Khan and both armies were facing each other at Chausa. There was delay for three months which was welcomed by Sher Khan. The result was that after three months, the rains started and the Mughal encampment was completely destroyed by flood. Humayun himself was washed away in the flood. He lost his beloved wife. Finally, he was saved with the help of a water-carrier.

Battle of Kanauj (1540)

In the battle of Chausa Humayun was defeated. He managed to reach Agra and called his brother to take revenge against Sher Khan. Kamran was prepared to help his brother and reached Agra with 20,000 troops but the assistance offered by his brother was not accepted by Humayun since Kamran was undependable man. Somehow Humayun raised a hugh army of 40,000 soldiers. In May 1540 the battle started between the two forces at Kanauj. In this battle also Humayun waited one month to begin the battle and by this Sher Khan made full preparation and attacked. The

Mughal artillery could not be utilised due to the rains. In this battle Humayun became a fugitive and Sher Khan became the master of Agra and Delhi.

Defeat of Humayun

(i) *Corrupt Officials*

When Sher Khan was raising his power and position, Humayun wanted to curb down his position. He sent his officials Hindu Beg and Sheikh Khalil to punish Sher Khan but the officials were bribed by Sher Khan. Further, the officials did not give the real strength of Sher Khan.

(ii) *Undependable Brothers*

When Humayun was defeated in the battle of Kanauj, he expected help from his brothers. But his expectation was not fulfilled. Hindal and Askari revolted at Agra which encouraged Sher Khan to fight against Humayun. Thus, the non-cooperation and faithlessness of his brothers of Humayun was one of the factors responsible for his defeat.

(iii) *Mistake of Humayun*

In the battle of Chausa, Humayun waited for three months. The rainy season started and the Mughal camp was devastated by flood. He was also carried away in the flood and he was saved by a water carrier. So also in the battle of Kanauj. He waited a month and by this time, his enemy gathered power and strength. So the mistakes committed by Humayun were one of the factors for his failure in the war.

Humayun's efforts to capture Delhi

After his defeat at Kanauj, he reached Agra and had to leave that place also. He tried to go to Kashmir but his arrival to Kashmir was blocked by his brother Kamran. So he was forced to go to Sindh. When he was wanderer he was invited by the ruler of Marwar and he was pleased to go over Marwar. But on his way he came to know that the ruler of Marwar changed his mind. So he proceeded to Sindh. On his way to Sindh, Raja of Amarkot extended his help by giving shelter where Akbar was born in 1542.

Humayun went to Persia

Finding his position insecure he went to Persia where he was promised to extend all possible help on the condition that he should become a Shia. Humayun accepted this condition and got the help of 14,000 soldiers for this invasion to recapture the throne of Delhi. He first marched towards India with huge army and captured Kandhar. He handed over Kandhar to the ruler of Persia as per the agreement reached among the two. Then he invaded and captured Kabul in 1544 from Kamran.

War with his brothers

After the capture of Kabul, he fell ill and taking this opportunity, Kamran recaptured Kabul from Humayun. Kamran was again defeated and forgiven in 1548. In 1549 Kamran again conquered Kandhar and in the third time Kamran was defeated. He ran away from the battlefield. Humayun did not show any kindness and sympathy. He ordered his eyes to be plucked out and sent to Mecca and finally Kamran died in 1557 at Mecca. His brother Askari was also despatched to Mecca and he never came to India. Hindal, the another brother of Humayun was killed.

Recapture of Delhi

Sher Khan who captured Delhi in 1540 was died. He was succeeded by Islam Shah in 1545. After Islam Shah, Mohammed Adil Shah was the ruler of Delhi. He was a weak monarch and pleasure loving man. His authority was challenged by Ibrahim Shah. Watching this chaotic situation, Humayun attacked India in 1554 and occupied Lahore in 1554. Then, he captured and seated on the throne of Delhi after a period of 15 years.

Causes for the failure of Humayun

(1) When he ascended the throne of Delhi, he would like to fulfil the desire of his father, Babur by giving various parts of his empire of his brothers and he did it. By doing so he weakened his position and strength. This was one of the causes for his failure.

(2) Another important cause for his failure was the hostility of his brothers with whom he had love, affection and kindness.

They did not lend their helping hand when Humayun was in trouble. However, this view was not accepted by Dr. Tripathi.

(3) When Humayun was ruler of Delhi, he did not take any steps to tone up the administration. He did not look after the welfare and well being of the people. He was always busily engaged in wars. So when he lost his empire, he was not helped by any people and he was forced to run away to Persia.

(4) He inherited a empty treasury from his father. He had to face financial crisis on and off. This was another cause for his failure.

(5) Humayun was not a good general. In the battle of Chausa, he waited three months for nothing. The rainly season started and due to heavy downpour, his army camp was destroyed by flood and he was carried away by the flood. Further, in the battle of Kanauj he selected a low land for encampment and remained silence for a month. As Sher Khan attacked all of a sudden, Humayun could not make use of his artillery and the result was his failure.

(6) Another cause for his failure was his own character and he lacked correct and accurate judgement and decision. He could not stick to a job. The result was that before anything was done completely, his mind passed on something else leaving the first one-half complete.

(7) He was open minded and plain hearted man. He did not suspect even his enemies. He believed in whatever he was told by anybody. The defeat at Chausa could have been averted if he had not believed the words of Sher Khan.

Death of Humayun

Humayun slipped down from the building known as Din Panah in January 1556 and died soon. According to Lanepoole, "He tumbled through life and tumbled out of it."

Humayun's Estimate

Love and affection

He loved his brothers very much. He was very kind, generous and highly outlined man. Dr. Ishwari Prasad writes, "Humayun was by nature a kind, gentle and affectionate monarch.

He was well disposed towards his kinsmen and treated them with generosity and leniency even when they conspired to bring about his ruins. When the nobles made an impassioned appeal to him to slay his arch enemy, Kamran, he replied though my head inclines to your words my heart does not and refused to stain his hands with murder of a brother."

Character of Humayun

(1) He was very polite in his conversation, decent in his behaviour and high degree of charity and munificence.

(2) He was a pleasure loving man. Lanepoole said that after the moment of victory, he would spend time in harem and in the opium eaters paradise, while his enemies were thundering the gate. When Bahadur Shah and Sher Khan were gaining power, he took delight in merry making and wasted his precious time.

(3) He was deeply interested in literature. He was unrival in the field of astronomy and mathematics and he wrote many essays on the nature of elements and celestial bodies. He was an expert in geography and delighted in the company of the learned people. Great decorum was adopted in his reception and a highly civilised and learned discussions were held in the most orderly hours.

(4) He was a duty conscious man. He was an ideal son, ideal brother, ideal father and an ideal husband. He was an intense pious man and true Muslim but he was not a fanatic of Islam. He followed the policy of religious toleration. His chief queen was a Shia and Bairam Khan was also a Shia. He used to follow the teaching of Islam but was not as staunch as the rulers of the Sultanate period.

(5) Humayun was a good soldier and was not afraid of the battlefield. He helped his father in the first battle of Panipat and the battle of Kanwah but he lacked exactness, clearness and clever judgement. He was not a great general and was cheated by his enemies frequently. As he had many weaknesses, he could not tone up the standard of the soldiers. The army proved superiority in the time of Babur lost its vitality and strength and it had many drawbacks.

(6) Humayun was not an expert in the administration. When he was the ruler of Delhi, he failed miserably to take steps to improve the administration. There was no concrete and solid reforms introduced by him. As he was deeply interested in merry making he had no administrative aptitude.

Dr. A.L. Srivastava remarked, "His considerable natural talent was greatly undermined by his addition to opium and by sensual indulgence. His overgenerosity and leniency towards his brothers and relatives whom he forgave again and again, proved to be impediments in the way of orderly and disciplined Government."

17

Sher Shah Suri and His Successors (1540-1546)

Birth of Sher Shah

The real name of Sher Shah, the lion king was Farid. His father's name was Hussain, Hussain entered the service of Jamal Khan of Punjab and when Jamal Khan was transferred to Jaunpur in the time of Sikandar Lodi, he handed over the Jagir of Sahsaram, Khawaspur and Tanda to Hussain.

Early life of Farid

Farid's father Hussain had married two wives and had eight children. As usual he loved his youngest wife. As Farid was the son of the eldest wife he was not happy in Sahsaram. So he entered the services of Jamal Khan at Jaunpur and earned the goodwill of his master. His master admired his ability and intelligence and as a result of the intervention of Jamal Khan Farid was appointed by Hussain to manage his Jagir and he did it successfully for 21 years.

Farid — the Jagir of Sahsaram

Due to his good administration and management Farid earned popularity which was not liked by his step mother who poisoned the ears of her husband against Farid. So Farid was driven out from Sahsaram for the second time in 1518. He went to Ibrahim Lodi and requested him to grant the Jagir of his father. But Lodi refused to grant it. When Farid's father passed away, Lodi appointed him Jagir in the place of his father.

His difficulties in the beginning

His step mother challenged the right of granting Jagir to Farid. The Jagir should be divided and his step brother should be given. It was mentioned by his step mother. She got the help of Mohammad Khan Sur of Chand in Bihar. To overcome this difficulty, he joined the service of Bahar Khan Lohani, the independent ruler of Bihar, who gave him the title Sher Khan, when he killed a tiger single handed. Sher Khan was appointed as tutor to Jallal Khan, the son of Bahar Khan.

Sher Khan got the help of Babur

Sher Khan got popularity in Bihar. The Afghan nobles and Lohani nobles did not like his popularity and as a result of their wording with Bahar Khan, Sher Khan was expelled. So, he jointed the services of Babur in 1527. When Babur invaded Bihar, he was much helped by Sher Khan to capture Bihar. As a reward of his help and bravery, his Jagir was restored in Bihar.

Sher Khan ruler of Bihar

During his service with Babur he closely watched the weakness and drawbacks of Mughal administration and knew the pitfalls then and there. Then he left the services and entered the service of Bahar Khan. After the death of Bahar Khan in 1528, Sher Khan was appointed as Deputy Governor of Bihar. He did many reforms and toned up the administration in Bihar. After the death of Dadu Bibi, the wife of Bahar Khan, Sher Khan became the actual ruler of Bihar.

Conquest of Sher Khan or Sher Shah

(i) *War with Humayun : Siege of Chunar Fort*

Chunar was a rock fort belonged to Sher Khan. Humayun led an expedition against the fort and the invasion lasted for 4 months and during this period Sher Khan was managed to defy the might of Humayun. Finally Humayun had to make a peace treaty with Sher Khan in 1533 as he learnt the news of trouble in Gujarat by Bahadur Shah. As per this treaty Sher Khan was the master of Chunar and he had to send a contingent of 500 troops for service in the Mughal army.

(ii) *Battle of Chausa, 1539*

After the treaty with , Humayun would like to proceed to Bengal. He captured Gaur and wasted his precious time in merry making for many months. During this period, Sher Shah established his authority from Bihar to Delhi. The communication to Delhi was absolutely under his control and he awaited an opportunity to defeat Humayun who was wasting his time in Bengal. In June 1539 rainy season started and the soldiers were unable to tolerate the severe cool climate. Further due to heavy downpour, there was a flood in which the army camp of Humayun was washed away. In June 1539 was fought the Battle of Chausa in which Humayun was defeated. The victory of Sher Shah made him *de facto* ruler of Bengal and Bihar and declared himself as king of Bengal and Bihar in 1539.

(iii) *Battle of Kanauj 1540*

The victory of Chausa made him the ruler of Bihar and Bengal. He had an ambition to sit on the throne of Delhi. But the defeat of Humayun in the battle of Chausa did not lose his courage and made up his mind to revenge Sher Shah. So Humayun collected a huge force and reached the place of Kanauj, situated on the banks of Ganges. Mirza Haider stated that the armies of Sher Shah and Humayun were standing against each other on either sides of river Ganges. Here also, Humayun repeated the same folly which was responsible for his defeat in the battle of Chausa. He did not attack Sher Shah for one month. It was Sher Shah who attacked the Mughals and in the battle of Kanauj, Humayun was defeated.

The delay of Humayun to start the battle of Kanauj, the non-co-operation of his brothers, the death of able and efficient generals of Babur in the natural course, or left for their home, the intolerable cool climate of Bengal to Mughal forces, Sher Shah's superior tactics, organisations and correct estimate of Mughal's army were the main causes for the victory of Sher Shah in the battle of Kanauj.

(iv) *Capture of Agra and Delhi 1540*

After the battle of Kanauj, Humayun was running from pillar to post to save his life. He reached Agra and Delhi somehow, but

Sher Shah chased him. When Sher Shah reached Delhi, Humayun ran away from Delhi to Lahore to get shelter from his brother Kamran. He was not prepared to risk a conflict with Sher Shah and did not help his brother by providing necessary helps and accommodation. So Humayun ran away from India.

(v) *Capture of Gakkhar territory*

When Sher Shah chased Humayun, he reached Punjab and annexed it. He led an expedition against Gakkhar territory and occupied it. He undertook this invasion to prevent re-entry of Humayun into India from North-West frontier. He also constructed a strong fort of Rohtas at Jhelum.

(vi) *Conquest of Malwa (1542)*

Malwa was now an independent country. Previously it was under the control of Humayun. So Sher Shah led an expedition against Malwa and conquered it in 1542. It was also stated that the ruler of Malwa was the leader of Rajputs and he crushed the Muslims authority. So Sher Shah attacked Malwa.

(vii) *Capture of Raisin (1543)*

Pooran Mal was the ruler of Raisin who had done cruelties to the Muslims. He enslaved the Muslim women. This was hated by Sher Shah and he invaded Raisin. But the fort was strongly defended by Rajputs. As the resistance was very severe, Sher Shah wanted to capture the fort by a clever device. He made a promise on Quran that if Rajputs were surrendered they would be offered good treatment and safe to their life. But contrary to the promise, when Rajputs came out of the fort, they were severely attacked. The children of Pooran Mal were captured alive. The daughter was made to dance in the street in the midst of the people. The boys were ordered to be castrated so that the race may be destroyed. In the words of Ishwari Prasad, "Such was the inhuman barbarity of Sher Shah towards an enemy who had relied upon plighted faith...."

(viii) *Capture of Multan and Sind (1543)*

Rebellion was started in these provinces. To crush the rebellion Sher Shah appointed Haibat Khan as Governor of these provinces who had to face a turbulent robber, Fateh Khan, a great Jat. Haibat Khan crushed the rebellion of Jat and occupied Multan and Sind.

(ix) *Capture of Rajputana (1543)*

Maldeo, the ruler of Marwar gave shelter to Humayun. So Sher Shah decided to invade and marched against Maldeo. As decided by Sher Shah, the victory of Maldeo was not an easy thing. The Rajputs put forth their combined strength. So Sher Shah made up his mind to win over the Rajputs through a clever device. A forged letter was prepared and circulated to create misunderstanding between Maldeo and his army. Maldeo was so much disgusted with all these affairs that he left the field. Though he left, the Rajputs put up a stiff resistance and it was extremely difficult to capture it easily. Sher Shah himself accepted "I have never lost the empire of Hindustan for a handful of Bajra (Millet)." Finally he captured Rajputana.

(x) *Seige of Kalinjar*

In 1545 Sher Shah seiged Kalinjar and the seige was prolonged for many months, Sher Shah decided to blow up the walls of the fort. Mines were dug and he was injured by the explosion of gun powder. The fort was taken by Sher Shah himself and he died in May 1545.

ADMINISTRATION OF SHER SHAH

Sher Shah was not only a great conqueror but also an administrator. He was a benevolent despot and not an autocratic king. He took keen interest to tone up the administration. He introduced many reforms which were greatly appreciated and had their own significance even during these days. "Sher Shah was the first who attempted to find an Indian Empire broadly based on people's will."

Central Administration

He was head of the administration. He had both civil and military powers in his hands. He always took measures for the welfare of the common man. As he was the guardian of the people, his duty was to protect the people. His administration was enlightened and vigorous.

Council of Ministers

She Shah was helped by his Council of Ministers and those were :

1. Diwan-i-Wizarat
2. Diwan-i-Ariz
3. Diwan-i-Rasalat
4. Diwan-i-Insha
5. Diwan-i-Qaza
6. Diwan-i-Barid.

Diwan-i-Wizarat. Diwan was the head of the Diwan-i-Wizarat. He was supervising income and expenditure of the State. He was head of other ministers.

Diwan-i-Ariz. Ariz-i-Mamalik was head of this Department. He looked after the recruitment, organisation and discipline of the army.

Diwan-i-Rasalat. This department was under a foreign minister who was incharge of the diplomatic relations with foreign nations. He was in close touch with ambassadors and envoys. He was also incharge of charity and endowment.

Diwan-i-Insha. The minister incharge of this department was supervising the Government records. He drafted royal proclamation and letters.

Diwan-i-Qaza. It was a judicial department. Chief Qazi was the head of this department. He had to deal with the appellate cases from lower courts.

Diwan-i-Barid. It was the Intelligence Department of the Government. It had many news writers and spies who were scattered all over the nation. With the help of the spies, Sher Shah was able to know the latest information of his country.

Provincial Administration

For administrative convenience, the country was divided into Sarkars, Parganas and Villages.

(i) *Sarkar*

It was the important unit of the division. There were 47

Sarkars in the country. Munsif-i-Munsifan or Munsif-in-Chief and Shiqdar-i-Shaqdaran or Shiqdar-in-Chief were the important high officials of Sarkar. The Munsif-i-Munsifan was a judge and supervised the works of Amins, whereas duty of Shiqdar-in-Chief was to maintain law and order in his jurisdiction. In addition to these administrators there were large number of clerks and accountants in each Sarkar.

(ii) *Pargana and its administration*

The Shiqdar, Amin, Treasurer, Munsif, and Hindu writer were the important officials in the Pargana. In addition to these officials, there were the Patwari, Chaudhari, and the Muquddam who acted as intermediaries between the subjects and the Government. Shiqdar can be compared to the Deputy Collector. He supervised the maintenance of law and order. He helped to collect the royal dues from the people. He presided over the law courts and settled the criminal cases. The duty of Amin of a Pargana was the collection of land revenue and he had to keep an account of income and expenditure of Pargana. The treasurer or Fotadar was the treasurer of a Pargana. He maintained the income and expenditure of the Pargana. Many clerks were appointed to help the officials and one of the clerks kept the accounts in Persia. Another clerk was maintaining the same accounts in Hindi for the convenience of the subjects. The clerks in Pargana were known as Karkuns. Though Sher Shah was head of the Government he freely allowed full freedom and independence to the officials of Pargana and he maintained correspondence with the Pargana officials through Patwaris and Chowkidar. The important officials in Sarkar and Pargana were transferred once in two years in order to avoid local rebellion or influence.

Village Administration

Village was administered by Panchayat in which influential men were taking part. It performed both judicial and administrative works in the villages. It was allowed to function freely and Sher Shah did not interfered in the administration of Village Panchayat.

Sher Shah's Army

Sher Shah's army was very strong and mighty. He had keen

interest in the recruitment, training and military techniques of his army. Highest posts were offered to the brave Afghan soldiers. During his reign, individual payment to the soldiers was put into practice and sometimes highest emolument was fixed to the extra-ordinary personnel on the basis of qualification and merit.

To root out the fraudulent ways in the army, Sher Shah introduced a new system of Dagh or branding of horses and chera or the preparation of descriptive rolls of the soldiers. He maintained permanent army at the capital. He gave importance to cavalry. The permanent army at the capital consisted of 1,50,000 cavalry, 25,000 infantry and 500 elephants. For convenience, army was divided into many divisions and each division was put under the control of a commander.

Taxes

Land Tax was the important source of income to the Government and taxes on commerce, presents, mint and khums were the additional incomes. Jizya was imposed upon the Hindus and heirless property was taken over by the Government.

Revenue Administration

Sher Shah changed the previous system and introduced a new system of measurement of lands. One-third of the total produce was levied as land tax either in cash or in kind and sometimes they were allowed to make payment at the treasury directly. There were three systems of assessment prevailed in the time of Sher Shah. Those were (1) Ghalla-Bakshi or Batai (2) Nasq or Muktai or Kankut (3) Naqdi or Zabli or Jamai.

Sher Shah instructed the officials to be lenient at the time of fixing up the taxes and rigid at the time of collection of taxes. He emphasised that while the army was moving, it should not destroy the standing crops in the fields. If any damage was done to the crops, the Government was to pay compensation to the owner of the field.

Defects of this system

The land tax was fixed at 1/3 of the average produce of the three kinds of land, *i.e.*, good, middle and bad. The result was that the bad land was overcharged and the good land was undercharged. The cultivators faced inconvenience due to the reason that settlement was made for one year. Further the officials in the Revenue Department were corrupt and did favouritism to the known cultivators in fixing the land revenue.

Judicial Administration

Justice was the most important wing of the good administration. Shah himself was the highest court. Punishment was offered to all without considering their status and influence. Gazi and Mir Adil were the head of the Civil Courts. In Sarkar Chief Munsif was the Chief of Civil Courts. The criminal cases were decided by Chief Shiqdars and Shiqdar. In the Parganas Amin was the head of the courts who delivered the judgement according to the rules and traditions of the land. The severe punishments were given not to reform the culprit but to teach a lesson so that others may not do the offence. Those Government officials who were not performing their duty sincerely were severely punished without showing any lenience to their status and position. Sher Shah was unbiased, in giving the judgement.

Police Administration

There was no separate Police Department during the period of Sher Shah. Soldiers were asked to do the duty of Police. Chief Shiqdar had to maintain law and order in Sarkars while in Pargana Shiqdar was incharge of this Department. Anti-social elements, thieves and robbers were closely watched. Sher Shah fixed up the responsibility of maintaining law and order in their jurisdiction and if any incident of murder or theft took place the concerned officer must detect the culprit failing which the official concerned must be hanged. In the villages the headman and other officers were required to make good the loss due to a theft or robbery if the culprits were not traced out. Abbas Sarwani, said that during the reign of Sher Shah travellers and way farers could move freely without fear to any corner of the nation in the midnight. People could sleep anywhere in the night after putting down their luggages. It was stated that an old lady could undertake a journey freely to any place carrying a basket full of gold ornaments on her head.

Currency System

Currency system was in a miserable condition. As there were many coins in the circulation, the ratio of the various coins had not been fixed up. Further debarring of the coins were common. Sher Shah put an end to this drawbacks of introducing a new system. New coins were circulated and the names of the coins were given in Devanagiri script. The ratio of exchange was also fixed up. Thus, the confusion prevailed in the currency was removed. Sher Shah also introduced gold coins in the circulation and thereby created full confidence to the people on the coins.

Mean of Communication

Sher Shah improved the means of communication by constructing four roads (1) Road from Sonargaon in Bengal to the Indus (2) Road from Agra to Burhampur (3) Road from Agra to Jodhpur and Chittor and (4) Road from Lahore to Multan. For the convenience of the travellers, trees were planted on either sides of the roads and Sarais were built at a distance of every Kroh. The Sarai's contained all facilities and separate places were provided for both Muslims and Hindus.

Postal System

Sher Shah introduced an effective postal system. Many messengers were appointed to send messages from place to place and in addition to the messengers, a lot of horses and camels were used for sending message.

Education System

Absolute freedom was given in the field of education. Granta-in-aid was given to the educational institutions. Scholarships were extended to the students on merit basis. For the education of Muslim, a maktab was attached to every mosque for imparting elementary education. Madrasas were started for higher education.

Intelligence Department

Sher Shah Introduced a network of spy system. He got appointed many news carriers and by means of them he got the daily news about the important incident happened in his country.

This system was so efficient that Sher Shah was able to get information from all parts of his dominion.

Religious policy

Regarding Sher Shah's religious policy there was no uniform opinion among the scholars. Generally he was tolerant in matters of religion and he separated politics from ethics.

Charity

Sher Shah started many charitable institutions such as Sarais, dispensaries and free meals.

Sher Shah was a good administrator. According to Tripathi and Dr. Saran, Sher Shah was merely a reformer and not an innovator. It is pointed that he merely revived the system of Ala-ud-Din-Khilji. Otherwise, there was nothing original in what he did.

18

Akbar, The Great (1556-1605)

Akbar the son of Humayun was born on 15th October, 1542 in Amarkot. His mother was Hameda Banu. When Akbar was born, Humayun was wandering from place to place. Akbar was one of the greatest rulers in Indian history.

Political conditions of India at the time of Akbar's accession

He came to the throne of Delhi in 1556 after the death of his father. At that time he was 14 years old. When Akbar was at Kalanuar, he got the news of his father's death and without further delay he enthroned himself and started his rule under the guidance of Bairam Khan. He had to face many problems in the beginning :

(1) The throne that he inherited was not a bed of roses. There was no law and order.

(2) The Rajputs increased their strength and power considerably. They wanted to crush the formidable enemy of Akbar. The important Rajput states were Mewar, Jaisalmer, Bundi and Jodhpur. Further the Rajputs wanted to achieve their past glory.

(3) Afghans were the greatest enemy of Akbar. Sikandar Shah Sur was having a large army in Punjab and wanted to suppress the powers of Akbar. So also Afghans in Bengal, Malwa and Gwalior made up their mind to attack Akbar. Thus, Akbar had lot of enemies on all sides.

(4) The economic condition was not sound. He inherited an empty treasury from his father. As the treasury was empty, he could not take any steps to weed out the enemies and this bad condition was still weakened due to famine which created a havoc in Delhi and Agra.

(5) The States of Gujarat and Malwa declared themselves independent and made diplomatic relations with other countries. Mirza Hakim, brother of Akbar wanted to sit on the throne of Delhi. The ruler of Kashmir also declared independence. The five states of Bahmini Sultans were absolutely independent. The rulers declared independence and did not owe any allegiance to the Sultans of Delhi.

Battle of Panipat (1556)

Hemu, the Prime Minister of Mohammad Shah Abdali of Bengal marched towards Agra on hearing the news of the death of Humayun. He captured it and moved again to Delhi. Tardi Beg, the Mughal Governor could not defeat Hemu and ran away from Delhi. Thus, Delhi also fell in the hands of Hemu. Hemu was a man of extraordinary personality. By sheer dint of his hard labour he raised his position to the level of Prime Minister. When Hemu captured Delhi, Bairam Khan advised Akbar to resist the aggression of Hemu. The advise of Bairam Khan was accepted and the armies of Hemu and Akbar met on the historic battle of Panipat in November, 1556. In the beginning Hemu was in upper hand in the battlefield. However, he was struck in the eye by an arrow and he became unconscious. On seeing this incident, the soldiers of Hemu fled away and Akbar got huge booty. Finally Hemu was captured and brought before Akbar who refused to kill an already dying man.

Causes for the defeat of Hemu

(1) He did not attack the Mughals at the appropriate time and he ought to have taken offensive against the Mughals just after the withdrawal of Tardi Beg.

(2) The artillery was captured by Ali Quli which disheartened the Hemu's soliders.

(3) Hemu should not have seated on the elephant in the battlefield. As he was sitting on the elephant the Mughals were able to concentrate upon him.

(4) As the elephants could not face the arrows of Mughals, they started destroying their own army.

(5) Finally there was no good leader after Hemu. When Hemu fainted in the battlefield, the soldiers ran away

and no commander came forward to lead the army against Akbar.

Results of the War

(1) After the second battle of Panipat, Akbar completely rooted out his formidable Afghan foes and he was the unquestioned monarch of Delhi-Agra.

(2) Sikandar Sur, the enemy of Akbar took shelter in Siwalik Hills, Bairam Khan sent his troops to capture Sur and finally Sur had to submit to the sovereignty of Akbar.

(3) In 1557, Mohammed Shah Abdali, also died in an encounter with the ruler of Bengal and thus Akbar was running the administration without any bottlenecks.

CONQUESTS OF AKBAR

Conquest of Gondwana (1564)

Gondwana was ruled by Rani Durgawati who was courageous and highly spirited lady. She was acting as regent for her minor son. Asaf Khan, Governor of Kara led an expedition against her and she died in the battlefield itself. Her country was devastated and a huge booty was recovered by the Mughals. Bir Narayanan, the young son of Durgawathi also died in the battle.

Conquest of Malwa (1561)

Akbar sent Adham Khan to punish Baz Bahadur who captured Malwa. In the battle Baz Bahadur was defeated. The booty seized at the time of the war was not given to Akbar by Baz Bahadur. Further he tried to take the possession of Rupmati, the wife of Baz Bahadur. She took poison and died herself in order to protect her chastity. Unable to tolerate the atrocities of Adham Khan, Akbar reached Malwa with huge force and dismissed him.

Revolt of Uzbegs (1564-1567)

Abdullah Khan, the trusted officer of Akbar took the lead to revolt against Akbar. He was supported by other Uzbeg chiefs. Ali Quli Khan, the hero of second battle of Panipat and Asaf Khan, the important officer of Akbar also joined hands with the Uzbegs. All the Uzbegs selected Khan Zaman as their leader and under his able command, they started rebellion against Akbar. They thought that Akbar had hatred against their race. Akbar crossed the Ganges with huge forces and suppressed the revolts of Uzbegs with firm hand.

Conquest of Chittor (1567-1568)

Rana Udai Singh was the head of Mewar State. He refused to recognise the sovereignty of Akbar. So Akbar led an expedition against Mewar and crushed the power of Rana Udai Singh who left the field leaving the army without leadership. Then the Rajputs under the leadership of Jai Mal fought with Akbar bravely and Chittor was finally captured by Akbar.

Conquests of Ranthambhor and Kalinjar (1569)

The fort of Ranthambhor was the strongest and highest rock fort. Akbar's army was standing on the top of the hill to invade the fort. The ruler of Ranthambhor realised favourable position of Akbar and decided to make truce with him. Then he handed over the fort and joined with the royal services.

Akbar sent a force under the leadership of Manjnum Khan to invade the fort of Kalinjar in Bundelkhand. When Raja Ram Chandra, the ruler of Kalinjar heard the news of the fall of the forts of Ranthambhor and Chittor, he himself surrendered the fort without encounter with Akbar in 1569.

Conquest of Jodhpur and Bikaner

Chandra Sen, the ruler of Jodhpur defied the sovereignty of Akbar. So Akbar attacked Jodhpur and brought under his control. So also the ruler of Bikaner recognised the authority of Akbar.

Conquest of Mewar (1572-1597)

Maharana Pratap was the ruler of Mewar. He was an ambitious man. He wanted to bring back the famous glory of Rajputs. He refused to accept the sovereignty of Akbar and hated the Rajputs who had matrimonial alliances with Akbar. Like other Rajputs, if he followed the policy of friendship with Akbar and accepted Akbar's authority his position would be nowhere and he would become a Jagirdar. So he did not like to be a subordinate ruler and declared himself an independent king of Mewar.

The Mughal forces were marched to invade Mewar and a fierce and gallant fight took place between Pratap and Mughals at Haldighati. The Rajputs put up a stiff resistance from the beginning of the battle and Mughals were completely exhausted their strength and energy. However, Pratap received a serious wound and retired to a hill and Mughals got victory in this war.

Though Mughals were victorious in the battle of Haldighati, Akbar was not satisfied about the activities of Man Singh and Asaf Khan because they did not pursue and capture Rana Pratap. So for some time they were excluded from the court.

Rana Pratap regained Mewar

Though Pratap was defeated he did not lose his heart. He gathered strength and again put up a stiff and gallant fight with Mughals and recovered the whole of Mewar except Chittor, Ajmer and Mandalgarh.

Death of Rana Pratap

When he was in death bed, he stated that even after his death his soul would not be satisfied if his followers abandoned the firm task of fighting with Akbar. In such circumstances, Amar Singh, the son of Pratap and his nobles took a pledge that they would continue fighting with Akbar after his death. Only then Pratap was satisfied and laid rest for ever. Rana Pratap was a brilliant star among the Rajputs. He was born for the motherland, lived for independent motherland and sacrificed his life for his motherland. No words of praise were sufficient for him. He was a great general, valiant fighter, good administrator, hero of freedom lover and protector of Hindus.

War with Amar Singh

After the dead of Rana Pratap, his son Amar Singh continued fighting with Mughals. There was a fierce battle once again in which Amar Singh was defeated. Though he was defeated, he consolidated his strength and again started his father's ambition of fighting with Akbar. Finally the fighting had to be stopped because Man Singh, the general of Akbar was asked to move to Bengal to crush the revolt of Usman Khan. Thus, Akbar was not able to have full control over Mewar.

Conquest of Gujarat

Akbar wanted to annex Gujarat because it was a commercially important place. Muzaffar Shah III, the ruler of Gujarat was a weak and inefficient man. This was the golden opportunity for Akbar to invade Gujarat. In 1572, one of the nobles of Gujarat invited Akbar to invade. So Akbar marched with a force towards Ahmedabad, the capital of Gujarat. He was honoured by many nobles and even keys of Ahmedabad was handed over to Akbar by Itimad Khan. Thus, Gujarat was easily captured.

Capture of Bengal (1576-1580)

Daud Khan, the ruler of Bengal captured the fort of Zanania. He defied the authority of Akbar which was a signal for him. So Akbar sent Raja Todar Mal and Khan-i-Khanna Munim Khan to teach a lesson to Daud. The siege continued for four years and they succeeded in capturing Bengal.

Annexation of Kabul (1585)

Hakim Mirza, the brother of Akbar wanted to capture Punjab and to punish his brother. Akbar sent his Prince Murad who defeated Mirza and allowed to retain only Kabul. Then after the death of Mirza, Kabul was also annexed with Mughal Empire.

Conquest of Kashmir (1586-1587)

Yusuf Shah, the ruler of Kashmir committed cruelties on Hindus. So Raja Bhagwan was sent to punish him. Yusuf was defeated and Kashmir was brought a part of the province of Kabul.

Conquest of Sind (1591)

With the aim of conquering Sind, Akbar sent Mirza Abdur Rahim who succeeded in his attempt and the whole of Sind was annexed with Mughal empire.

Conquest of Kandhar (1595)

The Shah of Persia was not able to suppress the strength of the Mughals. In 1595, Akbar completed the conquest and annexation of Kandhar.

Capture of Ahmednagar (1595-1600)

After capturing the whole of Northern provinces, Akbar paid his attention to Deccan. The Bahmini Sultans refused to accept the sovereignty of Akbar. So Akbar sent Prince Murad to Ahmednagar which was strongly defended by Chand Bibi with great courage. A truce was concluded between the two it did not last long and finally Ahmednagar was annexed to the Mughal empire in August 1600.

Capture of Asirgarh

It was a strong and well equipped fort in Khandesh which was under the control of Miran Bahadur. As Akbar found very difficult to capture it, he bribed the officials of the fort Asirgath, opened it and captured with great difficulties. Though Akbar wanted to conquer the whole of Deccan, he could not do so because of revolt of Prince Salim.

Akbar was not only a good ruler but also a great conqueror. He was engaged in many battles throughout his life. The empire that he inherited from his father was weak. But he established his control and authority over his empire.

RELIGIOUS POLICY OF AKBAR

Akbar was not a fanatic like Aurangazeb. He followed the policy of religious toleration and lenience towards Hindus. Unlike the Muslim rulers, he did not like to subdue the Hindus on the point of sword. All religions were treated equally and because of the policy of Akbar, he was able to get whole-hearted support from all subjects in his empire. His policy could be divided into five steps. Let us see the steps in detail one by one.

(a) Policy of Religious toleration

(i) *Matrimonial alliances*

Akbar married the eldest daughter of Raja Bihari Mal of Jaipur in 1562. In 1570 he married princesses from Bikaner and Jaislmer. The daughter of Raja Bhagwan Das was married to Prince Salim. This marriage healed the bitterness and produced a thick affinity and harmony among Muslims and Hindus.

(ii) *Removal of Pilgrim Tax*

Hindus had to pay Pilgrim Tax if they visited sacred places. When Akbar was in Mathura, he learnt it and immediately abolished it in 1563.

(iii) *Abolition of Jizya (1564)*

This tax was levied on Hindus and they had to pay this tax according to their income. In 1564 Akbar abolished this tax and both Hindus and Muslim became equal citizens of the State.

(iv) *Key posts given to Hindus*

As Akbar wanted to give equal treatment to Hindus, key posts were offered to them. Raja Todar Mal was appointed as Finance Minister. Raja Man Singh was given a mansab of 7000. Many Rajputs were taken into the Mughal empire. Out of his 12 Diwans of provinces, 8 were non-Muslims.

(v) *Abolition of forcible conversion*

He stopped the practice of converting non-Muslim to Muslim religion. He freely allowed the people to embrace their own religion. Before Akbar the prisoners were forcibly converted to Muslim. This was also stopped by Akbar.

(vi) *Great respect for Hindus*

Akbar had great respect for Hindu sentiments. As the Hindus worshipped cow, the killing of cows were forbidden. In 1590-1591 he prohibited the eating of the flesh of oxen, buffaloes, goats, horses and camels. Akbar himself avoided eating of garlic, onion and beef and for some time he did not move with people having beards. He took part in the Hindu festivals of Deepawali, Rakhi and Shivarathri.

He put tilak on his forehead. He was against the practice of sati and child marriage; widow remarriage among the Hindus was encouraged. Thus, he adopted a policy of reconciliation and lenience towards Hindus.

(b) Discussions on Various Religious Leaders

Akbar learnt many good Hindu concepts through his Hindu wife. With the help of Abul Fazl, he collected many books on history, religion, philosophy and literature and found out that there were many good principles in various religions. So he wanted to codify all the religions into one and for that purpose he constructed a building in 1575 known as Ibadat-Khana or House of Worship. Scholars from all religions were invited to take part in the discussion. The main moto was to trace out the true and genuine religions. The scholars were advised not to give room for their passions which would conceal the truth.

The discussion was taking place in a tense situation. The Mullas quarrelled among themselves and used abusive and intolerable words against one another. The quarrel reached optimum level that they would call one another fools or heretics. Akbar was greatly disgusted with all these affairs and he came to know that there was no fundamental difference in all the religions.

(c) Reading of Khutba

Finding the discussion was useless, Akbar wanted to combine in himself both political and spiritual powers. He removed chief Imam of Jama-i-Masjid and himself read the Khutba from the pulpit of a Fatehpur Mosque. The Khutba ended with the words of Allah-u-Akbar.

(d) Infallibility Decree (September 1579)

Infallibility Decree was prepared by Sheikh Mubarak in 1579 and as per the Decree Akbar was the supreme arbiter in political and ecclesiastical matters. The main points of the Decree were given below :

1. Obey God, obey Prophet and obey those who are invested with authority among you.
2. Surely the man nearest to God on the day of judgement is the Aman-i-Adil. Whoever obeys him, obeys thee and whoever rebels against him rebels against Thee.
3. The rank of Sultan-i-Adil is higher than the rank of Mujtahid.
4. Akbar is the most just, wise and God fearing king.
5. The emperor's decision was final provided that the decision was taken in accordance with the Quran and for the benefit of the nation.

"This document was written with honest intensions for the glory of God and the propagation of the Islam, and is signed by us, the Principal Ulema and lawyers, in the month of Rajab in the year nine hundred and eightyseven (987)."

Din-i-Ilahi (1581)

Akbar would like to create a national religion which would be acceptable to all the subjects. So he introduced his principles in the form of Din-i-Ilahi. According to Abul Fazl, "Akbar became the spiritual guide of the nation." Dr. Iswari Prasad said that "it was an eclectic pantheism containing the good points of all religions — a combination of mysticism, philosophy and nature worship."

Akbar was of the opinion that all the religions had some good concepts and the basic and fundamental points mentioned in various religions had been codified in the form of new religion called Din-i-Ilahi. The main concepts of this religion had mentioned below :

(1) The members of Din-i-Ilahi should follow a new method of greeting. When a man met with another man, he had to say Allah-u-Akbar and the another man used to respond by saying Jalla-a-Jallahu.

(2) The members of this religion should not celebrate death ceremony. Instead of celebrating death ceremony, they should prepare a dinner during his life time and gather provisions for his last journey.

(3) Each member should celebrate his birthday by giving a grand feast. He had to bestow alms and thus prepare provisions for the long journey.

(4) The members should abstain from eating flesh and at the same time they should not hate the flesh eaters.

(5) The members should not have relations or contact with butchers and hunters.

(6) "The members should not cohabit with pregnant, old and barren women; nor with girls under the age of puberty." Again "If any of the Darsaniyyah disciples died, whether man or woman, they should have some

uncooked grains and a burnt brick round the neck of the corpse, and throw it into the river, and then they should take out the corpse and burn it at a place where there was no water."

(7) The members should sleep in such a position that the head should be towards the east and the feet towards the west.

(8) There were four grades in Din-i-Ilahi and the grades were sacrifice of property, life, honour and religion for the sake of Emperor. Whoever sacrificed these four things, possessed the four degrees and who ever sacrificed one of the four possessed only one degree.

(9) Fire was considered as sacred to the members.

Members of this Religion

Though Din-i-Ilahi was the national religion, Akbar did not compel any man to embrace his religion. Even the nobles and the officials of Akbar refused to follow this religion. Further Muslim treated it as anti-Islamic and Hindus considered it as a modified from of Islam.

Criticism of Din-i-Ilahi

1. Akbar believed that he was a guide in spiritual matters and tried to heal diseases. This behaviour was not liked by the people.

2. It had no religious scripture or book, no defined or uniform prayer, no temple and no priests.

According to Sharma, the Din-i-Ilahi was "the crowning expression of the emperor's national idealism."

"It was nothing more than a tentative experiment in the process of fundamental synthesis; it was never forced upon any man."

According to Noer, the religion of Akbar was a sort of "Parsi-Sufi-Hinduism.

LAND REVENUE SYSTEM OF AKBAR

Land Revenue System of Akbar was not his original thinking. The system that he adopted was already practised by Sher Shah during his rule. So Sher Shah was the forerunner of Akbar in the field of Revenue administration. Before Akbar, Jagirdari system was followed and as this system had many defects, Akbar replaced this system and introduced revenue system of Sher Shah with necessary alterations and modifications. Akbar's long reign gave him ample opportunity to plan out, develop and perfect his system.

Early Attempts to Improve This System

To improve this system 10 Qanungoes were appointed. They completely studied the system and made some recommendation which could not be implemented due to Uzbeg rebellion. The previous system of Jagirdari was abolished and the nation was divided into 182 Parganas and an officer named Karori was put incharge of the revenue collection. As Karori was very corrupt and inefficient, this system could not be implemented properly.

Zabti System

In 1582 Diwan-i-Chief and Raja Todar Mal made drastic changes in the existing system of land revenue. In the previous system the revenue was fixed every year which resulted the state could not anticipate the possible income every year. To remove this drawbacks, Todar Mal made a change in the existing system. An aggregate of the rate of collection for 10 years from 1570 to 1580 was taken and one-third of them was taken as the basis of assessment. This new system was called as "Zabti System or Ain-i-Des-Sala" which was first introduced in eight provinces. Bihar, Bengal, Sind and Kashmir were not included in this system.

Measurement of Lands

Todar Mal ordered that cultivable lands should be measured. Before Akbar, the measurement was done by means of hampen-ropes. This measurement was not correct because this rope would expand in summer and contract in winter. Todar Mal removed this system and ordered to use a Jarib of bamboos joined together by the iron rings. Special instructions were given by Akbar to measure the lands honestly and no partiality was done to the cultivators in the measurement.

Gradation of Lands

Lands were divided into four grades, such as Polaj, Parauti, Chachar and Banjar lands. Polaj was a fertile land cultivated every year. Parauti was the land which was occasionally left uncultivated, probably for one or two years. Chachhar land was left uncultivated for 3 to 4 years and Banjar land was cultivated once in 5 years. The first two lands of Polaj and Parauti were further divided into three grades, *i.e.,* good, middle and bad.

Fixation of Land Tax

Fixation of land tax was done on the basis of category of the land, fertility of the soil and average produce of the last 10 years. Land tax was fixed at 1/3 of the average produce for Polaj and Parauti lands. For Chachar land the same was 1/15 of the produce in the first year and 2/15 in the second year. For the Banjar land, the state share was 1/26 of the produce in the first year and 1/13 in the second year. This share was also used to increase by progressive stages.

Mode of Payment

The farmers were asked to pay the tax either in cash or in kind. The cash rates were fixed by the officials and they were different in case of different crops. The rates of sugarcane was different from the rates of wheat.

Facilities of Farmers

Loans for agricultural purposes were given to the cultivators which could be repaid in easy annual instalments. The farmers were exempted from paying the taxes in bad seasons. The cultivators were given receipt for every payment. Voluntary payment was encouraged and force was used only in extraordinary circumstances.

Revenue Staff

Diwan-i-Ala was the highest revenue officer. Diwan and Amil were the highest officers in the province and Sarkar respectively. The Amil was assisted by officials of Bitikchi, Potdar, Qanungo, Muqaddam and Patwari. The Amil was expected to tour the villages to ascertain the exact cultivation of lands and he had to maintain crop statement for every year. The revenue collectors must send annual report about the work, character and integrity of the subordinate officials. The report of monthly income to the treasury must also be sent to the Government. The revenue officials were instructed that in measuring the land, not even a Bigha was concealed or overlooked. The treasurers were asked not to get extra coin from the peasants. In case there was bad monsoon or flood havoc to the crops or destruction of crops due to natural calamities, the situation must be reported for remission of taxes. The Qanungo was a Pargana Officer. Headman and Patwari were the officers in the village.

Estimate of Land Revenue System

It had many sound principles. The old system of Jagirdari was replaced. Maximum concessions were given to the peasants in fixing the tax. Akbar employed many persons to implement this system.

Sir Jadunath Sarkar has criticised the system in the following words :

> "The collection of revenue was always the result of a struggle between the Ryots and Sarkar and the arrears were seldom, if ever cleared".

On the whole this system was an efficient one and was for the welfare of the public. The peasants were quite happy and prosperous during the reign of Akbar.

THE MANSABDAR1 SYSTEM

Mansab is an Arabic word which meant office, rank or dignity. V.A. Smith and Dr. P. Saran had the opinion that this system had existed during the period of Babur and Humayun. But it was completed and put into practice during the reign of Akbar. In fact this system was borrowed from Persia. The object of Mansabdari system was to settle precedence and fix gradation of pay. According to Irvine "Mansabdar was that measure of status under the Mughal Government which determined a Mansabdar's (a) rank, (b) his salary and (c) his office in the Royal Court."

Grades of Mansabdars

There were many grades of Mansabdars. The persons who held the rank up to 12000 were called as Omrahs. Those who held the rank lower than that of 1000 but now below 20 were called Mansabdars. The figures given by Bernier was entirely different from this figure.

Abul Fazl had stated that there were 66 grades of Mansabdars. But in actual practice there were only 33 grades. In the beginning the highest rank was only 1000 but later it was enhanced to 12000 and 20,000. The ranks of Mansabdars were further sub-divided. They were (1) From 20 to 400, they were called Mansabdars. (2) From 500 to 25000, they were called Umra. (3) From 300 and above they were called Umra-i-Akbar (4) The holder of the highest Mabsab was called Amir-ul-Umra.

Maintenance of Troops

Every Mansabdars was fixed the number of troops to be maintained and in addition to the prescribed troops, he had to maintain horsemen, elephants, carts, camels, etc. For the proper maintenance of these a lumpsum grant was paid to the Mansabdars along with their salary.

Duties of Mansabdar

There was no fixed duty assigned to them. Sometimes they were assigned duty by the emperor and Mansabdars must successfully complete the duty given to them.

Nature of Appointment

There was no prescribed rules and regulation for the appointment of Mansabdars. If the emperor decided, he could appoint anyone as Mansabdar or any Mansabdar could be dismissed by him. He could promote any Mansabdar to higher rank without consulting anybody. All the officers recruited for discharging both civil and military duties were the members of the Mansabdari system. They were transferred from civil to military department and *vice versa.*

Salaries of Mansabdar

They were given very fat salaries. A Mansabdari of 5000

was paid from Rs. 28,000 to 30,000 per month and out of his salary, he had to spend Rs. 10,600 for the maintenance of troops and other obligation. A Mansabdari of 50 was given Rs. 250 and had to spent Rs. 185 for the maintenance of the soldiers, etc. According to some scholars that the Mansabdars were not paid for the whole year but this statement was strongly protested by Dr. Srivastava.

Nature of Mansabdar

Mansabdars were not duty conscious and led the life of pleasure. The properties of the Mansabdar were not given to the children after his death. The entire movable and immovable property would be confiscated by the Government. So they spent the money lavishly and led the life of luxury and comforts.

Zat and Sawar

According to Bluchman "Zat indicated the number of soldiers a Mansabdar was expected to keep and Sawar indicated the number actually maintained by him."

Irvine was of the opinion that Zat was the actual number of horsemen maintained by Mansabdar and Sawar was the additional honour showing the additional number of horsemen maintained by him.

R.P. Tripathi said that Sawar was the extra honour which a Mansabdar had. There were many opinions about Zat and Sawar among the historians.

Demerits of this System

(1) The Mansabdar did not keep the prescribed number of soldiers. In the later period, they brought people from streets in military uniforms and showed the strength. So Akbar had to take strong action against this practice.

(2) The Mansabdar did not maintain a regular force. They had their own kith and kins in the army which resulted there was lot of corruption and inefficiency in the force.

(3) The Mansabdars did not strictly observe the rules and regulations of Mansabdari system. So there were many malpractices among the Mansabdars.

(4) This system was very costly because Mansabdars were paid fat salaries.

(5) The military training and efficiency were varied from unit to unit. There was no co-operation and co-ordination between the forces of Mansabdars.

(6) Mansabdars were extravagant and inefficient. They spent a life of pleasure and enjoyments. They were not sincere and duty conscious.

(7) As Mansabdars had their own men as soldiers, they created trouble for the empire by raising revolts.

Though Mansabdari system had some defects, it was useful to tone up the administration of the nation. It replaced the Jagirdari system which created local rebellion. In this system the Emperor had direct control over the Mansabdars.

AKBAR'S RAJPUT POLICY

Rajputs were the important people in India. The policy adopted towards Rajputs was co-operation and peaceful. Before Akbar there was no smooth and cordial relation with the Rajputs. They were against the Mughals and followed the policy of hostility. But Akbar changed the hostile policy and wanted to win over the Rajputs by all means. Further he knew that sound administration could not be effected without the active co-operation of Rajputs. So the policy of reconciliation was adopted by Akbar and if he failed in this policy, he resorted to warfare. The Rajputs who refused the authority of Akbar were conquered and brought under his rule and those who accepted his sovereignty, concluded a peace treaty with Akbar. However, Mewar was the only state that always offered gallant resistance to Akbar. Let us see the chief features of his policy towards Rajputs.

Matrimonial Alliances

Akbar cemented his relation with Rajputs by matrimonial alliances. Raja of Amber offered his daughter for marriage and Akbar accepted this offer. Bihari Mal, Raja of Amber and his son were given Mansabdari rank and they entered into Mughal service. Akbar married the daughter of ruler of Bikaner in 1570.

Then Prince Salim married the daughter of Raja Bhagwan Das in 1584.

Freedom to Rajputs

The Rajaputs were given absolute freedom. The hostile policy of Mughals against Rajputs was stopped. Absolute independence was given to Rajputs in religious matters. Akbar abolished Jizya and Pilgrimage tax on the Rajputs.

Rajputs in the Royal Services

Efficient Rajputs were appointed in the Mughal service. They were given the posts according to their merit and ability. Many Rajputs were recruited to civil and military services. Raja Todar Mal, Raja Bhagwan Das and Man Singh were Rajputs who were given responsible position in the Mughal services.

War with Rajputs

Akbar tried to win over the Rajputs by making friendly alliances and in case he failed in his earnest attempt, he resorted to warfare. The State of Mewar refused to accept the sovereignty of Akbar. So he marched with mighty force to Mewar. The ruler of Mewar, Udai Singh put up a very strong resistance against Akbar and finally he ran away towards the hill leaving the defence of his fort Chittor in the hands of Jai Mal, who put up a gallant fight against the Mughal forces. The siege was continued for several months and Chittor was conquered by Akbar. Though Chittor was conquered, the Rajput fighters defied the authority of Akbar.

In 1572 Udai Singh of Mewar died. When he was in the death bed, he requested his followers to continue the policy of hostility with the Mughals even after his death. So after the death of Udai Singh, Maharana Pratap became the ruler of Mewar. He was a very brave and courageous man. He felt that it was disgraceful for Rajputs to surrender and he continued the struggle with Mughals. In 1570 Maharana Pratap was defeated in the battle of Haldighati. Though Rajputs were defeated, they never acknowledged the sovereignty of Akbar. Pratap was successful in recapturing the whole of Mewar except Chittor, Ajmer and Mandalgarh.

Significances of Rajput Policy

(1) Akbar utilised the services of able Rajputs in the Mughal empire. With their valuable advices, Akbar was able to establish a sound administration. Raja Todar Mal Bhagwan Das and Man Singh helped him a lot. (2) As the treatment given to Rajputs was cordial and friendly, Akbar was able to get the support of the Hindu community. The Rajputs were the military leaders of Hindus and when they joined the military service of Akbar, the Hindus also worked for the progress of the nation.

(3) During the rule of Akbar Hindus and Muslims came in close contact and exchanged their ideas and thoughts. So Hindu-Muslim cultures developed. The Hindus studied Urdu and Persian languages and Muslims studied Hindu literatures. A national school of art was created and both Muslims and Hindus joined hands for the development of Indo-Muslim art.

(4) As cordial relation was established between Muslims and Rajputs, Rajputs worked hard for the progress of the nation. They took part in political, economic, military and administrative development of Mughal empire.

Thus, the Rajput policy of Akbar was quite successful. The hostility of Rajputs was given up, which resulted a cordial affinity between Mughals and Rajputs.

ADMINISTRATION OF AKBAR

(1) The Emperor

Akbar was an autocrat. He kept all the powers in his hands and he was the believer of divine right theory of administration. He was all in all and his word was the law of the land. Dr. V.A. Smith remarks "Akbar was a teacher rather than the pupils of his ministers. He was the real authority in their appointment and he would dismiss any minister at any time he liked." He personally looked the administration of the empire. He was sitting in the court daily and got the petitions from the people. The troops of the Mansabdars were inspected by him. The Jagir was given by him and the foreign envoys had been received by him. It was stated that he worked more than 16 hours daily.

(2) The Ministers

There were many ministers who held direct discussion with the emperor about their departments. They helped to run the administration. Their term of office was not fixed and rules for promotion were not definite.

(1) The Vakil (Prime Minister)

He was next to the emperor. In the beginning Bairam Khan was working as Prime Minister. He had full control over the administration. But after Bairam Khan, Akbar took the entire administration in his hand.

(2) Diwan-i-Ala

He was the Finance Minister who kept the financial accounts of income and expenditure of the empire. He had powers to appoint financial officers in the provinces. Raja Todar Mal was the Finance Minister of Akbar.

(3) The Mir Bakshi

He was the Minister of Defence. He had to maintain a register showing the ranks of the Mansabdars. He helped the king in all military affairs.

(4) Sadr-us-Sadur

He was the Minister incharge of charities and endowments. During Akbar's rule this minister lost his importance because Akbar himself granted scholarships and religious grants to the subjects.

(5) Other Ministers

Darogha-i-Dak Chowki	—	Chief of Post and Intelligence department
The Mustaufi	—	Auditor General
Mir Atish	—	Chief of Artillery
Munshrif	—	Chief Admiral and Officer of the Harbours
Mir Barr	—	Superintendent of Forests.
Quzi-ul-Qazat	—	Lord of Chief Justice

Provincial Administration

The empire was divided into 18 provinces and all the provinces must be under the control of the Central authority.

Nazim (The Governor)

He was incharge of provincial administration. He had power to appoint and dismiss provincial officials. He had to maintain law and order in the provinces. The justice was to be dispensed by him. In short he was the ruler of province and he had to execute the orders received from the emperor. He must look after the measures of public welfare such as construction of roads, sarais, hospitals and wells. Akbar adopted the policy of issuing transfer to the governors once in two years so that they would not start rebellion against the emperor. The post of Governor was not a hereditory and it was given to the meritorious person.

The Diwan

He was the important officer in the province. He was incharge of agriculture and finance. He must keep a watch over the collection of taxes and deposit of money in the treasuries. Accounts had to be examined by him. Further agricultural officers had been supervised by him. In short he was incharge of civil and revenue affairs.

The Sadr	He was the supervisor of the lands granted for religious and charitable purposes.
The Qazi	He was the head of the judicial department

The Kotwal

He was the police officer in the province who looked after the law and order. He inspected bazaars and markets and he took steps to improve the health and sanitary conditions. Abul Fazl, in his famous look Ain-i-Akbari has given the following account of Kotwal : "The appropriate person for this office should be vigorous, experienced, active, deliberate, patience, astute and humane."

Sarkar and its Administration

Akbar divided province into Sarkars. The executive and military functions were performed by Faujdar. He had a small army to maintain law and order in the Sarkar. The works of Faujdar were supervised by the central authority. Amal Guzar was the revenue officer who was assisted by Bitikchi in the revenue administration.

He kept the revenue accounts and supervised the work of Patwari. There was an another officer called Khazandar who received the money from the people. He was the protector of the treasury in the Sarkars.

Pargana Administration

Sarkar was divided into Parganas. Shiqdar was the head of the Pargana and he had complete control over the administration of Parganas. Amil was the officer incharge of assessment and collection of land revenue Qanungo, the another officer had to maintain the records of land and its produce every year.

Village Administration

It was in the hands of Village Panchayat which had full control over the administration of sanitation, hospitals, irrigation, elementary education and other public works. There were two types of village — Zamindari and Rayyatdari. In the Zamindari village land revenue was collected by the Zamindar and paid in the treasury and in the Rayyatdari village the farmers paid the tax directly to the Government servants. Muqaddam was the chief officer of the village. Thus, Akbar built up an efficient system of administration in his empire.

Revenue administration

See the land revenue system of Akbar.

Military system

See the Mansabdari system.

Judicial Administration

Akbar wanted to give justice to one and all. He said, "If I am guilty of an unjust act I must rise in judgement against myself." He heard the cases in his judgement and delivered the judgement. He was the foundation of justice. The cases against the nobles and high officials would be heard in his court.

Central Court

Sadr-us-Sadur was the Supreme Court which decided the cases of religious character. Chief Qazi was the Chief Judge who tried the appeals from the lower courts. He was the appointing authority of the Judges in Sarkar and Parganas.

Provincial Court

Qazi was the Chief Judge in the province. Sipah Salar decided the criminal cases and Diwan tried the civil cases. The appeals came from the lower courts were also decided by them.

Courts of Sarkar and Pargana

Kotwal was the authority to decide the cases in Sarkar while in Pargana Faujdar was giving the judgement for both civil and military cases.

In the villages, the village Panchayat used to decide the cases of the village.

Punishment

Death punishment was given only by the emperor. For minor offences, the culprit was fined. Mutilation of limbs was another punishment given to the culprit. There was no written punishment.

Akbar's administration was really effective and good. He made a foundation for good revenue system. He also replaced Jagirdari system and introduced Mansabdari system.

19

Jahangir (1605-1627)

Akbar prayed God for an heir to succeed him and his prayer was fulfilled when he was at Ajmer. A son was born to him in August 1569 and he was named as Muhammed Salim.

Education

As Jahangir was born after many efforts, Akbar decided to give him maximum education. Akbar left no stone unturned to make him as much accomplished as he could be. Jahangir was taught Persian, Arabic, Turki, Hindi, Arithmetic, History, Geography and Sciences. Many teachers or tutors were appointed for this purpose and Abdur Khan-i-Khana, one of the versatile genius was the important tutor of Jahangir.

Marriage

Jahangir was getting married to the daughter of Raja Bhagwan Das at the age of 15. Khusrau was born after his marriage. In addition to this marriage, he married many women and it was stated that more than 800 wives were kept in the harem. In 1586 he was married to Jodh Bai, the daughter of Udai Singh.

Evil Habits of Jahangir

Though he was brought up in the right way, he developed many bad evils even during his early years. He was addicted to wine and liquor. His conduct and character were bad. Akbar tried to mend his behaviour but he failed in his attempt.

Revolt of Jahangir

He wanted to sit on the throne of Mughal empire. So when Akbar went to Deccan, he started open rebellion against his father and declared himself as emperor of Mughal dynasty. Akbar came to Agra and sent many warnings and threat. In spite of many efforts, Jahangir could not be surrendered. He acted as an emperor and executed Abul Fazi which made Akbar to be furious with Jahangir. So Akbar decided that his young son Khusrau must succeed the throne because he was handsome and blameless in private life. After hearing this news Jahangir realised his mistake and surrendered himself before his father. Akbar forgave his mistakes.

Accession to the Throne

When Akbar fell ill in 1605, there was a dispute in the royal court over the question of succession to the throne. Man Singh and his group supported Prince Khusrau to become the emperor where other group was in favour of succession of Prince Salim. But Akbar himself, before his death placed the imperial turban on the head of Prince Salim and recognised him as the successor in November 1605 at Agra amidst great rejoicing.

Early Measures of Jahangir

(1) *Liberal Steps*

To celebrate his succession to the throne, he forgave the opponents and they were given their previous status and dignities. He celebrated Naurauz for 17 or 18 days and distributed many gifts to the poor and needy people. He also gave prizes to the distinguished servants of the Mughal empire.

(2) *The Golden Chain of Justice*

Jahangir ordered to set up a chain of justice between the fort of Agra and a pillar fixed on the banks of Jamuna. The chain had 60 bells. If the aggrieved man would like to inform his matter with the emperor, he must pull the chain and on hearing the ringing bells, the emperor met the man and gave his judgement regarding his matter.

(3) *Ordinances of Jahangir*

Jahangir has written, "I established 12 ordinances to be observed and to be the common rules of practice throughout the empire."

1. He prohibited the levy of many cases called Tamgha, Mir Bahri, etc.

2. To prohibit highway robbery, Jahangir ordered to construct roads, sarais and mosques in various places.

3. The heirless property must be used for the construction of mosques, sarais and bridges. Further Jahangir ordered that the property of a dead man should be given to the heir without state interference.

4. By an ordinance Jahangir prohibited the sales of wine and intoxicating liquors to the people.

5. Jahangir ordered that hospitals should be set up in every big city and eminent doctors should be employed in the dispensaries or hospitals to attend the sick men.

6. No one was permitted to live in the house of another. The cutting of noses and ears of the criminals was also prohibited.

7. Killing of animals was stopped on Sunday and Thursday.

8. All the Mansabdars and Jagirs of Akbar were confirmed.

9. Prisoners for long time were set free.

10. Jahangir ordered to appoint officials to look after the poor people.

11. Jahangir said that Sunday was a very auspicious day. He used to believe that the whole creation began on this very day.

12. General pardon was given to the life prisoners.

Revolt of Prince Khusrau (1606)

Prince Khusrau was an ambitious youth who wanted to sit on the throne of Mughal empire. So he left Agra with 350 horsemen on the pretext of visiting the tomb of Akbar. He was joined by Abdur Rahim and Hussain Beg and they assured to help him in the event of revolt against his father, Jahangir. Prince Khusrau also got the blessings of Guru Arjun. After that he marched towards Lahore and besieged it. Lahore was defended by Dilawar Khan and hence could not be taken. In this time Jahangir marched to Lahore and defeated Khusrau in the battle of Bairowal and Khusrau ran away to Kabul along with his followers. However, he was captured, chained, handcuffed and brought before Jahangir. Everybody was moved by the sight but not Jahangir who ordered the prince to be thrown into prison. The followers of Khusrau were also severely punished. Prince Khusrau was put in the jail till 1616 and after that he was made over to Asaf Khan. Then Prince Khurram was incharge of Khusrau and finally he was murdered in March 1622.

Execution of Guru Arjun Dev (1606)

Guru Arjun Dev helped Prince Khusrau in starting the revolt against Jahangir. After crushing the revolt by Jahangir, Guru Arjun was declared as criminal and his property was confiscated. Further he spread out the Sikhism in the empire which was bitter for Jahangir. So Jahangir summoned the Guru and asked to give his explanation. He was meted with ill-treatment and finally he was executed. After the execution of Guru Arjun Dev, Sikhs made up their mind to give a permanent headache for the Mughal empire because he was the Guru of the Sikhs.

Jahangir's Marriage with Nur Jahan

Nur Jahan was the wife of Sher Afghan. She was very beautiful, clever, brave and shrewd lady and after the death of Sher Afghan, Jahangir married her in 1611 and the period from 1611 to 1627 was the period of Nur Jahan rather than Jahangir.

War with Mewar

Maharana Pratap, the ruler of Mewar was succeeded by his son Amar Singh who continued the fight with the Mughals. Jahangir first sent Prince Parvez to crush the power of Amar Singh but he did not achieve victory. So Mahabat Khan was sent with a big force and he was also not able to get victory. Finally Prince Khurram put on vigorous campaign against Amar Singh. The villages were set on fire. Children and women were captured and ultimately a peace treaty was signed between Amar Singh and Jahangir :

(1) As per the treaty Amar Singh acknowledged the sovereignty of Jahangir.

(2) Generous treatment was given to Amar Singh and all the countries conquered by him were restored to him.

(3) Karan Singh, the son of Amar Singh was raised to the rank of Mansab of 5,000.

(4) Amar Singh had no right to rebuild or repair the fort of Chittor.

"Some casual observers find fault with Amar Singh for giving up the struggle and entering into a treaty with the Mughals. According to them the restoration of Chittor was hedged with condition and therefore, was worse than useless. The sending of a Rajput contingent to the Mughal court from Mewar was a humiliation to the people of the state and betokened subservience."

Conquest of Kangra

It was a famous hill fort surrounded by many number of fortresses which were in the possession of hill chiefs. Firoz Tughluq and Akbar tried to capture the fort but failed in their attempt. Jahangir put up a strong fight and conquered this fort.

Capture of Kistwar

It was a part of Kashmir and an independent country. Delawar Khan the Governor of Kashmir invaded this place and captured it. Though Kistwar was captured people revolted and a peace treaty was made in 1622 and now it was the part of the Mughal empire.

War with Ahmednagar (1610-1620)

Ahmednagar was the part of Mughal empire during the reign of Akbar but it was an independent state when Jahangir ascended the throne so that he wanted to capture it. Malik Amber, the ruler of Ahmednagar was a man of extraordinary qualities, rare intellectual powers, riped experience in civil and military affairs and a great general. He introduced Raja Todar Mal's revenue system in Ahmednagar so that he got much influence and status in the society.

To capture Ahmednagar, Jahangir first sent Khan Jahan Lodi and later on Khan-i-Khana Abdur Rahim was sent to punish Malik Amber. Their attempts were failed. Then Prince Khurram was entrusted with the charge of conquering Deccan. When he marched to Ahmednagar with big force, Malik Amber submitted and accepted a peace treaty. Adil Shah, the ruler of Burhanpur met Khurram with presents worth Rs. 16 Lakhs and also promised to restore all the territory which had been seized by Malik Amber. This treaty was ratified by Jahangir who conferred the title of Shah Jahan and his mansab was raised to 30,000 Zat and 20,000 Sawar.

Loss of Kandhar

Kandhar was annexed by Akbar with the Mughal empire. But later on during the reign of Jahangir, Shah of Persia led an expedition against Kandhar. Jahangir ordered Shah Jahan to put a gallant resistance to Shah of Persia but he refused to go over to Kandhar due to misunderstanding with Nur Jahan. So Shah of Persia conquered Kandhar after the siege of 40 days.

Rebellion of Shah Jahan

When Shah of Persia invaded Kandhar, Shah Jahan was asked to go to Kandhar but he refused to do so because he did not like the interference of Nur Jahan in the administration. Further Nur Jahan was making her effort to put Shahryar, her son-in-law on the throne of Mughal empire. She was always in the helm of affairs and virtually the ruler of Mughal empire instead of Jahangir who was always under her influence. Shah Jahan hated the behaviour of Nur Jahan and raised the revolt against his father Jahangir who came out with huge army and defeated him at Balochpur. After the defeat Prince Khurram also known as Shah Jahan went to Deccan and had friendship with Malik Amber of Ahmadnagar. But most of his followers deserted him due to the fear of Jahangir and he wrote a letter to his father stating that his action must be pardoned. He also sent his two sons Dara and Aurangazeb to Mughal Darbar as hostages.

Death of Jahangir (1627)

The health of Jahangir was completely broken due to much drinking of liquor. To restore his health, he proceeded to Kashmir from Lahore. He could not stay there for long period due to severe cold. So he came back to Lahore with bad health and on the way he died in October 1627. His body was brought to Lahore and ultimately interned in the Jahangir tomb near Shahdara.

Foreigner's Visit

During the reign of Jahangir, Captain W. Hawkins and

Thomas Roe visited India. They came to India with a letter from James I of England to Jahangir. They were welcomed by the emperor and allowed to stay at the Mughal court for 3 years. The object of their visit was commerce and their mission could not be fulfilled on account of the intrigues of the Portuguese Jesuit Missionaries. Hawkins wrote about the condition of the people, administrative system of the empire, character of the emperor, his judgement, his duties, functions of the officials of Mughal empire, etc.

NUR JAHAN

The real name of Nur Jahan was Mehrunnissa. She was the daughter of Mirza Ghiyas Beg, a native of Tehran who came to India for job. He was helped by Malik Masud, a wealthy merchant and got a job in the Mughal empire. Owing to hard labour and honesty, he rose to the high position of Diwan of Kabul.

Marriage of Nur Jahan

Mehrunnissa also known as Nur Jahan was given in marriage to Ali Quli Beg Istagu at the age of 17. Ali Quli Beg was given a Jagir and the title of Sher Afghan. Considering the condition that Jahangir was a heavy drunkard, he raised the standard of revolt against him. So the Governor of Bengal was ordered to put down the rebellion of Sher Afghan. In the encounter Sher Afghan killed the Governor of Bengal. Later on Sher Afghan was also killed by the attendants of the Governor and Mehrunnissa, the wife of Sher Afghan was brought to Agra and kept in the place under Sultan Begum in 1607. In 1611 Jahangir married her and gave the title of Nur Mahal or "Light of the Palace." The title was changed later on as Nur Jahan or "Light of the World."

Was Jahangir Responsible for the Murder of Sher Afghan

Regarding the death of Sher Afghan there were many opinions. He met Mehrunnissa in fancy bazaar and after seeing her attractive beauty, he was so much attracted with her beauty. So he made up his mind to select her as his life partner. This was the opinion of many historians. Some scholars had the opinion that he was fell in love with Mehrunnissa even during his early period and with the idea of getting her married, Jahangir killed her husband and brought her to the palace.

Dr. Beni Prasad said that there was no concrete evidence about the love affair between Jahangir and Mehrunnissa. Based upon the contemporary chronicles and European records, he came to this conclusion.

Dr. Iswari Prasad is of the opinion, "The circumstances of Sher Afghan's death are of a highly suspicious nature." Jahangir was so much attracted by the beauty of Mehrunnissa and with the idea of marrying her, he might have killed Afghan. Dr. Prasad had mentioned many points to substantiate his argument.

Her Participation in the Administration

She was clever, intelligent and hard worker. She took keen interest in the administration of the empire. She was generous and kind to the poor and destitutes. Many orphan girls were brought under her custody and efforts were taken to get them married. She was the "asylum of all sufferers." "It was probable that during her reign no less than 500 orphans were married and portioned.

She extended her concession to her kith and kins by giving a special and high status in the empire. Her brother, Asaf Khan was given the first minister of the state and her son-in-law, Shahriyar was given maximum privileges in the administration. She took all possible efforts to succeed the throne after Jahangir. She tried to avoid unnecessary expenditure in the administration.

She impressed Jahangir very much by her attraction and he forgot the entire world. He always spent his time in the company of Nur Jahan. He remarked, "I have sold my kingdom to my beloved queen for a cup of wine and dish of soup." Nur Jahan was the virtual ruler of the empire and the entire administration was under her hand and the highest dignitaries approached her for favour.

Revolt of Mahabat Khan

Nur Jahan could not tolerate the growing power and influence of any man. It is clear from the treatment meted out to Mahabat Khan who was sent to crush the revolt of Prince Khurram. He did it successfully and his popularity created jealousy in the mind of Nur Jahan. So he was asked by her to surrender all the wealth that he captured in Bihar and Bengal. When he was about to meet the emperor he was publicly disgraced in the court and sent to prison with his hands tied to the neck. So Mahabat Khan could not tolerate it and brought a coup. He imprisoned Jahangir and Nur Jahan. Finally with great efforts and cleverness, she got herself and her husband freed.

Loss of Kandhar

In 1622, Shah of Persia laid siege to Kandhar and captured it. Khurram was asked to stop the aggression but he refused to do so. There was no denying the fact that the refusal of Khurram was due to her behaviour towards his father.

Revolt of Khurram

Khurram revolted against her because of her influence in the administration. She took measures in favour of his son-in-law to be successor of Jahangir instead of Khurram. So he raised standard of revolt.

Estimate of Nur Jahan

A foreign traveller writes: "Her unlimited domination over her husband, who loved her with a supreme devotion, is the most remarkable since who was no longer young when he married her in 1610 and Indian widows of thirty-four are usually widows indeed."

"She was a woman of versatile temper, sound commonsense and undaunted courage."

Dr. Iswari Prasad remarks, "Her devotion to Jahangir was unequalled, she loved him with all the intensity of her full blooded nature and so captivated him by her charms that he became a submissive tool in her hands.

She was the lover of art and beauty. New designs and fashions of ornaments were introduced by her.

Though she was talented, she could not tolerate the rising influence of others. Her interference in the administration was disliked and Mahabat Khan and Prince Khurram revolted against her.

20

Shah Jahan (1627-1658)

Birth and early life of Shah Jahan

Shah Jahan was born in January, 1592, at Lahore. He was the third of the four sons of Jahangir. His original name was Khurram. He was the most favourite of Akbar and so every care was taken to impart him good education. He was brilliant, smart and ambitious and he acquired adequate knowledge in Persian.

Royal patronage

As he was skilful in his work, he was put incharge of the capital while his father Jahangir went out of the capital to suppress the revolt of prince Khusrau. In 1607 he was given a Mansab of 8,000 Zat and 5,000 Sawar. In 1611, he got the Mansab of 10,000 Zat and 5,000 Sawar and then he was promoted to the rank of 30,000 Zat and 20,000 Sawar.

Revolt of Shah Jahan

Though he was given the highest position, he could not enjoy it forever after the marriage of Prince Shahriyar with the daughter of Nur Jahan. Nur Jahan supported Shahriyar for the throne of Delhi after Jahangir which infuriated Shah Jahan and so he revolted against his father. In 1625, an amicable settlement was made between father and son after an apology of Khurram.

Accession of Shah Jahan

When Jahangir died in October 1627, Nur Jahan invited her son-in-law Shahriyar from Agra to Lahore for the accession of throne. Asaf Khan, the father-in-law of Shah Jahan also summoned him for the same purpose. There was a war of succession for the Delhi empire in which Nur Jahan could not match with Asaf Khan. So Asaf Khan put Dawar Baksh on the throne as a stop gap arrangement and when Shah Jahan came to Delhi from Deccan, in February 1628, Dawar Baksh was removed from the throne and he enthroned the Mughal emperor. He assumed the title of Abdul Mujaffar Shahab-ud-Din Mohammad Shah Jahan. Khutba was read on his name and the coins were issued on the day of accession.

Revolt of Bir Singh Bundela

After the accession of Shah Jahan, the peace of the nation was disturbed by the revolt of Bir Singh Bundela who was gaining more strength and power. After his death, his son Jujhar Singh made encroachments on the Mughal empire which was unliked by Shah Jahan. So the army was despatched to crush his activities. There was some desperate fighting and ultimately Jujhar Singh surrendered. Shah Jahan got huge war indemnity and Jujhar Singh was allowed to have as much Jagir as could enable him to manage the Mansab of 4,000 Zat and 4,000 Sawar.

Rebellion of Khan Jahan Lodi (1628)

Khan Jahan Lodi was the Viceroy of the Deccan. He entertained an alliance with rules of Ahmednagar and enlisted the support of the southern people. Knowing this situation Shah Jahan wanted to suppress the rebellion and he himself went to Deccan. Khan Jahan Lodi could not stand against the ferocious attack of Shah Jahan and ran away from place to place. The allies of Khan Jahan did not help him and he failed in his attempt of getting co-operation from the rulers of southern chiefs. The chiefs instead of helping him, opposed him. At last, he was killed while fighting near the fort of Kalinjar in 1630.

Celebration of Nauroz of 1628

Shah Jahan celebrated Nauroz with great pomp and show. His sons were standing on the four corners of the throne of Shah Jahan and liberal gifts were given to the members of his family. In this auspicious day, the Mansab of Asaf Khan was raised to 9,000 Zat and 9,000 Sawar.

The misery of famine in 1630

A terrible famine took place in Deccan in 1630 which made untold miseries and calamities. Thousands of people were starved to death and suffering of the people was intolerable. The traders sold the flesh of dogs and mixed powdered bones with flour. Dead bodies were found here and there. According to Lahori, "Destitute at length reached such a pitch that men began to devour each other and a flesh of a son was preferred to his love. After the famine, pestilence came and many villagers started off their homes. Due to pestilence many people were died. Lanes were full of human corpses and there was much filth in the highways that it was practically impossible to pass through.

Death of Mumtaz Mahal

Mumtaz, the wife of Shah Jahan passed away in 1631. She was extremely beautiful and full of grace and charms. Shah Jahan was highly influenced by the beauty and impressive character of Mumtaz. She loved deeply her husband during those days when his fortune got a set back. She was a kind hearted lady and noted for her charity and helping nature for the poor and destitutes. She gave shelter to many miserable and oppressed men and women. Shah Jahan was deeply aggrieved on her sudden death and in memory of her death, he built Taj Mahal at Agra which is one of the wonders of the world.

War with Portugese

Portuguese who came to India for commercial purpose set up their factory at Hugli. In the course of time, they established their influence and imposed their own custom duties on the people. Further they captured orphan girls and converted them into Christianity. They indulged in all types of tyrannies over the poor people which were highly objectionable. Some of the Portuguese kidnapped two slave girls which were claimed by Mumtaz Mahal. In spite of the repeated requests the girls were not released. To remove these atrocities of Portuguese Shah Jahan directed Karim Khan, the Governor of Bengal to take action against the Portuguese. After a stiff resistance, the Portuguese surrendered and more than 10,000 people were died and 4,000 were imprisoned. Some of the captive Portuguese were agreed to embrace Islam and others were either imprisoned or tortured to death.

SHAH JAHAN'S REIGN — THE GOLDEN PERIOD OF MUGHAL HISTORY

The reign of Shah Jahan has been called the golden period of Mughal history. Mughal empire reached its glory and high water mark in his time. Many impressive and attractive big buildings had been constructed which proved the best architecture in the Mughal period. Literature, architecture, painting and music were flourishing all over the country. During this period many foreign travellers came to India and praised the rule of Shah Jahan. Hunter stated, "The Mughal Empire attained its highest union of strength and magnificance under Shah Jahan."

Political Condition

There was peace and prosperity in the country. Lanepoole stated that Shah Jahan was renowned for his kindness and benevolence which was liked by the poor people very much. There was no disturbances from the sides of Rajputs. They were loyal to the Mughal empire. Shah Jahan introduced a good administration. He appointed upright people as judges so that justice could be done to the people. He root out the corruption among the officials and established a perfect administration. According to Manucci, "He kept his eye on his officials punishing them rigorously when they fell short of duties." The judicial system was satisfactory and praiseworthy. Shah Jahan himself was a just ruler and he was impartial in his judgement. He heard the grievances of the people in person and settled them off amicably.

Financial Condition

The economic condition was quite sound and the revenue of the nation was 21 crores per year. The taxes were collected in proper way. The revenue of the nation was properly audited by the uncorrupt officers. Shah Jahan, though spent many millions of his Central Asian campaigns and spent a huge amount on buildings and administration, left behind surplus of 4 crores.

Trade and commerce were flourished. Portuguese set up their factories and started functioning which gave fillip to the prosperity of trade with foreign countries.

Architecture of Shah Jahan

He was called the Prince of builders. Many buildings had been constructed at Delhi, Agra and other places and his buildings were monumental evidences for his architectural taste and skill. He gave fresh life to the Indian architecture. Percy Brown remarks "Shah Jahan found the Mughal cities of stand-stone and left them of marble."

(1) Taj Mahal built in memory of his wife Mumtaz Mahal was the most famous building constructed by him and it was one of the wonders of the world. It was built on the bank of river Jamuna. It was stated that the model of the building was first made in wood and then it was constructed in marble. The cost of the building was Rs. 50 lakhs and more than 20,000 artisans and workers had employed in constructing Taj Mahal. It took 20 years to complete this beautiful building. According to Travenier, "It was completed in 22 years and cost more than Rs. 3 crores. It was called "Queen of architecture" and "Dream in Marble". Ravindra Nath Tagore has described it as "immortal tear on the cheek of eternity".

(2) Moti Masjid built at Agra was another famous building of Shah Jahan. It is to the north of the Diwan-i-Am and a sum of Rs. 30 lakh was spent on it. The construction was done from 1648 to 1652. It was considered as the purest and loveliest house of prayer in the world.

(3) Shah Jahan built many buildings like the Mussamman Burj, Jhanroka Darshan and Daulat Khana-i-Khas. These buildings were noted for their excellent grace and elegant style.

(4) He laid a foundation of a new city of Shah-Jahanbad. He knew well that the city of Agra was not suitable for imperial residence and made up his mind to transfer the capital to Delhi, the seat of many empires in history. With the help of the astrologers and architect, he built palaces, mosques, mausoleums, canals, gardens, paths, reservoirs, etc. He also built special

courts, marble halls and golden tomb — "all works of extra-ordinary elegance and splendour." On the occasion of the opening function of Shah Jahanbad there was lot of pomp and show.

(5) Red Fort was the another important building of Shah Jahan built on the bank of river Jamuna. This building was built by means of red stones. It has two spacious rooms called Diwan-i-Am and Diwan-i-Khas.

(6) Jama Masjid was a big mosque built at Delhi.

(7) The peacock throne built at a cost of Rs. 1 crore is also a fascinating monument. The other famous buildings of Shah Jahan are Jahangir's Tomb and Nizam-ud-Din Aulia's Tomb. His pleasure gardens such as Shalimar Garden in Lahore, Nishat Bagh, Shalimar-Bagh and Chashma Shahi in Kashmir are also famous.

Painting

Shah Jahan was a lover of painting and he patronised the painters. Mohammad Nadir Samarkand was the most distinguished painter. His son Dara, and his minister, Asaf Khan were deeply interested in painting. He has been described as Prince of Painters.

Music

He patronised singers and he himself was a good singer. Good musicians and singers were allowed to do their performances in the royal court. Jagan Nath Mahapatra, Sukh and Sur were the most distinguished singers during his reign.

Literature

He encouraged scholars and men of letters. He took interest in the company of educated people. He patronised Persian, Hindi and Sanskrit languages. In his court there were many eminent scholars such as Abdul Hamid Lahori, Mir Abdul Qasim Irani and others. An eminent historian rightly remarks .... "in the realm of architecture and the forms of art, it is unquestionable that the works of the highest quality in Mughal period belonged to the reign of Shah Jahan."

Foreign Travellers

Many travellers visited India during the reign of Shah Jahan. They gave full details about the economic and political conditions of India. Bernier, a French Physician wrote a book called, "The War of Succession of 1658," which mentioned the sufferings of Dara when he was being pursued by the armies of Aurangazab. Further he stated that the people were opportunists and time-servers. The Provincial Governors were rapacious, oppressive and ambitious. The people were demoralised and spiritless. The administration depended upon the will of the Mughal Empire.

The other sides of Administration

(1) The golden period of Mughal Empire could not be called so because people suffered very much. Many people died in pestilence and they had to eat the flesh of dogs. When the people were suffering for food, Shah Jahan did not take any steps to remove their miseries and he took interest in constructing buildings. He heavily taxed the people. Dr. Smith has remarked, "An insupportable burden was laid upon the agricultural and industrial masses."

(2) The administration of Shah Jahan was not sound and satisfactory. The officials were corrupt.

(3) Local Governors were tyrants and they never cared for the welfare of the people.

(4) Shah Jahan had little knowledge about army administration and he could not manage the large army which lacked discipline and co-operation. Further he wasted huge money in his unscrupulous campaigns in the Central Asia, which ultimately led to financial bankruptcy of the empire.

(5) Shah Jahan was a religious fanatic. He issued a royal edict by which he ordered to pull down all the newly built temples in his empire. The pilgrim tax which was suspended by Akbar was revived upon the Hindus and encouraged the conversion of Hindus to Islam. Thus, from the religious aspect the age of Shah Jahan was a terror.

Estimate of Shah Jahan

(1) Shah Jahan was a great ruler of Mughal Empire. He was

praised for his magnificent building. The important standing monuments are Taj Mahal, Moti Masjid, Red Fort, Jama Masjid, Peacock Throne and the City of Shah Jahanbad.

(2) He systematised the administration. He reduced the salaries of mansabdars and increased the land revenue by enhancing the state's demand from one-third to one-half.

(3) There was perfect peace in the country which increased the prosperity of trade and commerce. The economic condition was very sound and by means of good economy Shah Jahan constructed many marble buildings.

(4) According to Elphinstone, "Khafi Khan, the best historian of those time, gives his opinion that although Akbar was pre-eminent as a conqueror and a law giver, yet for the order and arrangement of his territory and finances and good administration of every department of the state, no prince ever reigned in India that could be compared to Shah Jahan."

21

Aurangzeb

Aurangzeb was staunch Sunni Muslim. He wanted to live as per the teachings of Quran. Dr. V.A. Smith has rightly remarked. "The puritan emperor aimed at the creation of a state in which Mohammad and Quran should be supreme and should guide the life of man." He was a fanatic and did not consider the feelings of other religious people.

Aurangzeb, the Puritan

1. He discontinued the use of the Solar Ilahi year for the purpose of counting his regional years.

2. The court singers were not allowed to do their performances and he disbanded them.

3. The usual practice of Jharokha Darshana was stopped by him which resulted that the people could not get their problems solved in person.

4. Aurangzeb stopped the practice of the weighing his body against gold, silver and other commodities.

5. He gave up his participation in the Dussahra celebrations of the Hindus.

6. In the beginning he put Tikka on his forehead if he called on Hindu Raja. But later he gave up that practice because it was a Hindu custom.

7. The royal astronomers and astrologers were removed from service.

8. Scent, burners of gold and silver were removed from the court.

9. Prostitutes and dancing girls were given the option of leaving the Mughal Empire or getting married.

10. Gambling was stopped.

11. Growing of beard was prescribed a fixed length. If the length was more than the fixed length, the excess would be cut off.

12. Dress of gold-cloth were disallowed and the length of the trousers was also prescribed by the state.

13. The practice of lighting lamps on the tombs of the saints and putting figures of birds and animals on the occasion of Hindu and Muslim festivals were stopped by him.

14. The celebration of Muharram was stopped in 1669. As the Governor of Ahmedabad celebrated Muharram, he was removed from service.

Destruction of Temples

Aurangzeb did not like the construction of new Hindu temples. So he issued orders to demolish all the new temples by the infidels. Later on he issued instructions for the destruction of temples in Benares, Gujarat, Mathura, Jodhpur, Jaipur and Golkonda. The important temples destroyed by him were Keshva Rai Temple in Madura, Viswanath temple in Benaras and Somnath temple in Kathiawar.

Imposition of Jizya on the Hindus

Jizya a tax on Hindus was re-imposed on the Hindus on April 12, 1679. Manucci is of the opinion that the object of the Jizya tax was two-fold, first to fill up the treasury and secondly to force the Hindus to embrace Islam. Sir Jadu Nath Sarkar clearly writes, "The Jizya was a commutation tax, charged from the non-Muslims in the feudatory states as well as in the empire, whether in the royal service or engaged in private vocation or agriculture for their non-embracing Islam and had to be paid by them in person with marks of humility."

Custom Duty

It was levied on Hindus and Muslims. The Hindus had to pay

5% whereas the Muslims had to pay 2.5%. This discrimination was made for the purpose of converting Hindus to Muslims.

Pilgrim Tax

The Pilgrim tax abolished by Akbar was re-imposed by Aurangzeb. If a Hindu undertook a pilgrimage for the sacred places, he had to pay tax for his journey which brought lot of income to the state exchequer. This tax was against the feelings of the Hindus.

Dismissal of Hindus from the Royal Services

The predecessors of Aurangzeb appointed many Hindus as Mansabdars. But Aurangzeb did not give importance to Hindus. The number of Mansabdars were reduced. The Hindus were not allowed to fill up the top level executive posts. He broke the monopoly of Hindus in the administration, particularly in the Revenue Department. Further Hindus were given employment only as clerks and lower than this grade. So many Hindus changed their religion and thereby bought the security of tenure of their office. Many Hindus were replaced by Muslims. The Hindus should not be the Heads of Department in which the Muslims worked.

Removal of Hindus from the key posts was not a good decision. The Hindus were efficient and uncorrupt in their duties and the administration could not be carried on efficiently without their services. So Aurangzeb had to recall Hindus at their previous posts.

Stopped Religious Preaching

In 1659, Aurangzeb knew the fact that religious preachings were taking place in the temples at Multan, Sind and Banaras. So to root out this practice, he issued orders for the punishment of those who were giving religious teachings in temples. "Orders in accordance with the organisation of Islam were sent to the Governors of all the provinces that they should destroy schools and temples of the infidels and put an end to their educational activities as well as the practice of the religion of the Kafirs."

Restrictions on the Hindus

Aurangzeb imposed many restrictions on the Hindus such as

celebration of Hindu festivals, riding on Arabian and Persian horses and elephants, burning of dead bodies on the bank of river Sabarmati, etc. Hindus were ordered that they must not look like Mohammedans. Hindus were also forbidden to carry arms. He also restricted Jharoka Darshan, the Hindu tradition envisaged by Akbar.

His step to embrace Islam

Conversion to Islam was recognised by the emperor and the converted persons were appointed in the high posts. If there was a dispute between Muslims and Hindus, regarding the property, the property would be given to Muslim without any inquiry. His method of conversion were 'iconoclasm, sacrilege, economic, bribery, forced conversion and restriction of worship".

Effects of Anti-Hindu Policy of Aurangzeb

(1) The Anti-Hindu policy of Aurangzeb was not liked by the Zats. So they rose against the atrocities of the emperor under the leadership of Gokal of Tilpat and killed many Muslims. Finally Gokal was arrested and put to death and after Gokal, the Zats continued their agitation under the leadership of Raja Ram, who gave stiff resistance till the last days of Aurangzeb.

(2) Satnamis were the highly orthodox Hindus and they raised the standard of revolt when a Government officer had killed a Satnamis. After a fierce battle with them, Aurangzeb put down their rebellion.

(3) The Rajputs raised the standard of revolt due to anti-Hindu policy adopted by Aurangzeb. Under the leadership of Bundhela Rajput, they engaged in fierce battle with Muslim and he succeeded in establishing a strong army in East Malwa. Chhatrasal, one of the four sons of Champat took this task and defeated the Mughals in many battles. He ruled as a free ruler till 1711.

(4) The Sikhs did not like the policy of Aurangzeb and they raised their voice against the emperor for the cruelties committed on the Hindus. Guru Teg Bahadur, the leader of Sikh was arrested and beheaded which added fuel to the fire. So Guru Govind Singh, son of Guru Teg declared war against the

Mughals and with his scanty resources and little force, he resisted the Mughals up to the death of Aurangzeb.

(5) *Economic Loss.* As a result of the religions policy of Aurangzeb, the state had to incur a heavy loss of income. The custom duty was exempted to the Muslim and many Hindu traders cheated the Government by telling that they were Muslims. Since many Hindu festivals were stopped, the income derived from them did not come which were a great source of income to the nation.

(6) *Deterioration in the Administration.* Due to the religious policy of Aurangzeb, many were thrown out of employment. The posts were filled up not on merit basis but on religious grounds. Many efficient Hindus whose services were indispensable were ordered to leave the post which created inefficient and weak administration.

Aurangzeb was doing all this to defend his own religion or to please his co-religionists in order to be called a Muslim King or to take revenge upon the Hindu Rajas, as the Marathas, Rajputs and Sikhs were harassing him and his co-religionists every now and then.

DECCAN POLICY OF AURANGZEB

Aurangzeb was an ambitious ruler and wanted to annex Deccan into his Kingdom. The important Deccan rulers of Bijapur and Golkonda belonged to Shia whereas Aurangzeb was a staunch Sunni. His Sunni fanaticism instigated him to take against Shia Kingdom of Bijapur and Golkonda. Further Marathas were often giving troubles by looting the neighbouring states of the Mughal dynasty. To arrest the Maratha's intruders, and to spread out Islam, Aurangzeb undertook an expedition to Deccan which continued for 25 years in his life.

Conquest of Bijapur (1686)

Aurangzeb sent Jai Singh to defeat Sikandar Adil Shah in 1665 but he was not able to defeat Adil Shah of Bijapur. In 1680, Diler Khan was sent for the same purpose and he was also failed in his attempt. In 1684, Prince Muazzam was sent with huge force against the ruler of Bijapur. He concluded a peace treaty with Adil Shah without war and returned. Finally Aurangzeb demanded the dismissal of Sharza Khan, the minister of Adil Shah. As his order was not complied with, he proceeded against the king in person and besieged Bijapur in 1685. A breach was made in the fortifications of the city and it fell in 1686. Aurangzeb annexed Bijapur with Mughal Empire and the ruler of Bijapur was taken into the Mughal service.

Conquest of Golkonda (1687)

Golkonda, the Shia state of Deccan was rendering help to the Marathas who looted out the property of the Mughals. So when the siege of Bijapur was taking place Aurangzeb sent a mighty force under the leadership of Muazzam to Golkonda in July 1685. Abdul Hassan, the Sultan of Golkonda made a compromise with Muazzam and as per the compromise the Golkoda Sultan acknowledged the suzerainty and promised to pay one crore in addition to regular tributes. This agreement was not satisfactory to Aurangzeb and he himself marched towards Golkonda and besieged it for 8 months. Though he used all his force to capture Golkonda, he could not do it. So he had recourse to bribery and gained admittance through the treachery of one of the officers of the garrison who opened a gate. Abdul Hasan was captured and made a prisoner. His kingdom was annexed in September 1687. Lanepoole said that the conquest of Golkonda and Bijapur, Aurangzeb considered himself master of the Deccan.

War with Marathas

Marathas were a powerful strength in Deccan and Aurangzeb wanted to crush the power of the Marathas. So he sent Shayista Khan against Shivaji in 1663. He could not capture Shivaji and could save his life with great difficulties. Later on prince Mauzzam and Raja Jai Singh were sent against Shivaji and Shivaji was forced to sign a treaty of Purandhar in 1665. As per the treaty, Shivaji attended the Mughal court at Agra in 1666 where he was arrested and kept in prison. However, he was managed to escape from the prison and reached his headquarters in the Deccan.

After Shivaji, his son Shambhaji continued the struggle with Aurangzeb. Sambhaji was imprisoned and put to death. Sahu, the son of Sambhaji was arrested and put in the jail. Though Aurangzeb put all his efforts to crush the mighty powers of Marathas, he failed in his attempt. Dr. V.A. Smith has said, "The Deccan proved to be the graveyard not only of Aurangzeb's body but also of his empire."

Effects of the Deecan policy

(1) *Annexation of Shia states was Blunder*

The annexation of Bijapur and Golkonda was not a good decision because these states acted as a barrier between the Mughal Empire and Marathas. By annexation of these states, Aurangzeb brought the Marathas face to face with Mughals.

(2) *Empty Treasury*

Aurangzeb was engaged in war for 25 years which emptied the treasury of the empire. He did not take any steps to tone up the economic condition of the empire. Further it is said that salaries for the soldiers and officials could not be distributed for three years which made the officials corrupt and incompetence in their duties.

(3) *Set back to Agriculture and Trade*

The Mughal army was huge in size and when it moved, it destroyed the paddy fields, trees and grass. So the agricultural output was reduced very much. The Marathas were often looted the wealth of the people and destroyed the standing crops and houses. They burnt the entire property by fire. According to Manucci, "He left behind him the fields of these provinces devoid of trees and bare of crops, their places being taken by the horses and men and beasts."

(4) *Poor Administration in North India*

As Aurangzeb was in the Deccan for 25 years, the administration in Delhi was very poor and inefficient. The important officials were transferred to South to look after the war activities which resulted in chaos and confusion in North India. The officers of the North were corrupt and openly defied the orders of the Central Government.

(5) *Revolt in North India*

As the emperor was absence in North India, there were many

rebellions. The Afghans revolted in Malwa and Mathura. The Jats, Satnamis and Mewatis raised their standard of revolt against the empire. The Rajputs under the leadership of Durga Das, the Sikhs under Guru Govind Singh and Marathas under Shivaji began to fight against the Mughals.

(6) *Loss of Spirit of the Soldiers*

The continuous war in Deccan for 25 years destroyed the strength and spirit of the soldiers. They felt homesick and wanted to go back to Delhi as early as possible. The morale and efficiency of the soldiers were broken, which resulted in the loss of the prestige of the Mughal Empire.

Thus we conclude that the Deccan policy of Aurangzeb was a complete failure and it led to the downfall of the Mughal Empire. J.N. Sarkar has rightly remarked : "All seemed to have been gained by Aurangzeb now; but in reality all was lost. It was the beginning of his end."

THE RESPONSIBILITY OF AURANGZEB FOR THE DOWNFALL OF MUGHAL EMPIRE

Though Aurangzeb was a good general and shrewd diplomat, he was mainly held responsible for the downfall of the Mughal Empire. Let us see the various causes for his failure in the administration of the Mughal Empire.

(1) Religious Intolerance

His religious policy was highly hated and objected by the non-Muslims. He was a fanatic and religious bigot. His religious policy of anti-Hindu was against the wishes of the people. He imposed Jizya and Pilgrim taxes on the Hindus and destroyed the Hindu temples. He issued royal edict for the compulsory conversion of non-Muslims to Islam. He adopted a double policy with Hindus and Muslims and thereby he lost the support of the common people of his reign.

(2) Aurangzeb — the Puritan

He was pure Muslim and embraced faithfully the important concepts of Quran. He used to follow the holy Quran word by word. He did fast regularly as mentioned in the Quran and never forget to read Namaz. During his reign, he disbanded the dancing girls, prostitutes, women, musicians and astrologers. He did not allow the celebration of any Hindu festivals in his kingdom. The practice of riding on Arabian and Persian horses and elephants, burning of dead bodies on the bank of river Sabarmati and lightening of lamps on the tombs of the saints were forbidden by him which infuriated all the people in turn against his administration.

(3) Deccan Policy of Aurangzeb

He was away from the capital for 25 years and engaged continuously in wars with Bijapur, Golkonda and Marathas. His Deccan policy drained the imperial treasury and lost the vitality and strength of the army. As he was absence in the capital, he could not have attention in the administration which resulted in many rebellions in North India.

(4) Revolts of Jats, Sikhs, Satnamis and Rajputs

They raised standard and revolt against the administration of Aurangzeb. When Guru Teg Bahadur was executed, the Sikhs were revolted against Aurangzeb and the Marathas turned against him, when they were forced to embrace Islam. Had he kept friendly relations with Shivaji, he would not have failed in his administration. Further Aurangzeb committed a blunder by alienating the support of Rajputs. During the reign of Akbar, the Rajputs had done creditable service of the Mughal Empire. They were good fighters and no ruler could be successful without getting their support. "The Rajputs who were the followers of the Mughal army and the strong bulwark of the empire were alienated forever. Their devotion and loyalty to the Mughal Empire were unquestionable. Aurangzeb lost these priceless allies forever."

(5) Neglect of Economic and Cultural Progress

Dr. A.L. Srivastava said, "He also wrongly imagined that successful rule implied only in the conduct of political, military and religious administration of a country and sadly neglected the economic and cultural and shunned music, painting and other fine arts. He did practically nothing to improve the architecture. Consequently an Indian civilization during his long rule of about fifty years declined greatly."

(6) Unworthy Sons of Aurangzeb

Aurangzeb had helped his father, Shah Jahan, to tackle the problem of the Deccan. Unfortunately, his sons did not help him at all. They were unable to share the administration with his father and Aurangzeb was left all alone to see the affairs of the country.

(7) Personalities of Aurangzeb

He was a good administrator and had great experience in the art of administration. So his ministers could not take any steps to tone up the administration because they were afraid that there would be any mistake, they would be severely punished. Further, Aurangzeb himself did all the details of administration and left the routine work with the Department Heads. They were treated as mere clerks, which resulted in the degeneration and confusion in the administration.

22

Downfall of Mughal Empire

Like all the empires, Mughal Empire had its downfall after the death of Aurangzeb. The rise and fall of the empire are the natural courses. The glory of this empire was peak and optimum during the rule of Akbar, Jahangir and Shah Jahan and began to decline after Aurangzeb. Regarding the downfall of Mughal Empire, Lane-Poole observes, "As some imperial corpse, preserved for ages in its dread seclusion, crowned and armed and still majestic, yet falls to dust at the mere breath of heaven, so fell the empire of the Mughals when the great name that guarded it was no more." Let us see the important causes for the downfall of Mughal Empire.

(1) Weak Successors of Aurangzeb

The successors of Aurangzeb were inefficient and poor knowledge in the administration. Bahadur Shah, the successor of Aurangzeb was an old man and the next ruler was Jalandhar Shah who was a big fool in statesmanship. They spent time in the company of women, so there was general degradation and deterioration in the character of the Mughal rulers. They became ease loving and cowardly. They went in palanquins and were hardly fit to rule a country where the mass of the people detested the Mughal rule.

(2) Weakness of the Mughal Army

Deterioration and demoralising of the Mughal army was another cause for the downfall of the Mughal Empire. The army was not trained and skilful. The soldiers took interest not in the battles but in their pockets. They enjoyed all comforts and facilities even in the battlefield. Further, the army consisted of various races and there was no unity among the soldiers and generals. The Mansabdari system of the Mughals had lot of defects. The soldiers cared for their immediate officers and Mansabdars and not for the emperor. Mr. Irvine said, "Excepting want of personal courage, every other fault in the list of military vices may be attributed to the degenerate Mughals, indiscipline, want of cohesion, luxurious habits, inactivity, bad commissionarit, cumbrous equipment."

(3) The Mughal Rule was Alien

The Mughals were not the Indians and they came from foreign country. Their way of life and customs were entirely different and their rule was thoroughly unpopular among the people. The will of the people was not considered and sometimes they acted as dictator except Akbar. So under these circumstances the fall of the Mughal Empire was inevitable.

(4) Economic Bankruptcy

The economic condition was not satisfactory and the rulers did not take any steps to improve the income of the state. Babur, the founder of Mughal Dynasty spent huge amount for the charity. Humayun was also bankrupt. Though Akbar introduced a new economic system, he could not do it continuously. Shah Jahan spent huge money in constructing buildings. Further due to failure of monsoon there was a dangerous famine which drained the economy of the state. Aurangzeb wasted huge amount in the Deccan expedition.

(5) Growth of Hostile and Rival Cliques in the Court

The growth of hostile and rival cliques in the court during the reign of later Mughals also undermined the strength of the empire. Nobody cared for the problems of the country. Every one tried to gain his own end. The various cliques always cared for their own benefit and the result that Nadir Shah and Ahmad Shah Abdali were able to attack this country and gave a great blow to Mughal Empire.

(6) Corrupt and Inefficient Administration

The officers became corrupt and inefficient. They accepted bribes for doing undeserved favours. Like the Officers, the emperor also adopted this practice. Aurangzeb had asked an aspirant to the title. "Your father gave to Sher Shah one lakh of rupees for adding Alif to his title and making him Amir Khan. How much will you pay me for the title I am giving you?"

(7) No Law of Succession

The law of primogeniture was not applicable to the Mughals. There was a war of succession after the death of a king among the brothers. Sword was the main arbiter and the mighty and powerful son would become the ruler of the dynasty. "Taking advantage of these wars of succession, the distant Provincial Governors lost no opportunity in setting up independent states for themselves."

(8) Rise of British Power

British who came to India for commercial purpose wanted to establish their supremacy in India. When Clive came to India, he knew the rivalry between the Marathas and Muslims and explained the feasibility of setting up a British Empire in India to the Prime Minister of United Kingdom. So they took up the full advantage of the rivalry of various tribes and Clive fought the famous battles of Plassey and Buxar in 1757 and 1761 A.D. respectively and with this victory British increased their strength and set up their empire in India.

(9) Causes for Aurangzeb's Responsibility (Refer Previous Chapter)

(10) The neglect of navy was the another cause for the downfall of Mughal Empire. The result was that the Mughals could not fight with the foreign soldiers who had strong navy.

(11) One might conclude by saying that "the Mughal State owes its decline and ultimate downfall to a combination of causes of which perhaps the most important one was uncontrolled domination of a selfish and extravagant bureaucracy and inequitable economic system which steadily improvised the revenue-production classes of the population."

23

Social and Economic Conditions of the Mughal Empire

The social and economic conditions of Mughal India are important like political history of Mughals. "The real history of the people in Mughal India that is of their social life and economic condition, is of greater interest and importance for us today than mere catalogues of political events or military campaigns" — V. Smith. Here we are discussing the important points of social and economic life of the people of Mughal India.

Social Condition

The foreign travellers who came to India during Mughal reign has given a vast account of the social condition of the people.

Division in the Society

The society was divided into nobility, middle and lower class of people. King was the head of the society. The Emperor, his courtiers and high officials belonged to privileged class and they enjoyed all the comforts and luxuries. They were allowed to marry more girls and enjoyed all facilities. Employees of the state and traders belonged to middle class people. They were sound in financial status but they could not enjoy the privileges of the privileged people.

Small traders, labourers, artisans, cultivators, slaves, shopkeepers were the lower class people. Their economic condition was deplorable and they were condemned to live hard and unattractive life. They were pessimists and they never tried to arise the standard of revolt against the imperial rule. The lives of the artisans were hard. They had to work in different villages to maintain themselves as there was no enough of work in one village.

Social Evils

The practices of Sati and child marriage were common among the people. Hindus and Muslims were believed in superstitions. Hindus believed that if they bathed in the Ganges, their sins could be washed away. So Hindus undertook pilgrimages to the holy places in spite of the difficulties of the means of communication and transport in Mughal Empire. Like Hindus, Muslims went to Mecca every year. Captain Saus wrote in 1612 that a ship that usually went from Surat to Mecca was unusually very big and carried as many as 1700 pilgrims who went to Mecca not for profits but out of devotion to visit Mecca and Medina. The use of liquor, opium, etc. was common and no effective check were put on them. Corruption was widely prevalent among the officials. Begging was very common and all the good principles of the society had gone away.

The Position of Women

The condition of women was highly deplorable. Polygamy was an acceptable practice in the society. The purdah system was prevailed and women were considered inferior to men. They were used only for the sexual pleasures of men. Prostitution was common and practically nothing was done for the education of women. In general, the women had lost their place which was given to them in the ancient India.

Festivals

Holi, Basant Panchami, Dussehra, Diwali, Shivaratri and Sankranti were the important festivals of the Hindus whereas Muslims celebrated Id-ul-Zuha, Id-ul-Fiter, Muharram and Milad-un-Nabi. Aurangzeb put a ban on the celebration of the festivals but he could not execute his order forever. In addition to the above festivals Nauroz was celebrated in the aristocratic circles with great pomp and show.

Dress

The Emperor and his servants in the palace and the privileged people spend huge money in dress which consisted of a large coat, light trousers, a turban and a silk scarf tied at the waist with ends handing down. They used many costly jewels and according to the financial status, the people used the dresses. The common man used only dhoti. Most of the people were virtually halfnaked. They managed to put on good clothes on festive occasions.

View of Foreign Scholars

Many foreign travellers came to India and wrote the social conditions of India which was the first hand information. Pelsart said that there were three types of classes in the society. The workers were paid little salary and they were forced to work in the field of the nobles. They took only one food a day and their houses were made up of mud with thatched roofs. The Officials were corruptive. Hindus and Muslims had faith in astrology. The general morale of the society had gone down during the reign of Aurangzeb.

Economic Condition of Mughal Dynasty

The economic life of the people during Mughal reign was satisfactory. Though there was much difference in income between the privileged people and lower class of people. Much information was not available during the period of Babur and Humayun. Sher Shah did lot of steps to improve the economic condition of the people. Like Sher Shah, Akbar introduced many economic reforms and measures such as Revenue System of Raja Todar Mal and Mansabdari system. From the economic point of view, the period of Jahangir and Shah Jahan was most glorious and it began to dwindle in the time of Aurangzeb. Manucci said, "All things are in great plenty here, fruits, pulses, grains muslin cloth of gold and silver."

Nature of Agriculture

Agriculture was the main occupation of the people. Sher Shah and Akbar did a lot for the improvement of agriculture. Further the peasants were willing to devote all their time and energy to produce more. The farmers were given all the facilities and all sort of things that are found in the Modern India were present during the days of Mughals. Rice, Barley, Wheat and Pulses were the significant crops. Cotton was cultivated in Deccan. Bengal was famous for high quality sugarcane. Lower quality of indigo was also cultivated in North India. The chief items of non-agricultural production were fisheries, minerals, salt, opium, liquor and indigo.

Industries

Cotton industry was flourished in Mughal India. The famous textile centres were Banaras, Jaunpur, Khandesh and Lahore. The dyeing industry was also on the road of progress. Leather products were produced in plenty. Lahore, Agra, Fatehpur Sikri were the important places of silk weaving centres and Akbar encouraged this industry by giving all the facilities to the weavers. The shawl and carpet weaving were also patronised by Akbar. Moreland said, "so much of cotton cloth was produced in the country that after clothing the people of India, the same was exported to Africa, Arabia, Egypt, Burma and Mecca. Precious and costly stones Industry was flourished and by means of these stone Mughal Emperors built many monuments including Taj Mahal, one of the wonders of the world. Metal industry was also grown in Mughal period and the metal swords, daggers and other tools were popular. As people used gold ornaments, gold and silver industries were prevalent during the Mughal period.

Export and Import in Mughal Period

Akbar took keen interest in the foreign trade. The important harbours were Cambay, Surat, Bengal, Malabar Coast, etc. India used to export all kinds of cloth and spices to other countries. The gold, silver, copper and other valuables were imported. The emperor took certain effective steps for the advancement of the trade. The nature of trade changed after the death of Akbar. During the reigns of Jahangir and Shah Jahan the Dutch and English set up direct trade between India and the West. Surat was the famous centre of European markets and they permanently set up their trade establishments in 1650 and before the end of the Mughal rule, the English controlled the whole trade of Surat. The Indian merchants had to face a stiff competition with the

English merchants and finally they established their monopoly over trade in the Mughal Empire.

Growth of Industrial Cities

As many industries were developed in the Mughal period, there was a growth of industrial cities such as Lahore, Agra and Fatehpur Sikri. Fitch writes, "Agra and Fatehpur Sikri are two very great cities, either of them much greater than London and very populous. Between Agra and Fatehpur are twelve miles, and all the way is a market of vegetables and other things." In eastern India, Banaras, Patna, Bardwan and Dacca were the prosperous cities. Kabul was the centre of the trade between Central Asia and India.

(For more details refer the Mansabdari system and Revenue system of Akbar)

ART AND ARCHITECTURE OF THE MUGHALS

The Mughals were great builders. Their magnificent and beautiful buildings have come down to us. They were really attractive and decorative. Fergusson said that Mughal architecture was of foreign origin. Persian influence was one of the features of Mughal architecture. The buildings were noted for its massiveness and simplicity and the buildings of Shah Jahan were known for decoration and delicacy. Let us discuss the development of art and architecture under various Mughal kings.

Babur

Babur built many buildings. As he did not know the Indian architecture, he had a mind to invite people from Constantinople. But his intension was not executed. "In Agra alone, and of the stone-cutters belonging to that place only, I every day employed in my places 680 persons; and in Agra, Sikri, Biyana, Dholpur, Gwalior and Koil there were everyday employed 1491 stone-cutters on my works." Among the buildings constructed by Babur, two buildings were existed. One building was the mosque in the Kabul Bagh at Panipat and another at Sambhal.

Buildings of Humayun

Humayun could not construct more buildings as he led a very

stormy life. A mosque at Fatehbad was constructed which was decorated with enamelled tiles in the Persian style. Din Panah, otherwise known as Humayun's Palace was constructed. It lacked durability and features of Mughal architecture.

Akbar

He adopted not only the Persian but also the Indian styles.

1. At Agra and Fatehpur Sikri he built palaces which were known for its excellent style of architecture.
2. The Humayun's tomb constructed in memory of his father in the year 1565 had four towers at the four corners of the building and marble was only used.
3. He laid the foundation of the new city in the honour of Salim Chisti in 1569 and many buildings were constructed there.
4. The Jama Masjid and the Buland Darwaza are the other buildings built by him. To celebrate his victory in the Deccan, he constructed Buland Darwaza which is one of the biggest and famous gateway in India. The Jama Masjid was called, "the glory of Fatehpur."
5. He constructed the forts of Agra and Lahore. The walls of the Agra fort are 75 feet high and possess a circumference of a mile.
6. The gates of Delhi and Amar Singh were constructed under his personal supervision and more than 5,000 buildings of red stones were also constructed between the two gates.
7. "Elephants and lion figures in the brackets and peacocks at the friezes from which it may be inferred that Hindu Craftsmanship predominated and the supervision of the Mughal overseers was of a very tolerant order."
8. The chief treasures of the architecture of Akbar's period were the extensive use of red stones, ideal synthesis of Hindu and Muslim styles, increased use of marble and construction of a huge and impregnable fort at Agra.

Jahangir

He was not interested in constructing beautiful building like his father. Itmad-ud-Daula tomb was constructed by Nur Jahan in memory of her father. Marble was used and the features of Indian architecture are found in this building.

Shah Jahan

Refer Shah Jahan.

Painting of Mughal period

The Mughal rulers were the great lovers of painting. Babur the founder of Mughal Dynasty got pleasure and happy in seeing the paintings of flowers, springs and streams in his palace. Painting was received great impetus during his reign.

Humayun

Humayun also took interest in painting. He invited two painters from Kabul in 1550. No painting of his period was existed as the reign period was short.

Akbar

Painting was given fillip during the period of Akbar, who created a separate Department for painting under the control of Khawaja Abdus Samad and for the promotion of painting a school called the "National Indian School of Painting", was established, Painters from various countries were invited. They belonged to different religions and castes and produced excellent and outstanding paintings. Akbar maintained an album of portraits. Daswant, Besawan, Sanwal Das, Tarachand and Jagannath were the important personalities of Hindu painters.

Jahangir

He gave an impetus to painting. It was stated that if any painting or a piece of painting was brought to his knowledge, he was able to identify the painters without any difficulty. "If any other person has put in the eyebrows of a face, I can perceive whose work the original face is and who has painted the eyes and eyebrows." A unique feature of realism was found in the painting. The natural objects of flowers, trees, hills, birds, beasts, clouds, etc., had been painted in an excellent manner and these paintings were extremely realistic and natural. The imaginary figures were replaced by the figures which depicted the real life of a man. According to Percy Brown, "With his (Jahangir) passing the soul of Mughal painting also departed; its outward form remained for a time in gold and lavish vestments : it lived on under other kings but its real spirit died with Jahangir."

Shah Jahan

As he was interested in constructing beautiful buildings, he lacked interest in painting. So the progress of painting was arrested during his period. The famous painters of the time of Shah Jahan were Mir Hasan, Anupa Chitra and Chitramani.

Music

The Mughals were the lovers and patrons of music. Babur not only liked music but also wrote poetry. Humayun was fond of music and set apart Monday and Wednesday for listening the music. Bachchu was the court musician of Humayun. Akbar was also a great lover of music. There were numerous musicians of various countries presented in the court of Akbar. Abul Fazl said that there were 36 singers and performers on various instruments.

Literature

Babur

He was a good scholar and writer. He thoroughly knew Arabic, Persian and Turki. His books were 'Memoirs' and 'Tuzk-i-Baburi' or 'Babar Nama.' He was called as "the Prince by the Autobiographers". Beveridge says that his book is considered as one of the priceless records. He was a good poet and learned man. Ghiasud-Din, Muhammad Khuda Mir and Shahab-ud-din were the important poets during his time.

Humayun

He was a learned man and a great scholar in many languages. He was a voracious reader. He wrote some Ghazals and Rubais in Persian tongue.

Akbar

Though Akbar was uneducated, he loved and patronised the

scholars and poets. He promoted the publication and translation of many books in Persian language.

The important historical books written during his period were given below :

(1) Akbar Namah of Abul Fazl.

(2) Ain-i-Akbari of Abul Fazl.

(3) Akbar-Namah of Faizi.

(4) Masir-i-Rahimi of Abdul Baqi.

(5) Tarikh-i-Alfi of Mulla Daud.

Among the books Akbar Nama of Faizi was the masterpiece. Abul Faizi was a courtier of Akbar and his account was more accurate. Badayuni was a historian who criticised the religious policy of Akbar.

He encouraged the poets and extended special privileges to them in the court. Ghizali, Faizi, Saiyyid Jamal-ud-din Urfi were the important poets.

Jahangir

He wrote his biography entitled as Tuzk-i-Jahangiri. He patronised the men of letters and he himself was an eminent writer. The important writings of his period were Zuld-ut-Tawarikh, Masiri Jahangiri and Iqbal Namah-i-Jahangiri.

Shah Jahan

Padshahnamah, Shahjahannamah and Amal Sabagh were the important works during his period. He was a man of letters and patronised the writers and the scholars.

It goes without saying that the art and architecture flourished during the reign of Akbar, reached its peak at the time of Shah Jahan. It began to decline at the time of Aurangzeb, the fanatic Muslim ruler.

24

The Deccan Policy of Mughals

Babur, the founder of Mughal dynasty had no Deccan policy. He came to India and conquered only North India and before capturing Deccan, he passed away. Humayun who had lot of problems did not think of conquering the Deccan. When Mughal Dynasty was founded, there were only two main kingdoms in the Deccan, *i.e.*, Bahmani and Vijayanagar. Let us see the Deccan policy of Mughal rulers.

Deccan Policy of Akbar

Akbar wanted to capture the whole of Deccan. The wealth of Deccan was so much attractive to him and he made up his mind to exploit the economic source of Deccan. The Bahmani States were ruled by Shia Muslims and Akbar wanted to subdue the Shia Muslims. The Portuguese were rising their power and strength in the Deccan and Akbar wanted to crush their mighty power. There were four independent states in the Deccan — Bijapur, Golkonda, Ahmednagar and Kandesh. Akbar sent his ambassadors to these states to accept his sovereignty but they refused to obey his order except Khandesh. So Akbar had to send his force to Deccan.

(1) Capture of Ahmednagar (1595-1600)

In 1593 Akbar sent a huge force under the leadership of Abdur Rahim Khan-i-Khana and Prince Murad to Ahmednagar which was strongly defended by Chand Bibi. A truce was concluded between the two but it did not last long. So there was a fierce battle at Supa in which the Mughals were victorious and finally Ahmednagar was annexed to the Mughal Empire in August 1600.

(2) Capture of Asirgarh

It was a strong and well equipped fort in Khandesh which was under the control of Miran Bahadur. As Akbar found very difficult to capture it, he bribed the officials of the fort, opened it and captured with great difficulties. Though Akbar wanted to annex the other states, he could not do so because of revolt of Prince Salim.

Deccan Policy of Jahangir

War with Ahmednagar (1610-1620)

Ahmednagar was the part of Mughal Empire during the reign of Akbar but it was now an independent state when Jahangir ascended the throne. So he wanted to capture it. Mailk Amber, the ruler of Ahmednagar was a man of extraordinary qualities, rare intellectual powers, riped experience in civil and military affairs and a great general. He introduced Raja Todar Mal's revenue system in Ahmednagar so that he got much influence and status in the society.

To capture it, Jahangir first sent Khan Jahan Lodi first and later on Khan-i-Khana Abdur Rahim was sent to punish Malik Amber. Their attempts were failed. Then Prince Khurram was entrusted with the charge of conquering Deccan. When he marched to Ahmednagar, with big force, Malik Amber submitted and accepted a peace treaty. Adil Shah, the ruler of Burhanpur met Khurram with presents worth Rs. 16 lakhs and also promised to restore all the territories which had been seized by Malik Amber. This treaty was ratified by Jahangir who conferred the title of Shah Jahan and his mansab was raised to 30,000 Zat and 20,000 Sawar.

Deccan Policy of Shah Jahan

Khan Jahan Lodi was the Viceroy of Deccan who made an alliance with the ruler of Ahmednagar. He enlisted the support of the southern people. Knowing this situation, Shah Jahan wanted to suppress rebellion and he himself went to Deccan. Khan Jahan Lodi could not stand against the ferocious attack of Shah Jahan and ran away from place to place. The allies of Khan Jahan did not help him and he failed in his attempt of getting co-operation from the rulers of southern chiefs. The chiefs instead of helping him, opposed him. At last, he was killed while fighting near the fort of Kalinjar in 1630.

Deccan Policy of Aurangzeb

Due to Deccan policy of the Mughals, a huge money was spent. Aurangzeb spent more than 20 years in Deccan which resulted in the neglect of the administration and he lost his control and authority in the rule. Further there were revolts and rebellions here and there and he could not root out all the outbreaks aimed against him. Thus, Aurangzeb's Deccan policy became of potent factor for the downfall of the Mughal Empire.

(For more details Refer Aurangzeb)

25

Frontier Policy of Mughals

The frontier provinces were a continued headache for the rulers of Delhi Sultanate. There were many independent chiefs in North Western frontier between Afghanistan and Delhi and these chiefs were the potential danger for the Mughal kings who had to fight with them. Let us see the frontier policy of the Mughals in detail.

Frontier Policy of Babur

Babur and Persian ruler had a look on Kandhar and both of them tried to conquer Kandhar and ultimately Babur established his supremacy in 1522 A.D. Thus, the North Western Frontier was safe during the reign of Babur.

Policy of Humayun

After the death of Babur, the country was divided among his sons and Kamran was the ruler of Kandhar and Kabul. When Humayun was running from Agra to Persia, he wanted to get the help of his brother Kamran but he did not extend his help. So Humayun went to Persia and with the help of forces of the Shah of Persia, he captured Khandhar. According to his promise, he gave Kandhar to the rulers of Persia and established his rule in Kabul in 1500. After the death of Shah of Persia. Humayun also established his sovereignty in Kandhar. However, due to his premature death, he could not have full control over the frontier provinces.

Policy of Akbar

Hakim Mirza, the brother of Akbar wanted to capture Punjab and to punish his brother Akbar sent his Prince Murad who defeated Mirza and allowed to retain only Kabul. Then after the death of Mirza, Kabul was also annexed with Mughal Empire.

The Uzbegs and Yusufzais revolted against the Mughal Empire. In 1586, a force was despatched to crush the revolt of Uzbeg but Yusufzais put to death 8,000 Mughal soldiers along with Raja Birbal. Now Akbar sent Raja Todar Mal along with Prince Murad to suppress the revolt. They succeeded in their task.

The Shah of Persia was not able to suppress the strength of the Mughals. In 1595, Akbar completed the conquest of Kandhar and annexed it with the Mughal Empire. The Mughal army returned to Agra. When the army was returning, it was attacked by the turbulent men called Hazaras in which about 5,000 men and 5,000 animals were put to death. The North-Western frontier policy of Shah Jahan was great failure and failure of his policy affected the prestige of the Mughals.

Policy of Aurangzeb

The turbulent tribes of North-Western frontier gave troubles by rising revolts against the Mughals under the leadership of Bhagu and Yusufzais but their revolts were crushed by the Mughal soldiers. Though Mughals were victorious against the turbulent chiefs, they could not have complete control over them. So Aurangzeb entrusted Mahabat Khan, Shayista Khan and Raja Jaswant Singh to deal with the situation and himself followed. The unity of the turbulent chiefs was broken and Aurangzeb tried to restore peace there. However, his ambition was not fulfilled. There was a big loss of men, animals and money. The Mughal's prestige was impaired.

The North Western frontier policy was not successful. Frequent rebellions were undertaken by the local chiefs against the Mughals which resulted in loss of men and money.

Policy of Jahangir

Kandhar was annexed by Akbar with the Mughal Empire. But later on during the reign of Jahangir, Shah of Persia led an expedition against Kandhar. Jahangir ordered Shah Jahan to put a gallant resistance to him but he refused to go over to Kandhar due to misunderstanding with Nur Jahan. So Shah of Persia conquered Kandhar after the siege of 40 days.

Policy of Shah Jahan

Shah Jahan decided to get back Kandhar from Shah of Persia. When Shah Jahan attacked Kandhar, the Governor of Kandhar sought the help of Shah of Persia but the later refused thinking that the Governor was playing tricks against him and finally the Governor had no other alternative but to surrender Kandhar to Mughals. Under Shah Jahan sent a strong force to capture Balkh under the head of Prince Murad. He captured it but before annexing it, he left the place. So Balkh was lost. In 1647 Shah Jahan sent Shuja and Aurangzeb to complete the task of capturing Balkh. There was a fierce battle and Aurangzeb showed great bravery and presence of mind. At last the peace was concluded.

Frontier Policy of Aurangzeb

The Muslim tribes in the frontier were always turbulent and a source of danger and trouble to the Mughals. They were poor and their poverty forced them to attack Punjab again and again. In the beginning the tribes were silenced by payments of money. However, "even political pensions were not always effective in securing obedience." In 1667, the Yusufzais who were dissatisfied about the reign of Aurangzeb, revolted against him under their leader, Bhagu. They crossed over the river Attock and plundered the district of Attock and Peshawar. But the rising of Yusufzais were suppressed within the next few months.

The Afridis revolted against the Mughals under the leadership of Akmal Khan, who declared himself as a king. He instigated his subjects to undertake a holy war against the Mughals. The Mughals put up a stiff resistance but they were defeated in the fierce battle at Ali Masjid. The victory of Akmal Khan enhanced his position and power. He recruited more people to the army and maintained a permanent army to check the aggression of the Mughals. Akmal Khan was joined by the Khattaks under their leader Khushall Khan who was "the leading spirit of the national rising and inspired the tribesmen with his pen and sword alike." In 1674, the Mughal forces attacked the rising powers of Afridis and their leaders were killed in the battlefield and thus the menace of Afridis was put an end.

The frequent troubles in the North-West frontier enabled Aurangzeb to understand the gravity of the situation and he made up his mind to settle down the troubles permanently for ever. He would like to restore peace either by means of diplomacy or force of arms. Many Afghans were brought under his control by means of presents, Jagirs, Persions and Offices. The Governor of Punjab followed a conciliatory policy towards the people. Thus, peace was restored in border areas. Though peace was restored, the frontier policy of Aurangzeb could not be turned a success. There was a big loss of men and money. The Mughal prestige was greatly impaired. The Mughal troops engaged in wars from Deccan were sent to the frontier line, this enabled Shivaji to pursue his aggressive designs with great success.

26

Rise of Sikhs

The Sikh movement played a significant role for the rise and growth of Sikh power during the Mughal rule in India. Later on, the increased strength and solidarity of Sikhs became a potent cause of the downfall of Mughal empire.

1. GURU NANAK

(i) His Early Life

Guru Nanak was born in October 1469, at Talwandi in Pakistan. His father, Mehta Kalu was a Khattri. Guru was very pious from his early days. He used to sing hymns pertaining to God. He was not interested in education. Anyhow he acquired knowledge of Hindi, Sanskrit and Persian languages.

Guru Nanak served as shepherd, farmer, trader and salesman for some time. He was married to Sulakhni, daughter of Mool Chand of Batala in 1488.

(ii) Enlightenment

Nanak showed very little interest in his family life, because he had a higher mission to accomplish in his life. It is said that one day when Nanak was bathing in a small stream in Sultanpur, he disappeared for some time in the water and he had an interview with the God. God said to him, "Go thou, spread love and devotion to God and glorify His name." Thus, he got enlightenment in 1494 A.D.

(iii) After Enlightenment

After this incident, Nanak wore a religious dress. He began to undertake long travels in order to preach true message to the people. From 1495 to 1530, he undertook religious tours in the North, the South, the West and East. He visited important religious centres of the Hindus, the Muslims and the Sikhs. In short he visited Mecca, Madina and Baghdad. His religious tours are known as 'Udasis'. During the invasion of Babur, Nanak was arrested by his soldiers and he was released soon due to his piety and saintliness.

(iv) His Settlement at Kartarpur

Nanak settled at Kartarpur near the river Ravi in 1530. It was founded by him. A large number of disciples gathered round him. He nominated his successor there. His name was Angad. He was a worthy disciple of Nanak.

(v) Death of Nanak

Nanak felt that his end was coming nearer at Kartarpur. He died in 1538 at Kartarpur. There was a quarrel between the Hindus and Muslims on the question of disposing his body. Finally they divided the covering sheet of the body into two pieces and one of the pieces was buried by Muslims and the other was cremated by the Hindus.

(vi) His Teachings

Guru Nanak had unique faith in God. According to him, "God is one; He is omnipotent....". "God has no shape, no sign and no colour, God is transcendent; He is glorious and merciful." Nanak used to say that self-surrender is the only way to please the God.

Guru Nanak gave more importance to the recitation of the name of God. He further gave too much emphasis to spiritual guide.

Guru Nanak was the firm believer in doctrine of Karma and morality. Everyone has to pay the price of his actions. Truth, sincerity and fairness in dealings are the symbol of good conduct. One should not tell a lie, steal or injure the feelings of others.

Guru Nanak preached Divine Love. He also preached universal brotherhood. He used to say, "There is no Hindu and no Mussalmans."

Guru Nanak condemned superstitious and unfounded practices among the people.

According to him the goal of a devotee is to attain the supreme bliss or 'Sach Khand'.

Thus, Nanak occupied a place of pride not only in the history of Punjab or India but also of the world.

2. GURU ANGAD (1538-1552)

Guru Angad was the successor of Nanak. He laid the foundation of Gurumukhi. He compiled the biography of Nanak in 1540. He maintained strict discipline and those who were rebellions, were severely dealt with.

3. GURU AMAR DAS (1552-1574)

Guru Angad was succeeded by Amar Das. He was a devotee of Vishnu. Later on he turned towards Sikhism. He took series of successful steps for the development of Sikhism.

Guru Amar Das constructed a Baoli at Goindwal which later on became the important place of pilgrimage for the Sikhs.

Guru Amar Das divided his empire 22 parts called Manjis. Each Manji was under the control of a devoted Sikh. Festivals like Holi, Diwali and Baisakhi were celebrated during his period. He prohibited the custom of Sati and condemned Purdah system.

4. GURU RAM DAS (1574-1581)

Guru Ram Das was the son-in-law of Guru Amar Das. He founded a new city known as Chak Guru or Ram Daspura. He introduced the Musand system. Their duty was to collect taxes in the country. By this they brought money to the Guru.

5. GURU ARJUN DEV (1581-1606)

Arjun Dev took certain steps like the construction of Harmandir temple and compilation of Adi-Granth which occupies a unique place in the development of Sikhism. He was highly responsible for the development of Musand system. He founded many new towns. The important of them are Tarn Taran. Kartarpur and Cheharta. He constructed a Baoli and Dabi Bazar at Lahore. He encouraged the Sikhs for horse trading.

Guru Arjun Dev had very cordial relationship with Akbar. But during the reign of Jahangir the relationship between the Emperor and the Guru became bitter. He was executed by Jahangir at the instigation of Chandu Shah. It gave new strength to Sikhs.

6. GURU HARGOVIND (1606-1644)

Guru Hargovind was the son and successor of Guru Arjun. Unlike his predecessors he kept two swords with him. They were called Miri and Piri. The former was temporal authority, the latter was his spiritual authority. Thus Guru Hargovind was not only spiritual guide, but also a military leader. He bore the title of 'Sachcha Padshah' and maintained a well equipped army.

Guru Hargovind erected a new building named 'Akal Takht' near Harmandir. It was the Guru's throne. He maintained a well equipped army. He fortified the city Amritsar and constructed Lohgarh fort.

Guru Hargovind introduced minor changes in the routine life of Guru.

There was cordial relations between the Mughal Emperor Jahangir and Hargovind. Later on he was arrested by Jahangir and was confined in the fort of Gwalior. Then he was released by him. After the death of Jahangir the relations between the Mughals and the Sikhs became bitter.

In 1628 the first battle between the Mughals and Guru took place. Shah Jahan considered the political and military activities of the Guru were dangerous for the Mughal empire. The battle was so fierce. The Sikhs won a glorious victory against the Mughals.

In 1631 the battle of Lahiva took place. During this battle both the sides suffered heavy losses. At last Guru succeeded in killing the Mughal leaders.

There was a fierce battle at Kartarpur in 1634. Painde Khan and Kale Khan were killed in the battle. Guru Har Govind was victorious in the battle.

7. GURU HAR RAI (1644-1661)

After Guru Hargovind, his grandson Guru Har Rai succeeded

him. During his period he maintained cordial relations with the Mughals.

8. GURU HAR KISHAN (1661-1664)

After the death of Har Rai, Har Kishan, a five year old boy became Guru. But he had an attack of small pox and died in 1664.

9. GURU TEG BAHADUR (1664-1675)

Guru Teg Bahadur was the 9th Guru. He was the son of Guru Hargovind. He had a large number of Hindu and Muslim supporters. But Aurangzeb's fanaticism led to his death in 1675. He refused to embrace Islam and so he met the fatal end. He was responsible for Govind Singh's vengeance upon the Mughals.

10. GURU GOVIND SINGH (1675-1708)

Early Life

Guru Govind Singh was the 10th and the last Guru of the Sikhs. He was born in December 1666, at Patna. He was the son of Guru Teg Bahadur. His mother's name was Gujri. From the childhood, he was bold and fearless. He was educated at Anandpur. Rajput soldier, Qajar Singh trained him as a soldier. He learnt Gurmukhi, Persian and Hindi. He was married to Jeeto, daughter of Harji Mal. Later on he married two more ladies, Sundari and Sahib Devan. He became Guru at the age of nine.

Achievements

(i) The most important achievement of Guru was the foundation of Khalsa. Before its foundation he made elaborate military preparation. It increased his popularity. The hilly Rajas of Bilaspur and Srinagar became jealous of him. In order to harm the Guru, they attacked Paonta Sahib. Guru Govind Singh inspired his soldiers to fight stubbornly against the enemies. The hilly Rajas were defeated. This victory greatly enhanced his prestige.

(ii) Guru Govind Singh constructed four fortresses in Anandpur — Anandgarh, Lohgarth, Keshgarth and Fatehgarth. A fierce battle took place at Nadaun between the Mughals and the

Guru. Mughals were defeated and repulsed. Aurangzeb decided to put an end to the activities of Guru. But the Guru continued his activities against the Mughals. Mirza Beg was sent to crush the Gnru. However, a compromise was reached between them. Prince Muazzam agreed to withdraw his expedition.

(iii) In 1699, Guru Govind Singh laid the foundation of Khalsa and prepared the Sikhs to fight against the Mughals. Accordingly he participated in the battle of Anandpur twice. He lost his two sons. In 1704, he fought against the Mughals in Chamkaur. In the battle, two remaining sons of Guru's were killed. But he managed to escape in disguise. He then fought the last battle with the Mughal forces in Khidrana in 1706. Though he lost all his followers in the battle, he succeeded in defeating the Mughals. After his victory he settled at Talwandi Sabo in Patiala.

Guru Govind Singh enumerated the following principles of Khalsa :

(a) The members of the Khalsa should call themselves "Singh."

(b) Every member of the Khalsa would be required to keep five things — *Kesh* (long hair), *Kirpan* (dagger), *Kachha* (underwear), *Kangha* (Comb) and *Kara* (iron ring round the wrist).

(c) They should have faith in God.

(d) It would be the sacred duty of all the members of Khalsa to exterminate the Turks and defend their religion.

By this Khalsa the Sikhs were brought under one umbrella.

Death of the Guru

In 1708 Bahadur Shah and the Guru marched to the south. Guru was stabbed by a Pathan on the way to the south on 7th October 1708 and died after some days.

Estimate

Guru Govind Singh is one of the greatest personalities of Indian history. He was not only a great Guru but also a great warrior and military general. He was an accomplished soldier.

Guru Govind Singh was an excellent man. He was tall and handsome. He was very strong and study. He had a charming personality. He was an ideal man; he was a loving husband; he was an affectionate father; above all he was a devoted son. Every job was very easy to him.

As a Guru, he occupied a prominent place among the Sikhs. He had a firm belief in God. His foremost aim of life was to worship God, spread his religion. Whatever money he got he distributed it amongst the needy. In short he was attracted by the Mughal Emperor Bahadur Shah, the son of Aurangzeb by his saintly character.

Guru Govind Singh was a brave soldier and great general. G.C. Narang has rightly remarked in the following manner :

> "Under his influence men had never touched a sword or shouldered a gun became heroes."

With great enthusiasm, the Guru fought against Mughals and inflicted defeat upon them.

As a social reformer he did a lot and earned a very good name and fame. He attacked the caste system. He worked for the unity of the Hindu society. He preached the lesson of self-respect and human dignity. He abolished the Masand system. He saved the Sikhs from the Brahmin exploitation.

The Guru was a great nation builder. By erecting the Khalsa, he struck a great blow to the caste system. He advised the people to follow the democratic lines and administered the baptism of sword to all the people. It created patriotism in the minds of the Sikhs. Thus, the Guru was responsible for an independent Sikh nation.

As a scholar Guru Govind Singh always liked the company of scholars. He followed a new style of Hindi poetry. He was well versed in Punjabi, Persian and Hindi. His masterpieces like 'Jap Sahib', 'Zafar Nama', and 'Vichittar Natak' are very famous in the literary field.

It goes without saying that the Guru was an immortal amongst the mortals by his memorable contributions to the Sikh community.

Banda Bahadur (1670-1716)

After the death of Guru Govind Singh, Banda Bahadur took up his task. His activities irritated the Mughals. So fierce battles took place between Banda and Mughal soldiers at Lohgarh and then at Gurudas Nangal. Finally Banda was arrested with his followers and sent to Delhi. There they were paraded in the bazaars and executed in June 1716.

27

Career and Achievements of Shivaji

The rise of Marathas in the South is considered as the most significant development of the Mughal period. Many factors were responsible for the rise of Marathas. They were (1) the physical features (2) Bhakti movement (3) the influence of literature and language (4) training in warfare (5) guerrilla tactics and (6) gallant leadership of Shivaji.

SHIVAJI

(i) Early Life

Shivaji was born on April 10, 1627, in the hill fort of Shivaner. His parents were Shahji Bhonsle and Jijibai. During his early age, Shivaji was influenced by Jijibai, Kondadev, Guru Ram Das and Tukaram.

(ii) Influence on Shivaji

Shivaji's mother Jijibai was a pious lady. She related to him the stories of Ramayana and Mahabharata and acts of brave Hindu fighters. She by "her examples and teachings did much to stimulate the zeal of her famous son in defence of Brahmins, cows and caste, the three principle objects of Hindu Venarations."

Dadaji Kondadev, an experienced Brahmin also played an important part in the career of Shivaji. He was the tutor of Shivaji. He imparted training in the art of civil administration. Moreover he brought Shivaji as an orthodox Hindu.

Guru Ram Das exercised a tremendous influence on Shivaji. He always advised him to do his best for uniting the Marathas.

Tukaram helped in building the character of Shivaji. He also asked him to love his country and countrymen above all the things of the world.

In his early days Shivaji made himself thoroughly familiar with the hilly country around Poona. The Mawali chiefs of his own age greatly helped him.

(iii) His Conquests

Shivaji started his career of conquests when he was 19 years old.

(a) In 1641 he became the Jagirdar of Poona. Taking advantage of the confusion prevailing in Bijapur due to the illness of Sultan of Bijapur, he captured the fort of Torna. It was followed by the capture of the fort of Chakanand the outposts of Baramati and Indapur. Then he captured the forts of Singharth, Kondama and Purandhar.

(b) In 1656 Shivaji conquered Javeli, the north western frontier of District Sitara by murdering Chandav Rao. Dr. A.L. Srivastava writes, "The conquest of Javeli was a landmark in Shivaji's career, as it opened a door for the conquest of the fresh territory south and west of his newly established kingdom...."

(c) In 1656 the conquests of Raigarh and Supa was successfully carried out by Shivaji.

(d) The activities of Shivaji had greatly annoyed the Sultan of Bijapur. At the same time Sultan imprisoned his father on 25th July, 1648, and confiscated his property. Shivaji was greatly perturbed on this incidence. The Sultan demanded two forts of Rangalore and Kondana for the release of his father. Moreover the Sultan sent a huge army under the leadership of Afzal Khan to bring back Shivaji dead or alive.

Afzal Khan came to the country and found that it was not easy to fight against Shivaji in the mountain regions. So he made up his mind to lure Shivaji the help of Krishnaji Bhaskar to bring Shivaji to meet him. Krishnaji met Shivaji and hinted his cunning idea. Hearing this, Shivaji decided to be on his guard. He promised to meet Afzal Khan.

Accordingly Shivaji and Afzal Khan met each other at a fixed place. Afzal Khan embraced Shivaji and then suddenly held his neck in his left arm with an iron grip and with his right hand tried to attack Shivaji with his dagger. However, Shivaji was saved himself with the help of an armour which he was putting on. In turn he attacked Afzal Khan. With the help of the "tiger claws" (Baghnakh) fastened to his left hand, he forced Afzal Khan to relax his grip and stabbed him with his dagger. Immediately there was a clash between Maratha soldiers and Bijapur forces. Afzal Khan was killed and Shivaji was victorious. In this way he acquired the territories to the south of Panhala and along the banks of river Krishna. Finally Sultan of Bijapur recognised Shivaji as an independent ruler.

(e) Aurangzeb appointed Shayista Khan as the Governor of Deccan in 1660. He also entrusted him the task of checking Shivaji. He marched against Shivaji according to the instruction of his master. He defeated Marathas at some places. Then he stayed in a house (Poona) where Shivaji had spent his childhood. So Shivaji hit upon a grand plan. Shivaji entered the city of Poona with his big army in the form of a marriage party on 15th April 1663. He immediately attacked the residence of Shayista Khan. At that time, he was fast asleep. Before his attack Shivaji reached the room and cut off the thumb of Shayista Khan. The son of Shayista Khan was also killed. After the work was over, the Marathas ran away. Aurangzeb was so much upset with this incidence and called him from Deccan and transferred him to Bengal.

(f) Shivaji plundered the city of Surat in 1664 and obtained a huge booty. Seeing this, Aurangzeb was greatly alarmed.

(g) Aurangzeb ordered Jai Singh to crush Shivaji. He was tactful and a brave general. He reached Poona in 1665. He immediately surrounded the forts of Purandhar and Raigarh with huge army. Shivaji was helpless. So he concluded the treaty of Purandhar in June 1665.

Accordingly Shivaji was to surrender 23 forts to the Mughals and retain only 12 forts for himself.

Sambhaji, the son of Shivaji was to be given a jagir.

Sambhaji had also to live in the Mughal court.

Shivaji also agreed to help the Mughals in their attack of Bijapur.

(h) Shivaji was invited to the Mughal court to meet Aurangzeb. He reached Agra where he was given a cold reception. In the Durbar he was not given proper respects. Shivaji protested against this. So he was arrested and imprisoned. Later on he managed to escape in a camouflaged basket.

Shivaji renewed his war with the Mughals. He captured the forts of Kondana, Purandhar, Mabuli and Nandal. From 1670 to 1674 Shivaji was successful in his campaigns against the Mughals.

(i) After his coronation in June 1674, he conquered Koli, Baglana and Khandesh. Then he turned towards Kolhapur. There he got a huge booty. He planned to attack Jinji and Vellore. In 1676, he attacked the remaining portions of Karnatic region and conquered a vast territory containing 100 forts, yielding an income of 20 lakhs of rupees.

(iv) Shivaji and Tanjore

Shivaji's grand coronation in June 1674 had greatly reduced his treasury balance. His conquests also were highly responsible for the deteriorating financial condition. He therefore, looked about for some fresh field of gain. He directed his attention towards the rich Karnataka plain or the Madras coast. It had enjoyed many years of peace and prosperity and whose wealth was fabulous. The Karnataka plain or the Madras coast was known in that age as the land of gold. It was an extremely tract, rich in agricultural produce, with a population that led to a life of primitive simplicity and consumed very little in food and clothing. There was brisk foreign trade. Thus, the annual addition to the national wealth was very large. From very early times the Karnataka has been famous for its buried treasure and attracted foreign plunderers.

From this land Samudragupta, and the Western Chalukyas, Malik Kafur and Mir Jumla had brought away vast booties. And at the end of the 17th century even after the recent raids of Mir

Jumla, Muhammad Adil Shah, and Nasrat Jung, the land still had enough wealth left in it to tempt the cupidity of Aurangzeb. To this real land of gold Shivaji's eyes were now turned.

The vast province of Jinji, officially known as Bijapur-Karnataka-Painghat, was divided into three bannias; one-third of it was held in Jagir by Venkoji as successor of Shahji and the remainder by two Muslim nobles of the Adil Shahi State. Shivaji planned to conquer these two Muslim fiefs, add to them one half of Shivaji's jagirs taken from his brother's hands and thus create a large East Coast Kingdom, which he would bequeath as an independent dominion to one of his sons, while his other son would inherit the territory of Maharashtra.

At this juncture there was chaos and confusion among the Hindu Nayaks of Jinji, Tanjore and Madura. The new Nayak of Madura at last seized the kingdom of Tanjore and beheaded its perpetually faithless ruler Vijaya Raghu in April 1674, Adil Shah was appealed by the son of the murdered king, and he ordered Venkoji to invade Tanjore and restore it to its old dynasty. But in 1676 Venkoji conquered the country, usurped the throne of Tanjore and crowned himself as an independent king.

The flood of Maratha invasion swept over the Karnataka plains. The southern half of the Bijapur's Karnataka plains was ruled by Sher Khan Lodi, a Pathan noble, with his seat of Government at Vali-Kandapuram. At that time Shivaji charged the confused and wavering range of the enemy and turned the retreat into a rout. Sher Khan flung himself with the remnant of his army into the fort of Tiruvedi in his rear. He tried to escape from it to Tevanampatnam a suburb of Cuddalore. Finally he was defeated by the Marathas. Shivaji himself appeared before Bonagirpatnam (Buvanagiri). Many forts were captured by the Marathas. Then Shivaji left the vicinity of Cuddalore, marched south across the Vellar river, cautioned his army for the rainy season at Tirumalawadi on the north bank of the Koleroon river 10 miles due north of Tanjore. The Nayak gave large booty and hence Shivaji promised to retire with his army.

At Shivaji's request, the Rajah of Tanjore had sent his ministers for a preliminary discussion. Shivaji opened his business.

There was serious exchange of words between them. So a partition by agreement was impossible. At last, when Shivaji uttered a hectoring tone, Venkoji told him that the only solution was to fight it out, for which he was ready.

In the meantime, Venkoji escaped from the sight of Shivaji and Shivaji ascribed it to the advice of the Tanjore Ministers. He placed them under arrest and threatened to send Janardhan Narayan Hanumante to take possession of the kingdom of Tanjore. Shivaji sent some of his officers to Tanjore to recall Venkoji, but they returned unsuccessful.

After a time the captive ministers of Venkoji were set free, and sent back to Tanjore with presents and robes of honour. Thus, Shivaji cleared himself in the yes of the public. But though he gave up the idea of invading the Tanjore territory south of the Koleroon, he seized the whole Karnataka north of that river, both the jagirs of Venkoji and those of Sher Khan, Vellore and Arni alone still holding out.

The French envoy M. Germain who spent three days in Shivaji's camp on the Koleroon, gives a graphic account of the Maratha King's spartan simplicity and efficient arrangements. He very easily captured Vanikamvadi (40 miles south-west of Vellore now it is Vaniyambadi), Arni and other places. After his march of Madras he had pillaged Porto Novo and made himself master of the South Arcot District. In 1678 the fort of Vellore surrendered. Thus, Shivaji became the great victor in the Karnataka plain of the Madras coast.

(v) Death of Shivaji

During his last days, Shivaji was greatly disappointed with the actions of his son Sambhaji. So he fell ill and died on April 13, 1680.

Shivaji's Administration

Shivaji was not only a great solider and conqueror, but also an excellent statesman and efficient administrator. According to Rawlinson, "Like nearly all great warriors — Napoleon is a conspicuous example — Shivaji was also a great administrator, for the qualities which go to make a capable general are those which are required by the successful organiser and statesman." He had all the qualities of a good administrator.

CENTRAL GOVERNMENT

(i) The King

The king was the head of the administration. He was also called Chattarapati. He was an aristocrat. He had all powers in his hands. He had ministers to assist him. But the main string of the policy were in his own hands.

The king had the following powers :

(a) Appointment of officers.

(b) Appointment of ministers.

(c) The issue of directions to the officers and ministers.

(d) General supervisicn of the entire administration.

In short Shivaji was an enlightened despot. He always took care to promote the welfare of the society.

(ii) Ashta Pradhan

Shivaji was assisted by the council of eight ministers known as the "Ashta Pradhan" in his day-to-day administration. The eight ministers were the following :

(1) **Peshwa of Prime Minister :** The main duty of the Peshwa or Prime Minister was to look after the general welfare of the state. In the absence of the king, he had to do all his works.

(2) **Amatya or Finance Minister :** His duty was to check and countersign all the public accounts of the kingdom. The income and expenditure of the country was under his control.

(3) **Mantri or Chronicler :** He was responsible for keeping a diary of the doings of the king.

(4) **Sumant or Foreign Secretary :** His duty was to advise the king on matters relating to foreign states. He was otherwise called Foreign Minister.

(5) **Sachiv or Home Secretary :** His duty was to look after the correspondence of the king.

(6) **Pandit Rao or Minister of Ecclesiastical Affairs :** His main duty was to look after the religious affairs.

(7) **Senapati or Commander-in-Chief :** He was incharge of recruitment, organisation and discipline in the army. He had to look after the disposition of troops in the battlefield.

(8) **Nyayadish or Chief Justice :** Judicial system was controlled by him. He was the highest Judge or Chief Judge of the kingdom.

(iii) Departments

During the time of Shivaji there were 18 departments of the state. Various ministers looked these departments. They worked under the supervision and guidance of Chattarapati.

(iv) Provincial Administration

Shivaji had two kinds of territories in his empire. They were (i) territories under direct control of the king; (ii) territories under the control of the Marathas which legally belonged to the Mughal empire. The former was called 'Swaraj'; the latter was called Mughal territories.

The Swaraj territories were divided into three provinces. Three viceroys were appinted for the administration of those provineces. Each Viceroy had to maintain peace and order in his province.

(v) District Administration

Each province was sub-divided into districts and parganas. Each pargana had a Collector with a contingents of troops under his command. Shivaji did not allow the hereditary office of the Deshmukhs.

(vi) Military Administration

Shivaji was a great military genius. He maintained a big well organised army. The strength of the army was very huge. There were 1,00,000 infantry, 40,000 cavalry and 1,260 elephants. Artillery was also a part of the army.

The Cavalry

The most significant part of his army was the Paga on state

cavalry. There were two classes in the cavalry, *viz.*, the Bargirs and the Shiladars. There were regular grades in the cavalry. The unit formed by 25 troopers. Over 25 troopers, there was a Havaldar. Five Havaldars were placed under one Jumladar and over 10 Jumladars, there was one Hazari, five Hazaris were under a Panj Hazari.

The Infantry

It was the next important branch of the army. There were three division, *viz.*, regiments, brigades and divisions. The smallest unit was formed by 9 soldiers. They were under a Naik. There was a Havaldar over 5 Naiks and a Jumladar over 2 Havaldars. Over 10 Jumladars there was Hazari and over 7 Hazaris, there was a Sari Naubat.

The Navy

Shivaji had a considerable fleet. It gradually developed into a very powerful force. In the middle of the 18th century, Maratha fleet was a great threat to the Portuguese and the English.

War Techniques and Discipline

Forts played a very important part in the military organisation. He had adopted guerrilla technique of warfare. It was a great boon to the Marathas for their success against the Mughals. Both Hindus and Muslims were recruited in the army of Shivaji. Strict discipline and morality was enforced among the soldiers. No woman was allowed to accompany the troops. Severe punishments were given for the violation of rules and regulations of the army.

Judicial Administration

The judicial system of Shivaji was not well planned. Hazir Majlis was the highest court. It was the court of the king. The most important cases were decided by this court. It was the final court of appeal.

The next immediate court was the court of Nyayadish or Chief Justice. Appeals from the lower courts were heard in this court. It had both civil and military jurisdictions.

Village Panchayats carried out the day-to-day administration of the justice. They had to deal with civil cases only.

The Patels were entrusted with criminal cases.

The punishments were severe. The culprits were fined even for small offences.

Financial Administration

Shivaji reorganised the land revenue system. His system was dated upon the principles laid down by Todar Mal and Malik Amber. For this purpose the whole kingdom was divided into "Prants". A Subedar was appointed for each province.

The Suba was divided into a number of "Tarafs". Havaldar was placed incharge of the Taraf.

The lowest unit was the village which was under a Patel.

The land was measured by means of rod known as "Kathi". The assessment was made after a careful survey. The share was 30 per cent of the total produce.

Besides, Chauth and Sardeshmukhi were collected by the state. They were collected from the regions outside the kingdom. The Chauth was 1/4th of the revenue of the district invaded, while the Sardeshmukhi was an additional tax 10 per cent on the gross produce.

There was income from forests. In addition to this profession tax was also levied during this period.

Estimate

Shivaji was not only a great fighter and conqueror, but also an excellent administrator. But the contemporary Muslim writer have described Shivaji as a tyrant and a robber chief. Khafi Khan describes him "as a father of fraud" and "a sharp son of the devil". The Maratha historians like J.N. Sarkar regard him as a "superman, a divine agency to free them from the yoke of Muslims".

Shivaji was a short statured man. As a man, he was very disciplined. He was a friend of the poors. He was gifted with extraordinary intelligence and supreme commonsense.

Shivaji was a great patron of learning. Many Brahmins were employed to collect synonyms for Persian words. He was a greatly religious minded man. He patronised Hinduism. He instructed his soldiers to respect mosques and other places of worship.

Shivaji strictly followed Hindu morals of those days. He was free from all vices of those days such as polygamy and concubinage.

Shivaji was a great military genius. He faced the mighty Mughals with great strength and courage. He was a master of war tactics. At the same time he was a matchless organiser.

As a ruler he was benevolent and stood for the betterment and welfare of his subjects. He was an excellent administrator.

Shivaji was a great nation builder. He claims a high rank in the pages of Indian History. He was responsible for the rise of Marathas. Writers like Grant Duff and K.M. Panikar have described him as a marvellous man. J.N. Sarkar has aptly remarked that "Shivaji was the last great constructive genius and nation builder that Hindu race has ever produced."

Thus, we may conclude that Shivaji was great in all respects.

28

The Coming of the Europeans

The coming of the Europeans in India was a significant event in the history of our country. The Portuguese were the first in the line. It was due to the great demand of the Indian commodities in European markets throughout the Middle ages. These things used to reach Europe either by land or by sea. The land route was practically closed by the Turks. There arose the necessity of finding a new route to India. Prince Henry of Portugal who is commonly known as the "Navigator" did a lot in this field. Diaz and Gama started their expeditions one after another. Gama reached Calicut in 1498. After that they were able to establish trading centres in India (*i.e.,* Calicut, Cochin and Cannanore).

De Almeida (1505-1509) was the first Viceroy of the Portuguese in India. He followed "Blue Water Policy" during his period. Both Almeida and his son were defeated and killed in 1509 by the Egyptians.

Albuquerque (1508-1515) was the second Viceroy of the Portuguese in India. He was a great conqueror. He conquered and annexed Goa in 1510. He built a fort at Cochin. He appointed a large number of Portuguese officers for the work of administration. Albuquerque was a great man. He was really be called the founder of the Portuguese Empire in India. After Albuquerque the Portuguese power began to decline.

Causes

(1) After the death of Albuquerque no strong person was sent to India to maintain their territories in tact. The result was that the Portuguese power began to disintegrate.

(2) There was corruption in the Portuguese administration in India. The salaries of the officials were low. Hence, they did not hesitate to accept bribes from any quarter.

(3) Since Portugal is a small country, its resources were not sufficient for the conquest of country like India. Moreover, it divided its resources between the Portuguese possessions in India and Brazil. So it failed in India.

(4) The religious policy of the Portuguese was also responsible for their ruin. The Hindus were ill-treated by the Portuguese. They used all kinds of methods for the conversion of the people of India to Christianity. They destroyed all the Hindu temples in the Island of Goa in 1540. The Franciscan missionaries became the centre of an immense propagandas.

(5) The rise of Dutch and the English power in India posed a danger to Portuguese power in the country. Gradually the Portuguese failed in their mission.

(6) The Mughal empire was also partly responsible for the decline of the Portuguese power in India.

(7) In 1580, Portugal came under the control of Spain. The result was that the Spanish interests predominated and the Portuguese interests were subordinated. Worthless Spanish officers were sent to the Portuguese possessions in India. These officers were irresponsible and irregular in their work of administration. Thus, they ruined the Portguese cause in the country.

(8) The early Viceroys of Portuguese in India were characterised by great individual courage, enthusiasm for conquest, personal and national pride. Later on the officers became cruel, factious and domineering. Moreover, inter-marriages were allowed. Unfortunately, the mixed race which came into existence was inferior to the original stock, less brave but not less arrogant, increasingly avaricious and corrupt. Hence, their empire in India became an insignificant one.

(9) According to Dod, "The Portuguese dominion was fast falling into decay because the officials were corrupt;

> the fortresses unrepaired and unarmed; trade was declining. Even more significant was the dissolution of Portuguese Union and solidarity...."

Thus, the Portuguese power disintegrated in our country.

CARNATIC WARS

After the Portuguese, the Dutch and the English established their trading centres. Later on the French also thought of trying their luck in India. Accordingly they established their trading centres in India. The French and the English companies fought the three Carnatic wars in the Deccan and these wars sealed the fate of the French in the Deccan.

First Carnatic War (1746-1748)

The first Carnatic War was merely an echo of the war of Austrian Succession which broke out in Europe in connection with the succession of Maria Theresa for the throne of Austria.

The then Governor of Pondicherry was Dupleix. He wanted to strengthen his position as against the English. Dupleix gave a suggestion for maintaining neutrality to the Madras Governor. The Governor was not willing to have such neutral relations. So Dupleix sought the help of Anwar-ud-Din, the Nawab of Carnatic. The Nawab told both the English and the French Companies not to quarrel and thereby not to break the peace of the country. The English did not like the idea of Nawab and proceeded with troops. On behalf of Dupleix, La Bourdonnais, Governor of Mauritius hastened to India with troops. In July 1746 the French and the British squadrons faced each other for some time. Then the French besieged Madras.

In the meantime the English sought the help of Anwar-ud-Din to direct the French to leave Madras and maintain peace. But in the end the French under La Bourdonnais, captured Madras. Difference arose between Dupleix and La Bourdonnais. La Bourdonnais, accepted a bribe of one lakh Pagodas and restored the same to the English for £ 40,000. Dupleix repudiated his action and recaptured Madras. The Nawab asked for the restoration of Madras to him. Dupleix refused to do so. So a battle took place between the forces of Nawab and the French. It was called the battle of St. Thomas or the battle of Adyar. In this battle, the French army defeated the Nawab's forces. The battle of Adyar is regarded to be one of the decisive battles of India.

Further Dupleix tried to capture Fort St. David also but failed. The English in turn tried to capture Pondicherry but the French defended the same successfully.

The war came to an end by the Treaty of Aix-la-Chappelle in 1748. According to this treaty :

(i) The English got back Madras.

(ii) The French got back Louisburg in North America.

(iii) Temporary negotiations were made between them to maintain their respective territories.

The Second Carnatic War (1748-1754)

The Hyderabad State was created by Nizam-ul-Mulk. In 1713, he was appointed the Viceroy of the six Subahs of the Deccan. After a long period of administration he died in May 1748. There was a struggle between his second son Nasir Jung and grandson Muzzafar Jung. Both of them desired to get the leadership of Deccan. So Muzzafar Jung joined hands with Chanda Sahib who wanted to be Nawab of Arcot. Chanda Sahib also opened negotiations with Dupleix. Accordingly he helped them. With the help of the French they defeated Anwar-ud-Din in August 1749 in the battle of Ambur. Anwar-ud-Din was killed in the battle; his son Mohammed Ali took refuge in the fort of Trichinopoly.

In the meantime the English helped Nazir Jung. He took the field in 1750. Muzzafur Jung was defeated, captured and imprisoned. Unfortunately a change took place. Nasir Jung was deserted by his troops and was captured and put to death. Chanda Sahib was recognised as the Nawab of Arcot. After the death of Muzzafar Jung in 1751, Salabat Jung was put on the throne by Bussy.

At this juncture Clive appeared on the scene and occupied Arcot. The French efforts failed to relieve Arcot; Chanda Sahib also failed to relieve Arcot. He had to give up the siege of Trichinopoly. Chanda Sahib was himself defeated and killed. The whole of the Carnatic fell into the hands of the English.

Dupleix met defeat after defeat at the hands of the English. So he was recalled in 1754 and he died in 1764.

Dupleix was succeeded by Godeheu. He arranged terms of peace with the English. According to the new treaty :

(i) Both the nations agreed not to interfere in the internal affairs of Indian states.

(ii) Both the French and the English retained their old positions.

(iii) The English got a town in Northern Circar.

Bussy remained in the Deccan and continued to exercise his influence. But the new treaty made the English stronger.

Third Carnatic War (1756-1763)

The treaty made by the French and the English Companies in India was a short-lived one. In 1756, the Seven Years War started in Europe. It echoed in India also.

The French Government sent Count Lally as the Governor and Commander-in-Chief. He reached India with great difficulty. He had some success at the start. He brought St. David under the French control. But he recalled Bussy from the Deccan. It was a great blunder on his part. As soon as Bussy left, the French influence ended.

In the meantime Salabat Jung went over to the English and gave them Northern Circars. Lally tried to get Madras but failed. He was compelled to retire to Pondicherry. He was defeated by Sir Eyre Coote in the battle of Wandiwash in January 1760.

The battle of Wandiwash was a decisive battle. It sealed the fate of the French. Bussy was imprisoned.

In April 1760, Karaikal was captured by the English. Lally surrendered at Pondicherry in January 1761.

In April 1761 Jinji was captured. Thus, the French had lost practically everything.

In Europe the Peace of Paris was concluded between the two powers in 1763. So also in India there was an exchange of prisoners of war.

Lally returned to France. But he was condemned and executed.

According to the Peace of Pairs the French territories were restored to them. But the French were not allowed to fortify them. It cannot be denied that the three Carnatic Wars completely destroyed their chances of founding French empire in India.

Battle of Wandiwash

The English and French had set up their settlements in India and there was a keen competition among these countries to have a permanent establishment which resulted a outbreak of hostilities in the Deccan. The three Carnatic Wars made the position of the English superior to that of the French Government. Let us see the causes for the battle of Wandiwash in January 1760.

The third Carnatic War was synchronised with the Seven Years War in Europe. Mr. Leynt, the French Governor of Pondicherry was succeeded by Count de Lally. He was appointed to tone up the administration of Pondicherry and expel the British from India. Though he was appointed in 1756, he reached Pondicherry only in 1758. He was a famous, brave and honest officer. But by the time he reached Pondicherry, English established their supremacy and domination over Bengal as a result of the battle of Plassey in 1757. Lally who came to India only in 1758 wanted to subdue the supremacy of the British which led to the war of Wandiwash in 1760.

Events of the War

(1) Lally, who came to India with the object of crushing the mighty of British attacked the Fort of St. David and captured it in 1758.

(2) Then he led an expedition to Tanjore to collect the arrears due to the French. On the way to Tanjore, he captured and plundered Nagore and then proceeded to Tiruvarur where he caught hold of the six priests of the temple and executed them. He was dangerous and ferocious in his attempt at Tanjore and people ran away to the forests from their homes. His cruel nature and sentiments made him unpopular and damaged his prestige. Soon after the attack of Tanjore he reached Pondicherry.

(3) Meanwhile two decisive naval battles took place between the English under George Pocuck and French under D'Ache.

Lally wanted to capture Madras and proceeded towards the Madras. The seige of Madras took place in 14th December 1758 which was strongly defended by the English Governor George Pigot. When Lally beseiged Madras, assistance was given from Trichy regiments and further an English fleet arrived at the coast of Madras to expel Lally from Madras. As the British got help in all directions, Lally retreated from Madras to Pondicherry.

(4) When Lally was retreating from Madras, there was a fierce battle at Canjeevaram in which the English were defeated by the French. Though the French got success in it, they could not get the required financial help from the mother country which led to mutiny among their soldiers.

(5) In September D'Ache was defeated and wounded in the naval fight with Pocuck. As he was sounded, he could not continue the war with the British, So he left the coromandal coast finally. Subsequently Eyre Coote came with reinforcement and on January 22, 1760, won a decisive victory over Lally at Wandiwash in North Arcot District. Bussy who took part actively in this war was taken as prisoner. This made Franch to establish their settlements only in Pondicherry, Mahe and Gingee. Thus in the battle of Wandiwash, the British defeated French in 1760.

In the words of Malleson, "The battle of Wandiwash shattered to the ground the mighty fabric, which Martin, Dumas and Dupleix had contributed to erect; it sealed the fate of Pondicherry."

Results of the battle of Wandiwash

(1) The French power was shattered. "The French were left without a foot ground in India."

(2) As a result of the War of Wandiwash, Pondicherry was blockaded by the British and captured on January 16th, 1761. Gingee and Mahe fell in the hands of the British.

(3) The City of Pondicherry was destroyed and economic condition was deplorable.

(4) The treaty of Paris was concluded in 1763 between the two countries. The French settlements in India were returned on condition that these would not be fortified again.

BLACK-HOLE TRAGEDY

Cause of the Tragedy

1. Weak position of the Nawab

Ali Vardi Khan died in 1756. He had ruled for about fifteen years. During his reign he could not consolidate his position. He was a good administrator and a virtuous man in his private life. He maintained a cordial relation with the English but at the same time kept them in check. He did not permit them to construct fortifications. After his death, Siraj-ud-Daula the son of his youngest daughter succeeded to the throne. Siraj-ud-Daula was a youngest of twentythree years with all weaknesses and vices of the harem-reared prince. He picked up a quarrel with the English.

2. English support to Shaukat Jung

Siraj-ud-Daula broke all the diplomatic relations with the British which resulted the English extended their support to the rival claimant, Shaukat Jung, his step brother, who was also supported by some nobles. As Siraj had all vices, he was not liked by the people also. The loss of support from the nobles, people and the English made him to an aggressive policy with English.

3. Construction of fort by British

British thought that there was a French danger to the existence of the English people in Calcutta and to safeguard their lives and trade privileges in Bengal, Britishers wanted to construct a fort which was disliked by Siraj-ud-Daula. Further the advice of Ali Vardi Khan before his death to Siraj was as follows :

> "Suffer them (the English) not, my son, to have fortification or soldiers; If you do so, the country is not yours."

He did not permit the English to build forts and other buildings. Due to the Seven Years War in Europe, the climate of war was imminent in India and England and France began to fortify their settlements. The Nawab did not like it and asked both to demolish the same. The French obeyed the advice of the

Nawab whereas the British refused to do the same. This infuriated the Nawab to adopt an aggressive attitude towards the English.

4. Affair of Kishan Das

He was a rich Bengali merchant who earned displeasure of the Nawab. He took heels from Calcutta with his family and treasure and got asylum with the British. The English refused to surrender the person and showed scant courtesy to the Nawab's messenger demanding his surrender.

5. Abuse of trade privileges

The English got some trade privileges from the Nawab and they began to misuse them which annoyed the Nawab for which he wanted to teach a lesson. He secured the support of the Hindus in the trade relations and showed harsh treatment with the British merchants.

6. Black-hole incident (1756)

The enraged Nawab wanted to expel the British merchants from Calcutta and attacked the English factory at Cossimbazar and then Calcutta with an army of 50,000 on 20th June. The English army consisted of 515 soldiers and they also ran away from the battlefield. The Governor of Calcutta, and the commander of the English army were incompetent. They sailed down the river and reached Falta with great difficulties. They despatched the news of their misfortune to Madras. Holwell, was asked to surrender the garrison after two days. After the surrender of Calcutta, Holwell and others were imprisoned.

"Black hole" is an incident in which 146 prisonars were lodged for a night in a room of about 18 by 14.10 feet. When the room was opened next day, 123 prisoners died by suffocation and the rest survived in a bad condition. The affairs of the Black-hole are chiefly based on the detailed account of Holwell written in 1757.

Controversy about Black-hole incident

(1) This incident did not happen because 146 persons could not be accommodated in a tiny room.

(2) The objectivity of this incident was not found in any

other contemporary Muslim and English sources, except the record of Holwell, who was a liar. He might have mentioned it for getting promotion.

(3) Of the 123 who were said to have died, only 56 names could be traced. So this tragedy was a myth unwanted by the interested Europeans to serve their personal ends.

(4) The 56 persons died, because of sickness and wounds in the battlefield and not of suffocation in the small room.

When the news of the surrender of Calcutta reached Madras, Clive and Admiral Watson set out their journey to Calcutta. They attacked the Nawab and succeeded in it which resulted in an alliance made between the two known as the Treaty of Alinagar. The provisions of the treaty were as follows :

(1) The company's settlements were to be restored.

(2) The Nawab accepted to offer compensation for the loss of the Britishers.

(3) Permission was granted to coin money and fortify Calcutta.

(4) The English got back their trade privileges.

Causes for the Success of the English and Failure of the French

(1) The English Company was a private enterprise. This created a spirit of self-reliance among the people. The servants of the company worked very hard to get more profit. As a result of this the English Company became prosperous. On the other hand the French Company as merely a department of the Government. It lacked self-reliance and completely depended upon the Government which in itself was rotten during the 18th century.

(2) The naval supremacy of the English was highly responsible for their success. On account of this, the English could send help to India whenever they pleased. There was none to check them on the way. On the other hand the French were not in a position to check their coming on the way.

(3) The English established their naval base in Bombay. It was a very suitable place for the English to begin their operation and also to repair their ships. The French had their naval base in the Isle of France which was very far off. The result was that they could not take immediate action.

(4) The English occupied three important places in India, *viz.*, Calcutta, Bombay and Madras. These three places were very important strategic places to them. If one of these places was conquered by the enemy, the other two remained. Even if two places were conquered by the enemy at one time, one place always remained with the English because the three places were far off from one another. It was very difficult to conquer these three places at one time.

The French had only one important station in India and that was Pondicherry. The other places like Mahe and Chandranagore could be conquered at any time and were always at the mercy of the English. The French lost all with the fall of Pondicherry.

(5) It cannot be denied that he French entered India from the wrong quarter. The Deccan was not fertile. It was absolutely unproductive. So the French enterprise was a failure. On the other hand, the English entered from the right quarter. They started from Bengal. It was a fertile area. The English had all sorts of help from there. So they succeeded in their attempt whereas the French failed in their mission.

(6) The English leaders were very brave and courageous. Lord Clive was more than a match for Dupleix. Lawrence, Sir Eyre Coote and other army leaders were highly responsible for the success of English. On French side there was no such men.

(7) There was unity and solidarity among the English men. It was not so in the case of French men. Moreover, the French officers often quarrelled among themselves. They did not work in co-operation. This brought disaster for them.

(8) Another cause of the failure of French company was that they subordinated the commercial interests to territorial ambitions. This made the French company poor. All their money was wasted on wars. The Government of French was busy in Europe and America. So they were not in a position to help Dupleix.

On the other hand the English always kept their eye on the sea and never neglected their commerce. Hence, their company became prosperous and rich.

(9) The French Government was rotten and it did not give due regard to the French officers. It did not even appreciate the services rendered by the French officers in India. But in the case of English officers, they were praised by their Government in spite of their defects. So the former failed and the latter succeeded in their attempt.

(10) The sea-route and the Gangetic valley were controlled by the English. It is fertile to lay stress upon the personal frailties of Dupleix. According to V.A. Smith, "Neither Alexander the Great not Napoleon could have won the empire of India by starting from Pondicherry as a base and contending with the power which held Bengal and command to the sea."

(11) According to Alfred Lyall the English gained victory over the French because of the sea-power and their control over sea.

(12) Dodwell in "The Cambridge Shorter History of India," says that "the main cause of the English success lay in the supremacy which the English squadron established at sea, permitting them to receive men, money and provisions from Bengal and England enabling transport and cover the operations of their forces, and depriving the French of their supplies." He further says, that the command over sea completely failed the designs of Dupleix, Bussy and Lally. Thus, the English met success after success whereas the French met defeat after defeat in India.

Estimate of Dupleix

Dupleix was one of the greatest of the Frenchmen who were sent to India by the French Company. He wanted to establish a French empire in India. He critically analysed the political condition in India and came to the conclusion that by helping one state against the other, the French could add to their resources and ultimately set up an empire of their own in the country.

Dupleix did well in the very beginning of his career. He was able to put Chanda Sahib on the Carnatic throne. Similarly he was sufficiently efficient to put Muzzafur Jung on the Deccan throne.

After the death of Muzzafar Jung he was able to put Salabat Jung in his place.

Dupleix was responsible for getting Northern Circars from Salabat Jung. It was due to him that the French influence was in its height in south India. When Clive appeared, things changed. He captured Arcot and thereby posed a danger to the French. Chanda Sahib failed to carry out the instructions of Dupleix. So he was defeated and the plans of Dupleix miscarried.

Dupleix was a good diplomat as that of Clive. But Clive was also a good soldier which Dupleix was not. It is true that Dupleix was no match for Clive. No wonder while Dupleix failed, Clive succeeded.

Dupleix did not get sufficient soldiers and enough funds at times of crises. It was a great handicap on the part of Dupleix. Hence, he failed miserably as against the English soldiers.

Moreover, the masters of Dupleix did not give him proper guidance to achieve glory as against the English. They ignored his sentiments. Nobody encouraged him, nobody appreciated him. So Dupleix will always remain a tragic figure in history. He was let down both by his fortune and by his countrymen. He rightly pointed that "he had sacrificed his youth, his fortune and his life. He had spent money out of his own pocket to finance the wars."

According to Henri Martin, the failure of Dupleix was due to the French Government and the Company.

Elphinstone says that, "Dupleix was the first who made an extensive use of disciplined sepoys in India."

Major Lawrence says that, ''Dupleix is a striking and brilliant figure in Indian History. His political conceptions were daring and imaginative and he aroused a dread in his English contemporaries which is at once a tribute to his personal power and testimony in their sagacity.''

According to Roberts, "Dupleix is a striking and brilliant figure in Indian history. For even if we give up the old uncritical estimate we need not deny his real claims to greatness...."

Malleson says that, "Dupleix was a great administrator and

diplomat which a wonderful capacity for organisation and great persistence and tenacity of purpose."

Sir Alfred Lyall admitted that, "Dupleix was a man of genius and political vision who strove gallantly against all those obstacles."

CAREER AND ACHIEVEMENTS OF ROBERT CLIVE

Early career

Robert Clive, the son of a clergyman namely Richard Clive was born in 1725. As a boy he was restless and mischievous. He displayed unusual daringness and bravery. He joined the service of the East India Company as a clerk in 1743 and reached Madras in 1744. When Dupleix captured Madras in 1746, he escaped to Fort St. David in disguise. He learnt the art of warfare from General Lawrence and diplomacy from Governor Saunders. He derived lessons from the failures of Dupleix and utilised them from the foundation of British Empire in India. The turning point in his career came during the second carnatic war. The grand victory of Robert Clive in that war enabled him to become a member of the Madras Council.

The Conquest of Bengal

Nawab Siraj-ud-Daula of Bengal found the servants of the company abusing their trade privileges and causing loss to the native merchants. Having realised the impending danger of British imperialism, Siraj-ud-Daula had captured the British settlements of Kasim Bazar and Calcutta. Robert Clive and Admiral Watson were sent and they recovered Calcutta. Clive concluded a treaty with the Nawab by which the company had restored its former position in Bengal.

Clive came to know that the disgruntled nobles of Nawab and his Commander-in-Chief, Mir Jafar, wanted to remove him. He hatched a plot against the Nawab.

Battle of Plassey

Clive wrote to the Nawab that he would place his complaints against him before his durbar at Murshidabad and marched to Plassey. The Nawab also reached there with his troops. A historic battle was fought near Murshidabad on 23rd June 1757.

The traitor Mir Jafar did not bring the main part of the Nawab's army into action. Clive gained a triumphant victory over the Nawab's army and proclaimed Mir Jafar as the Nawab of Bengal.

Mir Jafar granted the Jagir of the 24-Parganas to the company. Clive received a fabulous reward of 2,34,000 pounds. The Battle of Plassey decided the future course of Indian History. It made the company the *de facto* master of Bengal. Credit for this victory was given to Robert Clive by electing him as Governor of Bengal.

First Governorship of Bengal (1757-1760)

Robert Clive had three achievements to his credit during this period. Firstly Clive repulsed the attack of Prince Ali Gauhan against Bihar and consolidated the authority of Mir Jafar. The Nawab Mir Jafar out of gratefulness granted a Jagir to Clive. Secondly Clive sent Col. Forde from Bengal who captured Northern Circars from the French (1759). Thirdly Clive attacked the Dutch and routed them in the battle of Biderra in November 1759 and occupied Chinsura. This he did because he thought that the British victory in Bengal was incomplete as long as the Dutch remained strong in Chinsura.

Second Governorship of Bengal (1765-1767)

Clive left for England in 1760. During his absence the Calcutta Council replaced Mir Jafar by his son-in-law Mir Qasim. Mir Qasim granted the districts of Burdwan, Midnapur and Chittagong towards the expenses of the British troops. Soon, the Calcutta Council fell out with Mir Qasim and decided to make Mir Jafar Nawab once more. This led to war. Mir Qasim was driven away from Bengal and Bihar. He made an alliance with Nawab Shuja-ud-daula of Oudh and the Mughal emperor Shah Alam II. They attacked Bihar but were defeated by the English Commander Murae at Buxar in 1764. Clive returned to Bengal as Governor for the second time.

Treaty of Allahabad 1765

He settled the problem with the Nawab Shuja-ud-Daula of Oudh and the Mughal emperor Shah Alam II by the treaty of Allahabad in 1765. According to it :

(1) Shuja-ud-Daula got back his kingdom of Oudh except the districts of Kara and Allahabad on payment of fifty lakhs of rupees.

(2) The Mughal Emperor Shah Alam II was given the districts of Kara and Allahabad.

(3) He was to be paid Rs. 26 lakh annually.

(4) The Mughal Emperor granted the Company the right of collecting taxes in Bengal, Bihar and Orissa.

(5) The treaty of Allahabad throws light on the statesmanship and displomacy of Robert Clive. It is very important for several reasons :

(a) The grant of Diwani rights by the Mughal Emperor made the position of the Company legal in Bengal and Bihar provinces.

(b) The Nizam of Oudh became a dependent ally of the Company.

(c) Oudh became a friendly buffer state between the Company's possessions in Northern India.

Dual Government of Clive

One of the administrative measures introduced by Clive was the imposition of Dual Government in Bengal. "In the Dyarchy, the Company became Diwan and the Nawab became a pensioner of the Company. Thus, the English became the *de facto* rulers of Bengal. Clive wanted to set up a mashed system." The Company nominated two Deputy Nawabs. Muhammad Raza Khan in Bengal and Shetal Rai in Bihar, in whom were vested all Dewani and Nizamat functions, *i.e.*, collection of revenue, civil and criminal justice, police and general administration. As nominees of the Company they looked after its interest; the formal authority of the Nawab in the Nizamat affairs was recognised, but the string was kept in English hands. It was not really Dyarchy or Double Government; for the Nawab was tool rather than a partner of the Company. Its dominant feature was a divorce between power and responsibility; the English exercised full civil and military power without assuming responsibility for the good Government of the country. They "sucked the orange dry" but tried to create the impression that they "had not as yet devoured everything worth eating."

There were several reasons for adopting this system of Dyarchy :

(1) The Directors of the Company feared that the assumption of responsibility would consume profits.

(2) The Company did not have sufficient number of administrators for Bengal, Bihar and Orissa.

(3) The foreign powers could be told that the Company was not extending territories and thus, their jealousy was not likely to be roused.

The Dual Government led to the deterioration in the administration. The Nawab was not sanctioned the required money to run the administration. It led to the disastrous famine of 1770 when one-third of the total population of Bengal perished.

Dyarchy at work

The Amils or revenue collectors had to pay a fixed sum for the districts put in their charge. They had no connection or natural interest in the welfare of the country when they made the collections, nor had they any certainty of holding their places beyond the year. They tried to make as much profit as possible by squeezing the people. The appointment of English officers, called supervisors, to keep watch over the collection of revenue made confusion more compounded and corrupted more corrupt. Their participation in private trade was a crying evil.

Estimate of Clive

Clive was one of the greatest Englishmen who came to India. He combined in himself the qualities of a soldier and a statesman in a high degree. His system of Dual Government did not prove good but it was meant to be only a temporary measure. He never meant to make it permanent. The statesmanship and wisdom of Clive can be well understood from the Treaty of Allahabad of 1765. He laid the foundation of the British empire in India which in course of time came to include the whole of Indian sub-continent and lasted till 15th August 1947.

Robert Clive came to India as a clerk in the East India Company. He showed such remarkable military genius that he became commander-in-chief. It cannot be denied that his services to the British Empire in India were great.

Robert Clive was responsible for the capture and defence of Arcot in 1751. In collaboration with Lawrence he was able to frustrate all the designs of Dupleix.

During the second Carnatic War Clive appeared on the political scene of India and occupied Arcot. All efforts to dislodge him from Arcot failed. Even when Chanda Sahib sent half of his army under his own son to relieve Arcot, there was no better success than before. Clive's capture of Arcot proved to be the turning point in the contest between the French and the English. Clive has therefore been called as the "hero of Arcot," in the history of India.

Robert Clive from his early days was very interested in knowing things in the administration. He learnt his soldiering from General Lawrence and his diplomacy from Governor Saunders. In 1756, he co-operated with the Marathas to put down the pirate stronghold of Ghariah.

In 1757, Clive defeated Siraj-ud-Daulah supported by the French in the battle of Plassey. It was a glorious victory for the English. He laid the foundation of the British power in Bengal and provided the basis for further expansion into the interior of the country.

The period of second Governorship of Bengal of Lord Clive is remarkable for the successful handing of the political and administrative problems which confronted the Company in 1765. His masterly handling of the situation silenced all opposition and created an atmosphere of calm and quiet at least for some time. During this time he established Oudh as a buffer State. He was not only a great warrior but also a great administrator and statesman.

Lord Chatham compared Lord Clive with Frederick, the Great of Prussia.

According to Burke, Lord Clive settled great foundations. When he, "forded a deep water with an unknown bottom, he left a bridge for his successors over which the lame might hobble and the blind might grope their way.''

According to P.E. Roberts, in spite of his faults, there was the stamp of grandeur on all the words and actions of Lord Clive.

The system of dual Government of Bengal which was set up by Clive is not easy to explain. In the administration of Bengal he did a lot for the improvement of the Company.

It goes without saying that Lord Clive was the founder of the British empire in India. At the same time it cannot be denied that he was the architect of the ruin of the people of Bengal. ''The corruption, the oppression and the mal-administration under which they groaned for years were in no small measure due to him.''

According to one writer, ''Lord Clive's career in India may be briefly summed up as follows : first a merchant, then a soldier, and then a statesman.''

According to Dodwell, ''Clive was a man of insight rather than of foresight.''

Lord Macaulay says that, ''our island has seldom produced a man more truly great than Robert Clive, either in arms or in council.''

Warren Hastings

Warren Hastings joined the service of the East India Company as a writer at the age of 20. Later on he became the Resident at Qasim Bazar, where he showed his ability for the first time. He became a member of the Calcutta Council in 1761. He was appointed Governor of Bengal in 1772. By dirt of his shrewdness and ability he rose to the position of the Governor-General of Bengal in 1774, after the promulgation of the Regulating Act in 1774.

When Warren Hastings took up office as Governor of Bengal, he had to face many difficulties. There was chaos and confusion in the country in the field of politics, administration, justice and the financial conditions of the company.

Political conditions

(1) Warren Hastings wanted to continue the buffer state

policy towards Oudh. The Marathas rapidly recovered from the disaster of the Third Battle of Panipat and south to wreck vengeance on the Nawab of Oudh and Rohilkhand who joined hands with Ahmad Shah Abdali in that great battle. In 1769, they swept over Rohilkhand. Next year, they entered Delhi and invited Shah Alam II from Allahabad to occupy the throne. The Emperor was enthroned under Maratha protection. Hence, the Marathas had become a source of danger.

(2) Rohilkhand was put under jeopardy by the Marathas. Hafiz Rahmat Khan of Rohilkhand agreed to pay Rs. 40 lakhs to the Nawab of Oudh on the condition that the Nawab would extend his military help to repulse the Maratha invasion. In 1773 the Marathas actually invaded Rohilkhand but retired immediately when they saw the Nawab's armies. Hence, no actual war took place. Even then the Nawab demanded the said amount. Since Rahmat Khan evaded the payment, Warren Hastings had to despatch the British troops in support of Oudh armies according to the treaty of Benaras.

(3) The Maratha court at Poona was infested with internal rivalries. Death of Peshwa Madhav Rao in 1772 led to the succession of his brother Narayan Rao to the Peshwaship. But his uncle Raghunath Rao was ambitious of coming to power. He got Narayan Rao murdered in broad day light and ascended the throne. His usurpation was opposed by a regency headed by Nana Phadnavis. Raughnath Rao was defeated and driver out of Poona.

(4) Hyder Ali had acquired prominence as a military leader in Mysore. By dint of his military skill and qualities of leadership, he became the undisputed master of the Mysore State with Seringapatam as its capital. Hyder Ali had secured valuable aid from the French. He wanted to rout out the British from India. Another factor which strained the relations between Hyder Ali and the British was the hostility between Mohammad Ali and Hyder Ali. Besides, he was in league with Nana Phadnavis and was waiting for an opportunity to exterminate the British.

Under such political conditions Warrem Hastings took up the post of Governor of Bengal.

Administrative conditions

There was chaos in the country. There was practically no administration. The servants of the Company were doing havoc to the people; while the Company was getting nothing and its treasury was empty, its servants were making fortunes. There was no administration of justice worth the name. Everything required overhauling. Warren Hastings was the first beneficient administrator under the Company's rule. He wanted to give the administration a sound footing. He decided to establish a Government in Bengal based on its ancient laws and traditions and to govern the people in accordance with their own customs and manners.

The Dyarchy set up by Robert Clive resulted in administrative inefficiency and the great famine of 1770 in which 1/3 of the population of Bengal perished. People sold their sons and daughters and ate grass and leaves. Hence, Warren Hastings had to abolish the double Government and take up the whole administration into his hands. Hastings introduced a number of judicial, economic and administrative measures giving a new shape to the administration.

Revenue collection

During the Mughal rule, the right of collecting taxes was sold to the highest bidders who became hereditary revenue officers. Robert Clive auctioned the right of tax collection every year and made annual settlements. The work of tax collection was left in the hands of functionaries called Amils. The Amils were no better than contractors and the tenants suffered a lot. Although supervisors had been appointed in 1769, no improvement was made.

Judicial administration

Formerly, the Zamindars used to exercise judicial functions also in their jurisdictions. Hence, there was no actual judicial administration. People suffered from injustice and despotism of the Zamindars. The work of overhauling the judiciary was left with Hastings. As such, the most important reform introduced by Warren Hastings in Bengal in his capacity as the Governor of this province was his judicial reform.

Commercial conditions

There was the custom of the use of 'dustaks' by the officers of the company by virtue of which they used to have private inland trade 'duty free' under the permission of the Company. Hence, no custom duty was levied on the goods going into the interior of the land and armed by the servants of the East India Company. This dustak system was a very irksome and oppressive instrument of corruption. Besides this, there were a large number of custom houses or chowkies in the country and they acted as a source of great hindrance into the free coming and going of commercial goods into the interior parts of Bengal.

Estimate

Under such conditions, Warren Hastings assumed the office of the Governor of Bengal. He overhauled the entire administration. He introduced various reforms and set up a machinery of administration in Bengal before which there was none and over which the superstructure was raised later on by Lord Cornwallis. In modern India a regular system of administration started with the reign of Warren Hastings. It is therefore correct to say in the words of J.S. Cotton, "If Clive's sword acquired the Indian empire it was the brain of Hastings that planned the system of civil administration and his genius that saved the empire in its darkest hour."

29

The Rise and Fall of the Peshwas

The Marathas began to decline in their power and strength. There was political unrest and anarchy in the Maratha State. The Peshwas took this opportunity and rose to the highest leadership of the state from the poor and common family. Balaji Vishwanath was a shrewd man and established the Peshwa dynasty. He paralysed the powers of his colleagues and ultimately seated himself on the throne.

Balaji Vishwanath (1714-1720)

His ancestors were Deshmukhs. He worked as a clerk in the salt works at Chiplum and later on he was given job as a revenue clerk. He was appointed as Sar-Subah of Poona and Daulatabad. He joined in the service of the Mughals and Sahu. He took vital role in crushing the foes of Sahu, his master.

There were dissensions and intrigues in the Mughal Empire which was lossing its pomp and glory. The life of the Mughal Emperor, Sayyad was in danger. So to safeguard the emperor, Balaji Vishwanath was invited to Delhi. Though he came there Farrukh Sayyar was killed already.

The Treaty of 1719

Balaji Viswanath concluded a treaty with the Mughals in 1719. The following were the main provisions :

(1) Sahu's mother, his wife and other royal family members who were put in the prison at Delhi by the Mughals, were released.

(2) Sahu was recognised as ruler of Swaraj which would be created. He would become the ruler of Berar and Carnatic territories.

(3) Sahu was allowed to collect Chauth and Sardeshmuki from the six Deccan Mughal Subas, *i.e.*, Khandesh, Berar, Bidar, Bijapur, Golkonda and Aurangabad.

(4) Sahu would maintain a cavalry force of 15,000 horsemen and their service would be given to the Mughal Empire on demand.

(5) Out of the amount collected by Sahu, he had to give Rs. 10 lakh to Mughal Emperor every year.

This treaty increased the glory and power of the Marathas. They were legally accepted as the ruler or legal representative of the Mughal Emperor. After this treaty Balaji Viswanath, the founder of Peshwa dynasty died in 1720.

Estimate of Balaji Viswanath

(1) He solved the financial problem of the empire.

(2) He secured the right of Chauth and Sardeshmuki in the Deccan from the Mughal empire.

(3) He established the superiority of the Peshwas over other Marathas.

Baji Rao I (1720-1740)

Sahu appointed Baji Rao I, the eldest son of Balaji Viswanath as the Peshwa. He was young and energetic. When he assumed the power, he advised to Shah, "This was the right time for us, Hindus, to turn out Muslims from the Holy land. We have to strike the tottering tree." He further said that Sahu should be an independent ruler and obedience to the Mughal Empire should be stopped. "Strike, strike at the trunk and the branches will fall off themselves." He wanted that the Maratha banner should fly in the air in all the places. The Marathas should establish a strong power on the ruins of the Mughal Empire.

Battle of Palkhed (1728) — Causes

(1) The Nizam created dissension among the Maratha chiefs and he won over some of the Chiefs.

(2) He stated that Sahu should be replaced by Sambhaji and under his leadership, the Maratha power should develop. As Baji Rao was against the Muslim, he might have opposed his rule and

so he told Sambhaji plainly that he recognised only him (Sambhaji) as the only and rightful ruler of the entire Maharastra.

(3) Further the Nizam refused to pay Chauth to Sahu who got this right in the year 1719. Hence, the war was inevitable between the Nizam and the Peshwas.

War

The activities of the Nizam were against the interests of the Peshwas. So a war was declared by Baji Rao in the year 1728 against the Nizam. A fierce battle was fought in the battlefield of Palkhed in which the Nizam was beaten and he was forced to accept a treaty called Munji Shivgaon.

Provisions of the Treaty

(1) Sahu was recognised as the only king of the Marathas.

(2) The collection of Chauth and Sardeshmuki granted by the Mughal Emperor to Sahu was accepted by the Nizam.

(3) All the Maratha people kept in the prison of the Nizam were released and the Nizam accepted that in future he should not support Sambhaji against Sahu.

Battle of Bhilapur

Though the Nizam accepted the treaty of Munji Shivgaon, he wanted to subdue to the power of Sahu, so he induced the Commander-in-Chief of Sahu to revolt against the ruler. The Commander-in-Chief was given all the supports indirectly. On hearing the revolt of the Commander-in-Chief, Baji Rao got wild and at once he proceeded with a powerful army and crushed the power of the Commander-in-Chief in the battle of Bhilapur. Thus, the Peshwas was able to root out the enemy of Sahu and the plan of the Nizam was defeated.

Capture of Malwa and Bundelkhand

(1) Baji Rao was an ambitious man who wanted to extend the frontier of North. So he led an expedition against Malwa, ruled by Girdar Bahadur and it was captured in the battle of Amjhera in 1728.

(2) After capturing Malwa, the Peshwa turned his attention to Bundelkhand. The Governor of Bundelkhand was fighting with

the Mughal Governor, Mohammad Khan of Allahabad. So to defeat the Mughal Governor, the Governor of Bundelkhand requested Sahu to come to his aid. The Peshwa took this golden opportunity, advanced to Bundelkhand and occupied a greater part of Bundelkhand. In this expedition, the Peshwa captured an attractive and beautiful dancing girl by name Mastani. She loved deeply and used her influence over him.

Battle of Talkatora

Baji Rao knew that the Mughal Empire was shaking and failing down from its glory and strength. So he formed a 'Grand Hindu alliance' with the Hindu Rajas. He marched to Delhi and cut off the tottering trunk of the Mughal Empire in the battle of Talkatora. If the Peshwa wanted, he would have completely destroyed the capital city. But he abstained from leading such a disastrous expedition and deposing the Mughal Emperor from the throne.

Battle of Bhopal (1737)

The Mughal Emperor thought that the one person who could fight against the Peshwas was Nizam. So The Nizam was requested to come to rescue. The Nizam also felt that this was the right time to crush his staunch enemy with the help of the Maratha forces. But the decision of Nizam was not fruitful and he was defeated in the battle of Bhopal by the Peshwas. Consequently the Nizam was forced to accept a humiliating treaty with the Peshwas in January 1738.

Story of Mastani

She was a Muslim dancing girl. She was charming and beautiful to look at. She was a good musician and looked after Baji Rao like a devoted wife. This pretty girl fell into the hands of Baji Rao when he undertook the expedition of Bundelkhand. The constant company of Mastani with the Baji Rao was not tolerated by the Maratha Chief. So Mastani was arrested in Poona and operated her from Baji Rao who could not tolerate the separation and he died broken hearted on account of her separation on 28th April 1740. Mustani also passed away on hearing the death of her beloved Baji Rao.

Balaji Baji Rao (1740-1761)

After the death of Baji Rao, his son Balaji Baji Rao was appointed as Peshwa and this appointment was opposed by Raghuji Bhonsle, the nearest relative of Balaji Baji Rao but it did not materialise.

1. Full powers of administration of Peshwas. Sahu, the Maratha ruler passed away. He was the patron of the three generations of the Peshwas. Before the death of Sahu, he executed a will in favour of Raja Ram II and grandson of Tara Bai as his successor, which was highly resisted by Tara Bai. She used her strength and all efforts to regain the throne of Marathas but the attempt was not successful. Consequently Raja Ram offered full liberty of action to the Peshwa in the administration. As the Peshwa was extended maximum liberty, his position became more strong and Poona became the political and administrative capital of the Marathas.

2. Forming of Maratha Confederacy. All the Maratha States joined together and formed Maratha Confederacy. The Peshwa was the real ruler and there was no doubt that he Maratha Sardars were feeling restless under the Peshwa.

3. Holkar and Scindia were appointed as the wardens by Peshwa. They have been given full freedom to levy Chauth and Sardeshmurkhi.

4. Raghoji Bhonsle, the brother of Peshwa captured Central India and he attacked Bengal many times. Ali Vardi Khan, the ruler of Bengal was forced to give up Orissa to the Marathas.

5. In 1758, the Marathas occupied Punjab and the flag of the Marathas was unfurled on the fort of Attock.

Third battle of Panipat 1761

1. The Rohilla War

The Mughal Emperor Ahmed Shah appointed a new Wazir named Safdar Jung of Oudh who was an ambitious man. He developed misunderstanding with his neighbours, the Pathans, and the Rohillas. Consequently a war broke out between the Wazir and the Rohillas. Though the Wazir of Oudh had powerful force he could not defeat the Rohillas and the war was prolonged for many months. So he extended invitation to Holkar and Scindhia and the offer was fulfilled without any hesitation. With the help of the Maratha Chiefs, the Wazir of Oudh who was looking after the administration of the Mughal Empire made a crushing defeat on the Rohillas in the battle of Hussainpur in 1751. So in order to wipe out the disgrace of the Rohillas, they invited Ahmad Shah Abdali who readily accepted the offer and annexed the two provinces of Punjab and Multan in 1752 from the Mughal Empire.

2. Agreement with the Marathas

The loss of Punjab highly affected the prestige and position of the Mughal Emperor who held consultation with the new Wazir named Imad-ul-Mulk and concluded an agreement in 1752 with Scindhia and Holkar for the protection of the Marathas both from internal and external dangers :

(1) The Peshwas should protect the Mughal Empire.

(2) A sum of Rs. 50 lakh would be paid to the Marathas for their aid.

(3) The Peshwa should be given the right to levy Chauth in Punjab, Sind and Doab.

After the agreement, Scindhia and Holkar, the agents of Peshwa came back to South and informed the details of the agreement with the Peshwa who despatched a powerful army immediately to Delhi under the head of Raghunath Rao the brother of Peshwa. Now there was two parties against one another. Before Raghunath Rao reached Delhi, Ahmed Shah Abdali reached Delhi for the fourth time and devastated it. Then the Maratha forces entered Delhi and reinstated the deposed Alamgir II on the throne. The Maratha army proceeded to Afghanistan and occupied Kabul and Kandhar from Abdali.

3. Capture of Punjab

In 1758, the Marathas occupied Punjab and the flag was unfurled over the fort of Attock. The arrangements were made for the collection of revenue of the country up to the Indus.

4. Death of Dattaji

The capture of Punjab by the Marathas from Abdali was a

great insult and direct challenge to test the power and might of Abdali. So he wanted to wipe out the shame and to stop the penetration of the Marathas into his country. He prepared for a heroic struggle with the help of the Rohillas. At the end of 1759 Abdali made a sudden sweep into the Punjab and attacked and killed Dattaji by crossing the river Jamuna in Punjab. Ahmed Shah Abdali did not come to his country as usual. He stayed there, consolidated his forces and protected the Mughal Empire. It infuriated the Marathas who wanted to resist or challenge the authority of Abdali.

5. The Third Battle of Panipat (1761)

On hearing the death of Dattaji, the Marathas were ready to meet the challenge and the battle of Panipat took place in 1761. Ahmed Shah Abdali had 40,000 cavalry and 35,000 infantry. The forces of the Sadasiva Rao were 55,000 cavalary, 15,000 infantry and 15,000 Pindaris. A terrific battle took place between the two parties. Sadasiva Rao had full confidence over his forces and boldly entered into the theatre of war. Abdali cut off all the communications to the Maratha forces and all his diplomatic ideas and techniques of the war. In the beginning it was found that the Marathas had upperhand. But later on the upper hand of the Marathas was crushed and the important person, Sadasiva Rao was chopped off in the battlefield. Viswas Rao, the son of the Peshwa was also killed. Malhar Rao Holkar who took active part in the war took to heels and saved his life. Scindia became lame and thousand of warriors lost their life in the battle. The loss of the Marathas was countless. "Two pearls have been dissolved, twenty-seven gold mohars have been lost and of the silver and copper the total cannot be reckoned." After hearing the heavy loss of valuable good generals and huge wealth, Balaji Baji Rao rushed to Panipat with huge force but his arrival was too late. So he retired broken-hearted to Poona and died in 1761 a few days later.

Causes for the Defeat of Marathas in the Battle

1. Bhau Sahib, was arrogant, haughty and unyielding man. The actions of Bhau completely alienated the support of the Jats and Rajaputs to the Marathas. Further as he was unbending and

arrogant, he totally declined the guerrila tactics of war. He lost balance when he heard the death of his nephew Vishwas Rao who was shot dead in the battlefield. He made a mistake in dismounting the elephant to mourn over the body of his nephew. So the warriors took their heels from the battlefield.

2. There was perfect lack of unity and co-operation among the Maratha leaders. Personal jealousies and family feuds dominated among the leaders. Consequently, the Maratha leaders did not put an organised resistance and opposition to the foes.

3. The Jats and Rajaputs alienated their aid to the Marathas because they did not like the aggressive policy of the Marathas.

4. The Marathas failed to get the support of the Sikhs who were considered the good warriers in Asia. As Abdali was plundering and looting Punjab more than four times, the Sikhs were the formidable enemy of Abdali. But the Marathas did not enlist the support of them and they had full confidence only in their force rather than on Sikhs. It was a blunder of the Marathas.

5. The Marathas were the trained guerillas. Suraj Mal, Raja of Bharatpur suggested to Bhau Sahib that guerrilla system should be adopted for the easy victory over the forces of Abdali. But the suggestion was not carried out and decided to fight an open battle with Ahmed Shah Abdali.

6. Unlike the Marathas, Abdali was fully supported by Nawab Wazir of Oudh and the Rohillas. So they made a crushing defeat on the Marathas.

7. The Abdali's force was large in number and more efficient and skilful in fighting strength rather than the Marathas' forces. The Generals of Abdali were experienced and used their diplomatic ideas which suited to the time. They were brave and bold to tackle any problem which came across in the way. They were the born leaders of war. They were well trained and well disciplined.

Conclusion

The glory and influence of the Marathas was lost after the third battle of Panipat. It decided the fate of India. "The

Marathas and the Mohammedans weakened each other in that deadly conflict, facilitaing the aims of the British for Indian supremacy." "If Plassey had sown the seeds of British supremacy in India, Panipat afforded time for the maturing and striking roots.'' After this battle dissensions broke out among the Maratha Chiefs and the Peshwa never recovered his glory.